SERVICE SCIENCE

To remain relevant in today's world, practitioners should presume that they have two jobs: first, to do their work effectively so that they provide value to the organization; second, to improve how the work is done so that their organization remains competitive. This book offers clear guidance to excel at this ubiquitous second job.

Informed by an appreciation that most personnel who work in any firm, even firms that are manufacturing-oriented, routinely provide services as a key element of their jobs, this book explains how to provide and improve internal customer service, regardless of industry or role. It illustrates the common features, or service process "DNA," while providing a diverse set of examples to enhance understanding. Written by a pioneer in the development of principles and methodologies that address services in a structured and distinctive manner, this book stresses that service processes are distinctly different from manufacturing processes.

Rigorous and practical, this book will appeal to students and professionals alike, in business, hospitality, industrial management, public health, and other fields.

Online resources include Excel files that act as templates to help with quantitative analysis routines.

John Maleyeff is an educator, practitioner, and researcher who specializes in how organizations analyze, optimize, and improve the delivery of goods and services. He is currently Associate Professor of the Practice at Metropolitan College at Boston University, USA, where he teaches courses in business process analysis, supply chain management, and quality assurance. He was previously Associate Dean for Academic Affairs and Professor of Practice for the Education of Working Professionals portfolio at Rensselaer Polytechnic Institute. He has also held full-time positions at the U.S. Department of Defense, RCA's David Sarnoff Research Center, and the

Lego Group A/S (while residing in Billund, Denmark). He has traveled extensively while teaching and researching international operations, especially in Western Europe and China. He has provided consulting services to corporations in the areas of decision support, quality assurance, statistical analysis, computer simulation, and capacity planning. He has also developed training programs for practitioners, covering process improvement and statistical methods for quality analysis. These experiences have enabled him to leverage his knowledge and experiences to the benefit of his professionally-oriented university students.He holds an undergraduate degree in Mathematics, and M.S. and Ph.D. degrees in Industrial Engineering & Operations Research from the University of Massachusetts, USA. He has published his work in a diverse set of practice-oriented journals, including *International Journal of Business Intelligence and Data Mining, Journal for Healthcare Quality, Management Decision, Journal of Service Science and Management, Quality Engineering, International Journal of Educational Management, The TQM Journal, Benchmarking: An International Journal, Journal of Management in Engineering, International Journal of Production Research*, and *Journal of Healthcare Risk Management*. He researched the state of process improvement programs in governmental organizations across the USA and Canada, and authored a definitive guide (*Improving Service Delivery in Government with Lean Six Sigma*), available online from the IBM Center for The Business of Government.

SERVICE SCIENCE

Analysis and Improvement of Business Processes

John Maleyeff

Routledge
Taylor & Francis Group

NEW YORK AND LONDON

First published 2021
by Routledge
52 Vanderbilt Avenue, New York, NY 10017

and by Routledge
2 Park Square, Milton Park, Abingdon, Oxon, OX14 4RN

Routledge is an imprint of the Taylor & Francis Group, an informa business

© 2021 Taylor & Francis

Library of Congress Cataloging-in-Publication Data
Names: Maleyeff, John, 1955- author.
Title: Service science : analysis and improvement of business processes / John Maleyeff.
Description: New York, NY : Routledge, 2020. | Includes bibliographical references and index.
Identifiers: LCCN 2020004910 (print) | LCCN 2020004911 (ebook) | ISBN 9780367336059 (hbk) | ISBN 9780367336035 (pbk) | ISBN 9780429320750 (ebk)
Subjects: LCSH: Workflow–Management. | Reengineering (Management) | Business planning. | Organizational effectiveness. | Consumer satisfaction.
Classification: LCC HD62.17 .M35 2020 (print) | LCC HD62.17 (ebook) | DDC 658.5/3–dc23
LC record available at https://lccn.loc.gov/2020004910
LC ebook record available at https://lccn.loc.gov/2020004911

ISBN: 978-0-367-33605-9 (hbk)
ISBN: 978-0-367-33603-5 (pbk)
ISBN: 978-0-429-32075-0 (ebk)

Typeset in Bembo
by Swales & Willis, Exeter, Devon, UK

Visit the eResources: www.routledge.com/9780367336035

To Robert D. Davis, who taught me how to be an educator.

CONTENTS

FIGURES

TABLES

PREFACE

As an employee of a progressive organization, you will be expected to do your work effectively and to help improve how your work is done. Your job proficiency arises from education, training, and experiential learning. Playing a role in improving how your work is done will delight your supervisor and make you extremely valuable to your employer. You will be provided with more opportunities for career advancement. This book concerns the analysis and improvement of how work is done – called the *business process*. It looks at the types of business processes that may go unseen by the firm's customers. These processes are found throughout the firm, including departments like human resources, information technology, design, accounting, legal, marketing, engineering, analytics, and procurement. They exist in any firm that serves customers - manufacturing, banking, governmental, charitable, technological, educational, and healthcare organizations, among others.

The effectiveness of a business process can be hidden from view of the organization's leaders. More importantly, ineffective processes may remain unnoticed. Given the highly diverse nature of business processes, you would be well served by obtaining a scientific foundation that can be applied in a thoughtful and reliable way. *Service Science* provides this foundation. It will give you a fundamental set of principles, a formal methodology, as well as numerous techniques for evaluating a business process and making targeted improvements. It will help you understand and respond to root causes of problems rather than symptoms.

The goal of this book is to expose you to service science by presenting a structured approach for analysing a business process. You will learn to apply contemporary analysis tools and to monitor performance so that the process continues to operate reliably over time. This book stresses that these skills are valuable regardless of the type of firm within which you are engaged (manufacturing or service), regardless of your position (employee, contractor, or consultant), and regardless of the types of customers you serve (external or internal).

The book is structured to meet the needs of practitioners as well as students. It is geared towards anyone who is or will be a working professional. Although it applies traditional concepts alongside methods of Lean Management and Six Sigma, it is distinctive because it recognizes that business processes provide services that are fundamentally different from manufacturing processes. Many management approaches that apply in manufacturing simply do not work well in service-oriented settings.

Readers need not possess a strong background in mathematics or other science. Coverage and topics are accessible for anyone with common sense and a basic numeracy level. This book provides a wide range of examples in order to expose you to general principles, and scenarios that will closely resemble the types of challenges you will face as a practitioner.

Chapters are organized according to the closed-loop framework described in Chapter 1. Each chapter focuses on a distinct step in this framework while providing numerous practical examples. Many examples are continued over multiple chapters to illustrate the integration of the topics covered. When quantitative methods are employed, the calculations are presented in simple step-by-step fashion or implemented using an Excel template. The book's eResources provides these templates along with videos describing their use. Each chapter concludes with discussion questions or a set of quantitative problems. Answers to problem sets are included in the Appendix. A compressive set of case studies is included in the eResources. Instructors using the book as a course textbook will find these case studies particularly useful.

In an academic setting, this book will meet the needs of almost all university students (undergraduate and graduate) who will have a job upon graduation. Its target audience consists of full-time undergraduates and graduates, as well as seasoned professionals who are taking courses on a part-time basis. *Service Science* fits well in curricula found in business schools, hospitality departments, industrial management programs, engineering, public health schools, and other practice-oriented programs. The book can be used as a textbook in courses such as service operations management, business process management, or courses focused on process improvements such as Lean Production, Six Sigma, or Quality Management. It would be an effective supplement in more traditional broad-based operations management courses, taught in a business or engineering school. Finally, the book would be especially effective in schools that educate or train professionals in fields such as healthcare, law, accounting, finance, analytics, or human resources. In fact, any professional would gain value from understanding how to be a better practitioner by improving how their work is done.

This book aims to make a contribution by helping to develop a generation of service scientists who possess the ability to analyse and improve a business process, wherever it is found. It introduces readers to the unique management challenges posed by business processes that appear distinct but have many characteristics in common. You will learn to define value from the perspective of customers and evaluate business process flows relative to this definition. By applying methods associated with Lean management, you will be able to remove the activities that do not add value. In addition, you will learn to evaluate how a customer interacts with the business process before, during, and after the service, including their emotions during these interactions. This analysis will enable you to apply basic and innovative methods for reducing delays and customer frustrations, while seeking to provide additional value to the service offering. You will be exposed to basic analytical methods for determining capacity requirements that balance the need for a cost-effective business process with the desires of customers who seek responsiveness to their needs. You will also learn to create and analyse performance metrics for a business process, so that changes in performance can be identified quickly and their root causes found. The organization of a business process improvement program with associated infrastructure that motivates employee involvement to ensure its sustainability will be introduced. Finally, you will be able to holistically evaluate the benefits and risks associated with outsourcing or offshoring a business process.

Although this book addresses topics typically associated with *operations management*, it does not focus solely on core operations offered by service companies. It applies to *all* business processes found within any firm. The only types of employees who would not find the material in this book applicable would be those who are manufacturing products (cutting, forming, assembling, painting, treating, etc.), and those whose only job is to supervise these workers. However, those that support manufacturing, such as inspectors, trainers, material handlers, designers, and engineers all perform services that would be associated with the book's coverage.

On a personal note, I have written this book as an effort to integrate all elements that apply and support the application of business process analysis and improvement efforts. Although I started as a mathematically-focused engineer, I have grown to realize that no analytical method, however powerful, can be successful when it doesn't account for people. People are customers, people are workers, people are managers, and people lead the organization – a solution methodology must account for them in order for it to be successful. I have researched, taught and, most importantly, applied every method described in the pages that follow. I hope that the material is presented in an effective manner and that you, the reader, will benefit from the coverage contained within these pages.

ACKNOWLEDGEMENTS

Many individuals assisted me in this endeavor. I express my sincere thanks to Frank C. Kaminsky for what he taught me about statistics and the Deming philosophy of management, and for being a good friend over many years. I am also indebted to Robert D. Davis who taught me how to work hard, enjoy my work, and value my friendships. My many conversations with David L. Rainey taught me a great deal about management in the presence of uncertainty and sustainable leadership. Edward D. Arnheiter and I share a passion for Lean management that enhanced my understanding and provided many practical examples. My thanks to Tiange Shen, who assisted me by researching many of the examples, and creating supporting documents and Excel templates. Thanks to Alexander Maleyeff for his unofficial copy-editing support that corrected my many writing flaws. Finally, I thank Meredith Norwich at Routledge for her support before and during this effort.

My professional and personal life has been enriched by many individuals who are no longer with us, including Joseph Cavanaugh, J. Byron Nelson, Poul Dalsgaard, John Maleyeff (Sr.), and, especially, Emily Kenney Maleyeff. I hope this book honors their memory.

1

SERVICE SCIENCE

Service Science Foundations

Service Science is an emerging academic discipline created in response to the need for organizations (businesses, industries, non-profits, governments, etc.) to better understand how to create, manage, and improve services for the benefit of consumers, internal entities, and external partners. The term *science* is used because service science researchers use observation and experimentation to describe fundamental underpinnings. This knowledge leads directly to a better understanding of how a business can effectively manage, analyse, and improve the services it offers and how best to deliver those services.

This book makes contributions to the field of service science by studying the structure of services from a process-oriented perspective derived from Lean management and Six Sigma principles. It avoids copying methods that work well in manufacturing settings because, at their core, service processes are structured in unique ways. Services need to be considered using a distinctive set of principles, methods, and tools.

Service science is, by necessity, a multi-disciplinary subject. It includes elements of industrial engineering, computer science, marketing, information technology, and business analytics. It is also known by the acronym SSME (Service Science, Management, and Engineering). Service science was initiated around 2002 at the IBM Almaden Research Center in conjunction with Professor Henry Chesbrough of the University of California at Berkeley. As IBM transitioned from a manufacturing-oriented to a more service-oriented business, many of its leaders were concerned that their management system needed to change accordingly. It became apparent that a better appreciation of how to design and deliver services to maintain profit margins at acceptable levels was necessary.

Any service organization with either internal or external customers can benefit from a better understanding of service science, especially those that experience the following challenges:

- Service quality is good but costs are high or the services takes too long.
- Service quality is inconsistent across customers or across service providers.
- Service delivery has been automated but problems remain or new problems are created.
- Cross-departmental information handoffs take too long or are prone to errors.
- Workers are frustrated with inadequate cooperation from other business functions.
- Workers often resort to *fire-fighting* which ineffectively uses resources.

Manufacturing Vs. Service

The study of manufacturing as a science began with the 1909 publication of *The Principles of Scientific Management* by the American engineer Frederick Winslow Taylor (1856–1915). Taylor advocated for the simplification and standardization of production work. He determined the most efficient approach to each work task using structured workplace experiments. An oft-cited example is Taylor's shovel experiments, which resulted in specialized shovels that corresponded to the task at hand (for instance, a larger shovel for ash and a smaller one for iron ore). He performed similar "time and motion" experiments to determine standard work for bricklayers based on studying the motions required to build brick structures. This work also was used to document specific requirements that personnel departments used to hire workers. Taylor's research was possible because so many tasks in manufacturing settings are machine-based or require humans to perform repeated, identical tasks (in fact, many of the tasks done in Taylor's era are now automated).

In the years since Taylor's work, additional advances to the state of knowledge in manufacturing management have taken place. Many of these advances have originated in university research departments (e.g., mathematical models for forecasting, inventory management, and optimization). Significant breakthroughs have been initiated by practitioners (e.g., Lean production which originated at Toyota; Six Sigma which originated at Motorola). Advances in information technology have resulted in new approaches, especially in the management of manufacturing supply chains (e.g., material requirements planning and enterprise resource planning).

Today, manufacturing management is a mature discipline. The applicability of most manufacturing management approaches from firm to firm is enhanced due to the commonality of characteristics across manufacturing systems. With a few exceptions, manufacturing processes deal with tangible items whose physical characteristics are changed (e.g., size, shape, color, hardness, etc.) as a result of the process. For example, not only is a plastic molding process very similar from firm to firm, but plastics molding processes share common traits with machining, painting, or curing processes for metal. They all require setup before production can begin, they all change the physical nature of the inputs to outputs; the amount of time to perform a task is constant or near constant, and success can be easily measured. Therefore, methods for control and improvement are essentially the same across all manufacturing processes, regardless of their product type, location, and customer traits. That is why university degree programs in mechanical, manufacturing, or industrial engineering prepare students to be experts across all types of manufacturing processes.

Services, on the other hand, vary a great deal from process to process (a detailed description is included in Chapter 2). Professionals who perform jobs such as consultants, accountants, actuaries, human resource professionals, auditors, salespersons, lawyers, insurance adjusters, nurses, and data scientists all deliver services. However, expertise in any of these fields is only focused on learning the skills needed to perform the necessary tasks. Little or no time is spent on optimizing the business processes involved in delivering these services. Lacking a scientific approach, these services would appear to have little in common. Hence, the approach to the design and management of service delivery tends to be ad hoc and inconsistent.

Service Science Practitioners

According to the Bureau of Labor Statistics, less than 10% of U.S. workers are employed within a manufacturing firm. But, most workers in a manufacturing firm have jobs classified as overhead, including those working in service departments such as sales, marketing, engineering, design, accounting, finance, information technology, human resources, analytics, planning, research & development, legal services, logistics, and various other support functions. With over 90% of workers employed by non-manufacturing firms, and most workers in manufacturing firms delivering services, one can estimate that service science is relevant to almost all jobs in the United States (this characterization would be similar in most developed economies and lower in developing economies).

It is also apparent that many (probably most) workers who deliver services have customers who are internal to their employer. For example, accountants provide financial reports to headquarters, designers provide blueprints to manufacturing, human resources hire workers for other departments, and forecasters deliver sales projections to the supply chain manager. Often, the effectiveness of these services are "hidden" because all costs associated with their operation are aggregated within the general, selling, and administrative expense line on a profit-and-loss statement. Consider a data scientist working within a marketing department. It has been reported that data scientists spend 50-80% of their time collecting and cleaning up data sets before they can be used to perform useful analyses. To a service scientist, rather than accepting that the time they spend as a "data janitor" is a necessary evil, an effort should be made to reduce this percentage for future projects.

During the course of their workday, most workers routinely encounter similar situations where much of their time is wasted. It has been reported that at least 20% of marketing budgets were spent on wasted efforts and that 50% of their budgets were spent on generating sales leads that were never pursued. Human resource managers reported that the ineffective efforts finding job candidates for technical jobs takes time away from other critical activities such as engaging and interviewing candidates. Some business processes are expected to be less than 100% effective in creating value. Innovation processes, for example, generate some ideas that create value and others that do not create value. But, a study showed that some firms' innovation processes were much more effective than others [1]. These differences can be attributed to more effective business process management.

Unfortunately, this wasted time translates to higher than necessary spending, much of which is also hidden from view of a supervisor or manager. Based on observation alone, they may not be able to distinguish valuable time from wasted time, or they may accept the situation as normal. In time, a service worker's job satisfaction is negatively affected, which impacts service quality and customer satisfaction.

Many other workers in service processes spend considerable time on activities that, in an ideal setting, would be unnecessary. They include: (a) an auditor waiting to meet with a client regarding suspicious transactions, (b) an accountant calling a division manager to clarify confusing ledger entries, (c) a human resource manager interviewing a perspective candidate who is not qualified for a position, (d) a product designer revising a blueprint because the manufacturing department cannot make a product that conforms to its design specifications, and (e) a proposal writer waiting for pricing information from the sales department. It may not seem critical if each worker spends an average of one hour per day on these unnecessary activities, but this one hour corresponds to over 240 hours per year (30 working days) of lost opportunity to use that worker on tasks that could positively impact an organization's profitability.

Evolution of Business Process Management

Business Process Management (BPM) is not precisely-defined. It is rooted in a number of disciplines, including operations management, marketing, computer science, information technology, and strategy. For purposes of this book, the evolution of BPM from the perspective of operations management (OM) is most relevant. OM itself has broadened from focusing on production and inventory control to focusing on production management based on the realization that manufacturing effectiveness requires a system that integrates management, processes, and technology. As the service economy grew, OM became the preferred title of the discipline that included both manufacturing and service OM principles.

Today, OM consists of a combination of academic (mostly analytically-oriented) methodologies and industry (most practice-oriented) methods. Unlike many other scientifically-oriented disciplines, OM has always been influenced by business leaders and their firms. Henry Ford (1863–1947) invented the automobile assembly line around 1908. This innovation enabled him to produce the black Model T at lower costs and expanded his consumer base due to its affordable selling price. The quest for economies of scale characterized OM practice for many years. In 1909, Ford was quoted as stating "Any customer can have a car painted any color that he wants so long as it is black." This statement effectively describes a limitation of the economies of scale approach.

In the years after the Second World War (1939–1945) a fundamental paradigm change took place, led by Taiichi Ohno (1912–1990) and Shigeo Shingo (1909–1990) at Toyota Motor Corporation in Japan. Their approach, which forms the basis of the *Toyota Production System* (TPS), achieves productivity improvements by studying the creation of value and removing all activities that do not add value for customers. Their approach is described in many publications, starting with *The Machine That Changed the World* [2]. Although sometimes referred to as the TPS, this approach is more commonly referred to as Lean production.

As productivity-focused advancements were evolving, a parallel effort existed that concerned quality management. As manufacturing moved from craftsman style approaches to systems with interchangeable parts, the need to ensure that quality standards were met became more important. In the U.S., methods of sampling inspection were developed during the Second World War by Harold Dodge (1893–1976). Later, these methods, which focused on separating good from bad items, were replaced by approaches pioneered by Walter Shewhart (1891–1967) and popularized by W. Edwards Deming (1900–1993). The new approach attempts to ensure quality by focusing on the processes that create products. Maintaining control of the production process became the goal, with various statistical and problem solving methodologies employed for this purpose. This new approach, originally called *Total Quality Management*, has become known as *Six Sigma*.

While the practice of manufacturing operations management matured, most developed economies became increasingly dominated by service-based industries. In response, the discipline of service operations management (SOM) was born. SOM focused on firms that delivered services as their core mission, such as hotels, retailers, airlines, and restaurants. SOM methodologies include some that were variations of production management and others that combined service marketing, information technology, and project management.

Little attention has been paid to the management of the secondary or internal services commonly referred to as business processes. A strategy known as Business Process Reengineering (BPR) was popular in the 1990's. BPR practitioners advocated the design of business processes to account for new realities, such as modern information technologies, increased competitiveness, and the increase in speed within the global economy. The most important tendency in business processes has been the proliferation of outsourcing. Today, it is common for corporations to outsource many business processes, including information technology, human resources, analytics, legal, medical image analysis, call centers, copy editing, and audio transcription. There has, however, been somewhat of a backlash in recent years as the hidden costs of outsourcing have become more apparent and the additional value of insourcing business processes is better understood.

The application of methodologies commonly referred to as Lean and Six Sigma to services has taken place. It is not uncommon to find books with titles such as *The Toyota Way to Service Excellence* [3], *Lean Hospitals* [4], and *Lean Six Sigma for Service* [5]. This book attempts to unify the commonly used methods into a straightforward, applications-oriented but technically sound set of principles, procedures, and tools.

Structure of the Book

Before a business process can be effectively managed, it must be well understood. The approach detailed below evaluates the business process either as a routine endeavor or as a component of an improvement effort. Practitioners who believe that their business process has been optimized are encouraged to follow these steps, the outcome of which may have surprising implications.

Chapter 2 sets the stage for effective business process analysis by defining a business process, focusing on the diversity of processes that offer services of all types to internal or external customers. It describes characteristics that business processes share, such as intangible inputs and outputs, cross departmental interactions, and highly variable activity times. The coverage provides guidance to help readers distinguish between various types of processes, especially seemingly dissimilar processes that share common underlying characteristics. These processes can have common solutions to problems affecting their performance. Additional coverage describes the various challenges faced by business process managers due to the special characteristics that exist in their business process.

The remainder of the book describes a closed loop procedure for analysing and improving a business process. Each chapter provides a formal development

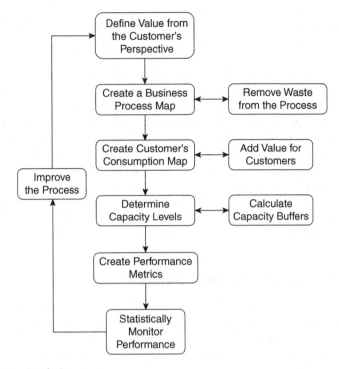

FIGURE 1.1   Book Construct

of various methodologies and includes a roadmap for applying the methods (including Excel templates where quantitative methods are applied). The chapters are organized in a framework summarized in Figure 1.1 and described below.

Define Value from the Customer's Perspective (Chapter 3)

The business process should meet the needs of customers rather than the desires of service providers or the business process manager. Unlike customers of products, who judge quality mainly based on well-defined physical characteristics, service customers deal with an intangible process output and often interact with service providers. This interaction provides important information that impacts the work and affects process effectiveness. Customers need to fully understand business process output in order for the process to be completely effective (e.g., a call center's explanation, a physician's instructions, or an analyst's report). Service managers need to appreciate that, although a written report (e.g., proposal, market study, statistical analysis, accounting statement, etc.) is tangible, its value consists of intangible information.

Business processes for external customers, such as call center support, proposal writing, and appointment making, have satisfaction levels that are disproportionately affected by the "weakest link" in the service delivery process. There is usually an inverse relationship between the salary of workers and the amount of interactions with external customers. For example, a low paid receptionist or call center representative spends more time with external customers than does a firm's executive leadership. Business processes with internal services, such as hiring, forecasting, and software development, are most effective when customer needs are fully understood. Nuisances cause preferences to vary across customers. Ensuring internal customer satisfaction is challenging because organizational structures can hinder process effectiveness. For example, although a marketing department may be incentivized to generate leads, the sales department may be less effective if a high proportion of leads does not translate to sales opportunities.

Create a Business Process Map (Chapter 4)

The most effective way to evaluate a business process is to create a display that is easy to understand and provides a complete unbiased representation of its activities. These *process maps* may take many forms and need not have a standard format. The only important attributes are their accuracy and clarity. That is, they need to show every activity that can reasonably be expected during operation. They include planned process steps as well as unplanned or unnecessary activities such as correcting errors, organizing data, waiting for information, and other potentially unnecessary events.

It is important that the process map shows what actually happens, not just what should happen, during operation of the business process. It needs to include interactions with other processes, including those managed by other departments. For example, a process map of an accounting statement development process should show each department that provides data, as well as the actions necessary to contact the data supplier due to late submissions, confusing information, or incorrect data. Analysis of the process map will identify places where time or effort is not devoted to adding value for customers. These activities are referred to as wasteful activities and should be removed from the process.

Remove Waste from the Process (Chapter 5)

The elimination of wasteful activities will result in a faster service for customers with fewer errors. The cost of providing the service will be reduced by utilizing workers more productively. Usually, the elimination of wasteful activities does not require excessively technical solutions. Often, an analysis of the process map will identify *low hanging fruit*, which are problems that are relatively easy to solve. Unfortunately, the challenges faced by managers attempting to remove waste is complicated by organizational issues, such as when the recommended process change involves another department or function.

The main methods of removing waste include standardizing tasks so that consistency is maintained, preventing mistakes from occurring, using visual mechanisms to keep everyone informed in real time, and keeping the workplace orderly so that time is not wasted finding documents or other information. Although *resistance to change* is often noted as an obstacle for improvement, if the workers within the process are involved in the development of improvement ideas, they are much less likely to resist changes that better the process.

Create Customer's Consumption Map (Chapter 6)

Customers play a unique role in a service process that is unlike the role played by manufacturing customers. Often, customers need to provide information that initiates the service and the quality of this information is associated with the quality of the service ultimately provided. Customers can also play a role during service delivery, for example by clarifying their desires or desorbing a problem. And, they need to fully comprehend service output, such as a report or set of instructions.

By mapping the customer experience, a service provider will be able to determine where customers experience inconvenience, frustration, confusion, and other undesirable emotions. In addition, the service provider will identify opportunities to provide customers with additional value by extending the service backwards (before the service begins) or forward (after the service ends). For example, if an accountant knows specifically how an executive uses an accounting report, they can add value by performing additional ad hoc analyses for specific executives.

Add Value for Customers (Chapter 7)

Adding additional value is often relatively easy for service providers once they understand their customers' experience. When customers are external customers, adding value results in more revenue or greater market share. For example, many aircraft manufacturers offer maintenance service to airlines who purchase their engines. When customers are internal, adding value benefits the firm because work is done more efficiently. The managers and workers of the business process will be seen as more valuable within the firm, thereby reducing the motivation for the firm to outsource the service.

The creation of innovative ideas that result in added value for customers can be enhanced by helping an analyst or project team think *outside the box*. Because many innovations are developed by interdisciplinary groups, the generation of innovative ideas is enhanced by artificially creating cross disciplinary thinking. One method involves the use of a random word generator, where the introduction of seemingly unrelated concepts enable a project team to think of innovative ideas by temporarily forgetting what they know about the current service offering or business process. In this way, new ideas can take root.

Determine Capacity Levels (Chapter 8)

Capacity planning for many services is an informal exercise based on budgets, past experience, and convenience of service providers. However, effective capacity planning ensures that important (and often expensive) resources are utilized when demand for them exists. The intent is to have workers available so that prompt service is provided to customers. Effective capacity planning also ensures that important resources are not idle when no demand exists. Operations managers carefully plan capacity for core operations, and this ability needs to extend to business processes. The targeted assignment of extra capacity is often needed when demand is uncertain or when activity times vary, and both are common in a business process.

Most capacity planning for business processes concerns workers. The determination of resource requirements requires matching forecasted needs with resource availability in ways that minimize labor costs. Shift scheduling can become complex due to the hour-by-hour changes in customer demand, but effectiveness can be enhanced by flexible staffing systems. As a final strategy for maintaining customer satisfaction in the presence of congestion, strategies are available to inform, distract or entertain customers so that their time spent waiting is not a cause of significant unhappiness. An Excel template for capacity planning is included in the book's eResources.

Calculate Capacity Buffers (Chapter 9)

Services typically exhibit activity times that vary from customer to customer. For example, the length of time to verify a financial transaction will vary from transaction to transaction due to differences in their complexities and the length of time necessary to find required verifications. Although customer demand for many services exists at a predictable rate, service providers cannot predict with precision when each customer will present themselves for service unless appointments are made. For example, we can often predict the rate at which customers contact a call center but not the precise time at which each call will arrive.

Because of the variation in customer arrival and/or service times, the business process manager should plan capacity levels so that customers do not experience long waiting times. A *capacity buffer* is the extra capacity that is reserved in the presence of arrival or service time variations. When a capacity buffer is employed, planned resource utilization will be somewhat less than 100%. Rules have been created to determine the capacity buffer size (5%, 10%, 15%, etc.) based on the amount of variation present in the system. These values can be used as rules of thumb or specific buffer sizes can be developed by use of a queuing model template, which is included in the book's eResources.

Create Performance Metrics (Chapter 10)

Once waste is removed, more value is added for customers, and capacity requirements are determined, the business process needs to be monitored to ensure that it performs as expected and that new problems are identified promptly. Although quality assurance systems are common in most firms, they tend to focus on core production or services for external customers. For example, a hotel will typically have a system in place for monitoring the cleanliness of its rooms. The same level of rigor should be applied to monitoring performance of any business process.

Business processes are sometimes monitored, but often the metrics focus exclusively on financial considerations and do not account for the customer's needs. For example, a purchasing department may be monitored using a purchase price variation metric where the intent is to motivate lower costs for purchased goods. However, a customer of the purchasing function, the manufacturing function, defines value based primarily on the quality of goods purchased. It is incumbent on the firm's leadership to ensure that customer needs are considered when monitoring the performance of any business process.

Statistically Monitor Performance (Chapter 11)

Performance data will be generated from internally-derived metrics and externally-derived customer satisfaction surveys. These data should drive decision making by determining if a process is succeeding in satisfying customers and by identifying changes in process performance. Their analysis is made challenging due to the presence of random variations. For example, the number of mistakes made per proposal will vary from proposal to proposal, even when the proposal writing process is unchanged. Business process managers who are ignorant of the presence of variation risk taking actions for no reason, which wastes their time and can increase tension among workers.

The analysis tool should account for random variation and, therefore, statistical methods are employed. Basic statistical control charts are used to analyse performance data. These charts ensure that action is taken when changes in data exceed limits that would be attributed to the natural variation expected in process outcomes. Control charts are a mainstay of statistical quality management. They are easy to understand and interpret. An Excel template for their creation is included in the book's eResources.

Improve the Process (Chapter 12)

The performance management system will identify systemic problems and isolated detrimental process changes that affect process outcomes. In response, a process improvement effort should be initiated. A structured framework is required to ensure effectiveness of the effort. This framework should be based on principles and methods that are sound and that remain consistent over time. A contemporary approach, based on a combinations of Lean and Six Sigma methodologies, can be successfully employed for managing process improvement projects using the tools described in earlier chapters.

The recommended approach applies what most practitioners refer to as continuous improvement, although improvement actually takes place in discrete increments motivated by issues and challenges that are continuously monitored. The recommended project structure involves carefully defining the problem, creating process maps and obtaining data to measure important process characteristics, analysing the process maps and available data, recommending changes to improve the process or add value for customers, and developing a mechanism to ensure that changes are effective and that they are sustained.

Supporting Infrastructure (Chapter 13)

A firm that seeks to implement a rigorous system for analysing and improving their business processes needs to create a foundation that supports these efforts. It is critically important that the organization appreciate that the best improvement ideas are generated by workers who have first-hand knowledge of the process and its customers. This appreciation must extend to formal policies that motivate participation. Organizational structures, including how workers are incentivized, need to be consistent with the goals of ongoing process improvement. For example, workers should not fear that their job would be in jeopardy as a result of a successful process improvement effort.

A system for process improvement requires a consistent approach that incorporates a sound set of methodologies. These methods need to apply well to the types of processes to be evaluated and the knowledge of process workers. Organizational leadership needs to be assertive in its support of the program by maintaining a supportive culture within the firm. Process improvement programs are most successful when workers derive personal benefits (i.e., their work life is improved). Those affected by the improvements should be made aware of the efforts, which helps generate goodwill and encourage future participation.

Outsourcing Opportunities and Risks (Chapter 14)

Many firms outsource certain business processes to minimize labor costs and take advantage of specialized skills. This practice is effective only when customer needs are fully understood. For example, customers of software development processes may value customized solutions that are more difficult to achieve when communications take place across many time zones. Offshoring a business process can have the financial benefits associated with lower labor costs, but they can present a myriad of risks that need to be considered.

Each risk factor that will potentially affect a business process can be quantified using a formal procedure. The method employed would consider each risk factor's likelihood of occurrence, its potential impact on process performance, and the chance that the issue will be discovered before customers are affected. Various strategies can be utilized that help the business process manager avoid a risk or mitigate its effect. These methods need to be carefully applied in light of the myriad of risks, so that only those risks that are likely to disrupt the process significantly are addressed.

Summary & Key Takeaways

This book concerns the analysis and improvement of business processes. It concentrates on those processes that may not be given sufficient attention in traditional operations management textbooks, either because they do not produce products or they are not core operations at a service firm. The book's mantra is that every professional employee has two jobs – to do their work and to improve how their work is done. It is the latter idea that the book addresses by introducing the reader to concepts and tools that apply to any business process in any firm, as long as the process provides a service. The book stresses that almost everyone in the organization is doing a job that is relevant to the book. In summary, the key takeaways from Chapter 1 are:

1. *Service Science* is a systematic approach that creates knowledge about service processes by developing underlying explanations for observable phenomena. By establishing a scientific foundation, problems can be solved more quickly and without significant effort to "reinvent the wheel."

2. This book is relevant to the great majority of professionals because most workers in any enterprise are service providers, even those who work for firms that are manufacturers. Some business processes exist within service-oriented firms while others provide services to customers who exist within their firm.

3. A business process manager should apply the framework described in this book to ensure that a business process operates as planned, and that it has

sufficient capacity to serve customers, so that no time wasted on activities that do not add value for customers.

4. Process improvement is motivated by deviations in performance or new problems. A formal approach re-applies the book's framework within the context of an organization whose infrastructure supports the efforts. Key requirements include motivating workers to participate and eliminating barriers that do not support departmental interactions.

Discussion Questions

1. List some jobs that you have had and define the business processes that you took part in:

    (a) Who were the customers?
    (b) How did you know that customer needs were met?
    (c) Was your boss equally familiar with how well customer needs were met on an ongoing basis?
    (d) What were the main problems you encountered in delivering these services?

2. Have you ever worked at a job where you played a role in how a business process was improved? If so:

    (a) What motivated the need for improvement?
    (b) How would you describe the effort: formal or informal?
    (c) Was the effort successful in the long term? Why or why not?

References

1 Furseth PI, Cuthbertson R. The right way to spend your innovation budget. *Harvard Business Review*. 2018. Available from: https://hbr.org/2018/08/the-right-way-to-spend-your-innovation-budget/
2 Womack JP, Jones DT, Roos D. *The machine that changed the world*. New York: HarperCollin; 1991.
3 Liker JK, Ross K. *The Toyota way to service excellence: lean transformation in service organizations*. New York: McGraw-Hill Education; 2016.
4 Graban M. *Lean hospitals: improving quality, patient safety, and employee engagement*. Boca Raton: CRC Press; 2016.
5 George ML. *Lean six sigma for service: how to use lean speed and six sigma quality to improve services and transactions*. New York: McGraw-Hill; 2003.

2

THE BUSINESS PROCESS

Business Process Definition

An enterprise, or *firm*, can be defined as a collection of entities that work together to meet the needs of their customers by providing them with products and/or services for which the customer has a need. The firm is usually referred to as a business or a company, and its members would include a collection of departments, functions, partners, subsidiaries, employees, and suppliers, among others. As a firm's size increases, so does its dependence on separate functional units that operate under separate (but coordinated) management structures. In these cases, workers tend to possess more specialized skills than they would in smaller firms. A firm could take a variety of legal forms, such as for-profit or not-for-profit, and may be product-oriented (including agriculture, fishing, and mining) or service-oriented. The entity could also be either public or private.

In order to serve their customers, all firms operate a *system* of interrelated *business processes*, each of which consists of a set of interconnected *activities*. Most business processes are classified as either a manufacturing or a service process. A *manufacturing process* is a set of activities that create a physical transformation of a tangible item. A *service process* is a set of activities designed to solve a customer's problem that is not based on a physical transformation. Simply put, a service process is any process that does not change the physical characteristics of a tangible item. All firms, even those that manufacture products, operate a set of service processes. Some of these processes provide their customers with services that supplement their products (e.g., troubleshooting, installation, and maintenance). But most of these processes provide services to support the operation of the firm (e.g., accounting, information technology, and marketing).

Customers of a business process may include *external customers* who exist outside the firm. Examples include retail consumers, consulting clients, and hospital patients. A business process often has *internal customers* who are entities within the firm. Examples include an employee hiring process whose customer is a department's management, an accounting process whose customer is a company executive, and a design process whose customer is the manufacturing department. These services are often referred to as internal services. Most employees in medium and large firms provide services to internal customers. This chapter concerns business processes that create services for either external or internal customers.

Business Process Example: Jet Engine Manufacturer

Consider a jet engine manufacturer that designs, produces, tests, and maintains jet engines that it sells to various aircraft manufacturers, who represent its main set of external customers. In addition to the engines, the firm delivers many services to its external customers such as assisting with new jet engine designs, making changes to existing engine designs, testing engines under unusual conditions, troubleshooting performance problems, repairing engine malfunctions, maintaining engines on a routine basis, training installers, providing installation instructions, and assuring regulatory requirements. Like many jet engine manufacturers, most component manufacturing is outsourced. Therefore, a considerable number of workers and managers are devoted to providing services to external customers and a large number of business processes with external customers are service-oriented.

In this jet engine manufacturing firm, most of the employees serve internal customers. Although a few isolated exceptions may exist, every business process in the following departments would be classified as a service process:

(a) Human Resources (recruiting talent, interviewing candidates, orienting new employees, training existing employees, managing talent, overseeing benefits, etc.);

(b) Engineering (planning projects, creating new engine designs, modifying current engine designs, troubleshooting manufacturing problems, communicating requirements to procurement, etc.);

(c) Procurement (budgeting, identifying potential suppliers, validating supplier quality, negotiating contracts, troubleshooting supplier problems, etc.);

(d) Sales & Marketing (researching new industry trends, maintaining sales data, creating advertising materials, maintaining social media sites, etc.); and

(e) Accounting & Finance (creating routine financial statements, developing standard cost estimates, processing customer payments, paying suppliers, etc.).

Finally, in addition to the jobs listed above, various employees will work on cross-departmental teams. They work on projects of importance to all business units, such as new business development, enterprise software implementation, and supply chain quality management.

Business Process Transformations

The essence of any business process can be described by the *transformation* that takes place as the activities are executed. A process is likely to be characterized as one of the six transformations:

1. **Physical**: Physical properties of a tangible item are changed (e.g., manufacturing, assembly, painting, packaging);
2. **Physiological**: Properties of a living organism are changed (e.g., medical practice, psychologist, therapist, veterinarian);
3. **Exchange**: One commodity is replaced with another commodity (e.g., insurance, bookstore, supermarket, pawn shop);
4. **Informational**: Intangible content is provided to a customer to solve a problem (e.g., software, education, consultation, troubleshooting);
5. **Locational**: The physical location of an entity is changed (e.g., airline, taxi, trucking, mail delivery, distribution); and
6. **Storage**: Entities are held for use at a later time (e.g., banking, hotel, warehousing, library).

With the exception of the physical transformation, all others exist as service processes. Service processes are significantly diverse in character. For example, taxi and logistics firms provides location transformations by moving an entity from one location to another. Physicians and school nurses provide physiological transformations when treating a sick person. Retailers and life insurance companies provide exchange transformations when customers pay for goods or services. Warehouses and hotels provide storage transformations by keeping an entity safe from damage or harm. Finally, consultants and computer programmers provide informational transformations when they give advice or write computer code.

Many, if not most, organizations include processes that encompass more than one type of transformation. A hospital includes processes that can be classified as physiological (e.g., medical treatment), exchange (e.g., billing), informational (e.g., medication instructions), location (e.g., patient movement), and storage (e.g., hospital room). A ride sharing service includes processes that can be classified as informational (e.g., connecting passenger and driver), location (e.g., customer transport), exchange (e.g., bill payment), and storage (e.g., the automobile).

Although many firms consider their core competencies most important, it behooves any business practitioner to appreciate that it provides many transformations that customers deem valuable. Otherwise, the firm may risk losing customers or missing opportunities to attract new customers. For example, consider a pre-school located in an urban setting. It includes an informational transformation (educating children), along with a location transformation (transporting children to a playground), a physiological transformation (providing treatment for minor injuries), an exchange transformation (billing customers for its service), and a storage transformation (keeping children safe from harm). In fact, the processes associated with the storage and location transformations may be the two about which customers care most. Management can also generate improvement ideas (in some cases, innovative ideas), by observing how disparate firms provide similar transformations. For example, many hospitals have improved patient satisfaction by adopting practices that are known to be effective in hotels (e.g., comfort of rooms for overnight stays).

Informational transformations are the most likely transformation for a business process, including those whose customers are internal or external. One study showed that as many as 90% of services include informational transformations, with internal services showing an even higher percentage [1]. Information is often a key transformation even when a visible indicator of the service appears. For example, consider a hiring process, where the job candidates are certainly tangible. It is the information about their qualifications and experiences, and how these relate to a job description, that constitutes the service flow. Almost every department providing services to an internal customer constitutes an informational transformation. Some processes provide other transformations, such as the movement of an incoming part from a supplier, the repair of a mechanical device, and the dispensing of drugs by a pharmacy. In almost all of these services, however, information is an important secondary output that needs to be managed effectively.

Effectively managing informational transformations can be a challenge. For example, consider a customer who contacts a call center with a problem. The customer seeks information and, if successful, the customer is more knowledgeable after the service is complete. There may be no visible manifestation of the success or failure of the service, because the customer would appear the same regardless of the quality of the information provided to them. The intangibility of a service makes it more difficult to precisely define quality and create standard work processes.

Service Process Description

The activities that make up a service process differ depending on the nature of the process. A convenient approach to begin analysing a process is by incorporating a common framework for its description. Every service process has five essential components, as described below:

Inputs are provided by suppliers, who may be customers or another business process. The inputs may consist of tangible items (e.g., a person to be moved, a part to be stored or a sick patient), or intangible information (e.g., a problem description, an accident report, or a taxi destination). A tangible input, such as an accident report, is considered intangible because it is the information in the report (rather than its physical manifestation) that is important to the process.

Flow Units "move" through the process. They can also consist of tangible items or intangible information. The term *flow* does not necessary imply that entities are moving. For example, an analyst uses data (as inputs) to perform an analysis using their expertise and a software application. Here, flow refers to the transitioning from raw data to a structured data set, then to an analysis, and finally to a recommendation.

Activities are the main tasks that take place to transform inputs to outputs. For most tangible items, activities are usually those that change them. However, in some cases, activities are designed to not change the items (e.g., a storage transformation). For intangible information, the key activities are those that transform information to another form.

Resources refer to the people, tools, equipment, and facilities that are used to create the transformation. Effective process planning ensures that resource capacity (amount of work that can be performed) is in line with predicted resource demand (amount of work necessary). Resources are often shared over multiple product or service types, and they can be shared across more than one business process.

Outputs are provided to customers. Like inputs, they may consist of tangible items (e.g., a person having been moved, a part after storage, or a treated patient), or intangible information (e.g., a solution, an insurance claim, or a drop off location). When specifying service outputs, it is best to list outputs in specific terms (e.g., proposed work, schedule, and budget) rather than the tangible manifestation of the output (e.g., the proposal document).

Any of the three services provided as examples below (software troubleshooting, talent hiring, and blood testing) could exist to serve external or internal customers. For example, a software troubleshooting process may serve a firm's employees or consumers of a commercially-available application or both.

Software troubleshooting:

- **Inputs**: The problem
- **Flow Units**: Information
- **Activities**: Answer call, confirm customer ID, listen to problem, identify potential solutions, evaluate each potential solution, explain to customer

- **Resources**: Telephone network, technician
- **Output**: The solution

Talent hiring:

- **Inputs**: Job description
- **Flow Units**: Information
- **Activities**: Obtain job description, search external job database, evaluate internal candidates, contact candidate, arrange for interview, interview candidates, evaluate results, make recommendation
- **Resources**: Human resource personnel
- **Output**: Recommended candidate

Blood testing:

- **Inputs**: Blood sample
- **Flow Units**: Blood, information
- **Activities**: Receive blood sample, confirm patient ID, confirm specified tests, setup equipment, insert sample, run test, document results, deliver report
- **Resources**: Lab technician, chemicals, equipment
- **Output**: Test results

For business processes providing a service, customers often play a role in service delivery by providing inputs. Their participation can have both positive and negative effects on the outputs. For both the software troubleshooting and talent hiring processes above, customers initiate the process by providing key information. Software troubleshooting is especially prone to ineffectiveness when the customer's knowledge is not sufficient to provide helpful technical information. Internal customers (e.g., in talent hiring) are better equipped to play an effective role because they are likely to use the same terminology as the service providers, and they can be trained to provide information using a standard format.

Differences in Manufacturing Processes

As discussed in Chapter 1, manufacturing processes differ from service processes in many respects. Among the most notable differences are that tangible items flow through a manufacturing system while services are usually intangible. The difference in the nature of flow units is extremely important. In manufacturing systems, demand uncertainty can be mitigated by making some products before they are requested by customers. These *inventory buffers* are an important element of traditional operations management. For intangible services, the creation of inventory is usually impossible. For example, consider a troubleshooting call center. With the exception of a list of frequently asked questions, it would be impossible to solve customer problems prior to their call. Therefore, in a service system, buffering for uncertainty is accomplished by allocating more resources than would usually be necessary. This practice is referred to as *capacity buffering*. Because capacity buffering will generally result in some worker idle time, managers are often reluctant to use this tactic and, as a result, many customers experience long lead times for service delivery.

Service Process Classifications

Since about 1964, efforts have been made to classify services. The main intent of these classification schemes is to enhance a practitioner's ability to take advantage of common structures, especially for seemingly different processes or similar processes found in dissimilar firms. This approach helps to avoid the inefficiency associated with considering every problem as unique. Many approaches to service classification exist. For example, services have been classified based on the level of customer contact or the level of labor intensity. To be effective in service process management, however, the classification must not be too broad, and should focus on the types of activities that take place within the service process. Therefore, classifying a business process based on visible characteristics (e.g., number of customers, key resources employed) will not be as effective as a classification that is based on types of activities that take place.

Six types of service processes that involve informational transformations are shown below. This classification scheme is based only on the types of activities that take place. It is useful due to the predominance of informational transformations among service processes. The six types of informational-based business processes are:

Gathering: The process summarizes information for use by others.

Examples include writing installation instructions, creating maintenance guidelines, generating accounting statements, reporting health and safety data, or creating environmental compliance reports.

Evaluation: The process determines if a standard is met.

Examples include conducting an auditing, testing blood samples, inspecting products, confirming bill payment amount, or testing an employee's knowledge.

Analysis: The process performs an analysis to support decision making.

Examples include writing a proposal, evaluating statistical data, making a sales quote, analysing marketing study data, or developing a new business opportunity.

Troubleshooting: The process is devoted to solving a unique problem.

Examples include helping an employee with software installation, treating an emergency room patient, repairing a consumer's appliance, conducting an accident investigation, or resolving a customer complaint.

Consultation: The process provides professional expertise to assist customers.

Examples include designing tools, forecasting innovative product demand, developing software, selecting suppliers, providing logistics support, or determining a patient's treatment options.

Planning: The process predicts, tracks, or controls projects or other activities.

Examples include planning for software integration, forecasting project timelines, tracking metrics, orienting employees, recruiting talent, or prioritizing jobs.

As the examples show, it is clear that many seemingly dissimilar service processes consist of similar sets of activities. For example, an audit to determine if a worker is following standard protocol and the testing of a material to determine if it meets specifications both involve evaluation of actual performance against a standard.

These classifications are designed to help manage business processes by ensuring that the organization avoids the need to "reinvent the wheel" when a problem takes place or a change is contemplated. Practitioners should be aware that a service process may include more than one business process that differs in its classification. For example, consider the writing of a proposal in response to a RFP (request for proposal). Although this process mainly involves analysis, it also includes the collection of data and other information from prior work, which constitutes a gathering process. Or, consider the project planning for a construction project. Although this work mainly involves planning, it also includes solving problems that occur during the project itself, which constitutes a troubleshooting process. In both of these cases, it should be unlikely that confusion will exist because the process mapping procedure (covered in Chapter 4) would clearly delineate activities associated with each type of process.

Challenges of Service Process Management

The characteristics that make service process management challenging are discussed in this section, along with a discussion of why they are too impactful to ignore. Business process managers will need to be aware of them and ensure effectiveness of efforts to analyse and improve their business process. These tendencies are common across most business processes, including all of the classifications listed earlier:

1. Prevalence of information as a key flow unit;
2. Process flows that cross functional boundaries;

3. Activity duration variability; and
4. Hidden costs and benefits.

These common challenges provide a basis for developing a scientific understanding of underlying elements of a service process. There are few "one-size-fits-all" solutions in business process management, but recognition of these tendencies will facilitate more effective approaches.

Prevalence of Information as a Key Flow Unit

The most common transformation that takes place within a service process is informational. This characteristic is often overlooked when physical manifestations of the service act as a communication device. Examples include a written report, website, or blueprint. An engineering drawing, for example, is valued for the information it contains rather than the paper on which it is written. Focusing on the physical form of information is tempting to those with experience in manufacturing, where optimizing part flow is a common goal. It is usually impossible to guard against demand uncertainty using inventory, as would be the case in manufacturing. For services, uncertainty needs to be accounted for in other ways when determining capacity requirements that minimize resource costs while meeting customer needs for quick and high quality services.

Managers familiar with quality analysis methods associated with tangible items may become frustrated by the somewhat subjective nature of intangible quality measurement. In many cases, organizations rely on senior staff to review process outputs prior to their delivery to customers. Examples include checking accuracy of calculations, editing final reports, and listening to a "dry run" of a presentation. These practices should be discouraged for several reasons: they increase costs, they are not effective at finding the root cause of an error, and they delay subsequent activities. These reviews can be replaced by an alternative approach that ensures valid information at its source. For example, consider proposal writing for an architectural firm, where senior management reviews each proposal prior to its submittal in response to an RFP. Rather than focus efforts on inspection as a means to assure quality, a more effective effort would focus on ways to prevent mistakes from occurring. The development of a standard format with templates for required calculations could reduce errors, especially for inexperienced proposal writers.

Process Flows that Cross Functional Boundaries

Service processes tend to flow in ways that traverse departmental or functional boundaries. This characteristic results in a myriad of connections across entities within a firm, mostly consisting of information exchange. For example, an analyst who creates a customer quote in response to an RFP will gather information from finance, operations, information technology, and marketing before submitting the quote. A business process manager is presented with a challenge because firms are often organized as quasi-independent business units. This arrangement is commonly referred to as *functional silos*. Each silo is evaluated by the firm's leadership based on metrics that apply to the type of work performed. Employee actions tend to be incentivized according to the metrics assigned to the department. For example, a computer programmer's merit pay may be based on the number of lines of code generated rather than their role in helping an analyst from another department estimate IT support costs. Similarly, an operations manager may be incentivized to produce parts with good quality and on time, while maximizing resource utilization. Helping with an RFP would likely not affect these incentives in a positive way, and may take time away from the manager's primary work focus.

Data from a study of almost 200 service processes concluded that an average of five functions were involved in service delivery [1]. This characteristic is consistent across service process types, and for manufacturing and service oriented firms. The number of functions per service process was somewhat higher for larger firms because they tend to create specialized departments.

When functional lines are crossed, the numerous *handoffs* of information will often have a detrimental effect on business process performance. Sometimes the definition of a term or phrase may have different meanings in different departments. Consider the term *forecast error*. A forecasting function may define forecast error as past deviations between the forecast and actual sales. A planning function may define forecast error as anticipated future forecast uncertainty. A miscommunication regarding higher forecast errors may cause planners to create higher inventory levels when, in fact, sales are lower than forecasted.

A related problem occurs when important information is not communicated well across functional units. Consider the case of changes being made to a product or service, where related functional units are not notified of the changes. In these cases, customers may experience outdated web sites, incorrect assembly instructions, or other forms of confusion. Other internal departments, such as the call center, may experience overload (due to higher call volume) or ineffectiveness (due to lack of training regarding the new offerings).

When functional lines are crossed, individuals performing a set of process activities may be unfamiliar with the overall service process. They may be unaware of the need for prompt action when necessary. For example, an accountant may delay providing information to a proposal writer even when the proposal's due date is approaching. This problem can be mitigated by having the entire service team play a role in developing and improving the service process. Some firms also make use of highly visible displays to show the status of work so that everyone involved gets a sense of the relative priorities of activities that they need to accomplish.

Activity Duration Variability

The duration of a service process activity (i.e., the time required to perform the task) is usually highly variable. This tendency is unlike manufacturing activities, which are often machine-paced, automated, or use standard work processes to make activities (such as assembling parts) consistent. Service activities tend to respond to customer needs in ways that by necessity differ across customers. Consider the time required to triage (determine level of severity) for a department that troubleshoots software problems. Although the triage process may take an average of 5–6 minutes per problem, the range may extend from a minute or two to 15–20 minutes. The duration of other activities in the troubleshooting process would vary as well, including determining the warranty policy, researching alternative solutions, creating testing protocols, evaluating potential solutions, documenting results with instructions for customers, and answering customer questions.

Although much of the variation occurs because customer needs vary, other activities that should have consistent duration are subject to uncertainty from other sources. The prevalence of information flows often leads to misunderstandings, such as the interpretation of customer-provided information. Variations also occur due to the experience level of the service provider or the customer. When functional boundaries are crossed, other forms of uncertainty exist especially when the information supplier resides in a different functional unit. Information may be late in arriving because of the information supplier's lack of urgency. The information can be inaccurate or incomplete because of the lack of concern on the part of the information provider.

Higher variation in activity duration has three implications for service process managers. First, it is likely that the statistical nature of the variation will be unknown, except for the average duration in some cases. Not accounting for these variations can lead a manager to take action when, in reality, no real cause other than the normal variation associated with the service process has occurred. These reactions are at best a waste of time and at worst can lead to counterproductive actions. Second, service managers need to find ways to reduce activity duration variation when practical. They may segment similar customers according to their needs to create a bifurcated service process. Although segmentation can be costly, it will help mitigate the negative impact of activity duration variation. Third, it is rarely possible and usually unwise to attempt to synchronize activities in a service process. This idea may appear reasonable for a process manager with experience or education in manufacturing, where systems like assembly lines can be very effective. The effectiveness of synchronization is predicated on predictable and reliable timing for each task and therefore this approach would not be effective in a service process.

Hidden Costs and Benefits

Service process management is challenging because of the *hidden costs* and benefits associated with service delivery. In this context, hidden refers to the lack of transparency on standard accounting statements and routine performance metrics. For example, the income statement category called Selling, General, and Administrative (SG&A) expenses includes most of the services performed for internal customers. A reader of the income statement would not be able to see inefficiencies and other problems associated with most internal services, such as those found in the human resources, accounting, marketing, or IT departments. Many performance metrics focus on costs of each functional silo. For example, a key metric in purchasing is purchase price variance, which is the difference between budgeted and actual amounts paid to suppliers. The cost associated with poor quality of manufacturing can often be traced to a new supplier who may have been the least expensive of the candidate suppliers for that part. This impact may be hidden and the purchasing process would likely continue a practice that may be detrimental to the firm.

Benefits of superior service can also be hidden, because service customers can derive benefits in unexpected ways. For example, an especially helpful call center worker may delight a caller, resulting in more revenues than would have occurred otherwise. An especially friendly bank teller may create better customer satisfaction than an unfriendly bank teller, even when both perform transactions quickly and accurately. A reader of the income statement would have no way of realizing these impacts on revenues. Sometimes cost cutting (e.g., downsizing) disproportionately affects business processes because managers fail to appreciate these hidden benefits.

Manufacturing process managers also experience hidden costs although manufacturing accounting is fairly accurate and inclusive, with direct labor and materials highlighted on the income statement. The calculation of standard unit costs for products is common. It is usually possible to observe manufacturing workers and note if they are making parts, setting up a machine, or waiting for late parts to arrive. But, these managers have less opportunity to derive hidden benefits by delighting customers because process output is precisely defined through formal product specifications.

Example: Monthly Accounting Reports

Consider the "third day" monthly reports that an accounting department creates at a large firm. Their name is derived from the report's deadline, which is three days after the month ends. Customers of the reports, mainly senior executives, may be happy with the accounting statements in terms of their accuracy. They may also be satisfied that the "third day" deadline is rarely missed. In addition, these customers may be pleased that the department responds quickly when questions are raised. While not entirely displeased, getting the statements a day earlier would suit many of the executives because their staff need about a day to run certain special calculations. If the accounting department had known about the special calculations performed by some customers, they could consider making them part of the routine reporting system. In fact, other customers may also benefit from the additional calculations. As this example illustrates, managers of a business process whose output takes a physical form should focus on whether or not the information provided is completely consistent with the entire span of customers' needs.

Illustrative Simulation

A simulation was created to help a student or practitioner experience the effect of activity duration variation on the effectiveness of a service process. Simulations are useful because they mimic real systems and show how factors of interest affect performance without need to experiment with the actual process. When uncertainties are included in a simulation's logic, it is sometimes referred to as a *Monte Carlo* simulation. Monte Carlo simulations can be either physical or computerized. When physical, a device such as a coin, die, or deck of playing cards is used to generate random events and a physical representation of the process is used to mimic the real system (similar to a board game). When computerized, software creates the random events using a random number generator and logic is programmed so that operation of the real system is represented accurately.

Mortgage Application System

The computerized simulation described here mimics a mortgage approval process. The process evaluates an application in six steps, each located in a different department. The simulation can apply when departments are in separate locations, including in places around the world. A reader can imagine the six departments as pre-approval, credit check, home appraisal, title review, preparation for underwriting, and underwriting.

A simulation enables an analyst to repeat the operation of the service process many times so that a specific effect can be isolated. One *iteration* of the mortgage approval simulation consists of 4 weeks with each week consisting of 5 workdays. In total, the simulation is run for 20 days, which would be referred to as one month (in reality, with holidays and other shut down periods, many firms operate about 20–22 days a month). It is assumed that each department moves all completed applications to the next department in time for processing the following day.

The most important outcome of the simulation is the number of mortgage applications completed in one month. The simulation is repeated for a large number of iterations (i.e., months) so that the average, standard deviation (i.e., variation), and distribution (i.e., pattern of variation) of the applications completed in one month can be analysed. The service system being simulated is shown in Figure 2.1 with the six departments labelled A through F.

To simulate uncertainty, the simulation uses a random number generator. The daily demand for new applications is assumed to be uniformly distributed between 1 and 6 (this uncertainty can also be simulated physically using a six-sided die). To simulate a perfectly balanced system, the same distribution (uniformly distributed integer from 1 to 6) is assumed for the number of applications completed each day by each department. The system is perfectly balanced because the average daily demand is 3.5 applications per day (the average of 1, 2, 3, 4, 5, and 6) and the number of mortgages completed in each department averages 3.5 per day. Based on these averages, one might expect the system to complete an average of 70 applications in a 20-day period (i.e., one month of the simulation).

The daily variation of new applications is realistic because the number of customer requests would be subject to uncertainty. No one would expect the number of new applications to be the same each day. The variation in the number of applications completed per day (1 to 6) in each department can be explained as follows. A value "1" would mean that the first application chosen required an entire day to complete, because it was complex or some event (sickness, lost forms, mistakes, etc.) caused only one application to be completed. At the other extreme, the value "6" would mean that the first six applications were simple and no other mitigation occurred. Values 2–5 represent other possibilities depending on the complexity of the application and the other relevant events.

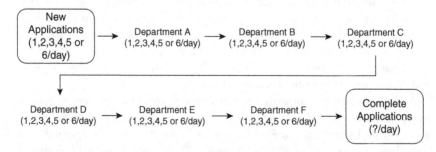

FIGURE 2.1 Mortgage Application Processing Simulation Setup

In the simulation, each department's "inbox" (application queue) will start each month with 4 applications needing review. Unlike inventory in a manufacturing system, these initial inbox levels cannot be directly controlled. They are the result of the system's design and all of its uncertainties. In an actual mortgage approval system, the beginning of a month would start with inboxes left unprocessed the last day of the previous month. Hence, it would be inaccurate to start the simulation with no applications in every inbox. Although the assumption of 4 applications in each inbox can be changed when running the simulation, it is reasonable to start each inbox with 4 applications.

Simulated System Output

The simulation was developed in Excel and it is included in this book's eRe-sources, along with a video illustrating its use. The simulation was run for 200 iterations (i.e., months). Figure 2.2 shows the variation in the number of applications completed per month. The sample average was 53.6 applications and the sample standard deviation was 4.2 applications. The distribution (i.e., pattern of variation) resembles a bell-shaped (i.e., normal) distribution. For a normally distributed variable, 95% of outcomes will fall within two standard deviations of the average. Hence, we can expect that, in 95% of months, between about 45 and 62 applications will be completed (53.6±8.4). This range is evident on the histogram.

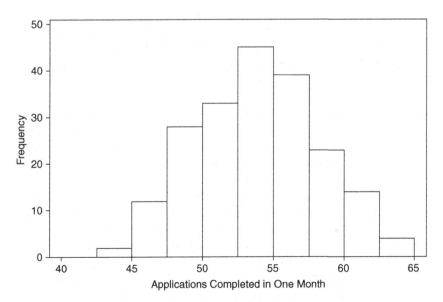

FIGURE 2.2 Example Simulation Results (200 Months)

The result of the simulation is surprising, and it illustrates a concept that is vitally important for a business process manager. The system's demand averaged 3.5 applications per day, or 70 applications per month. However, the number of applications completed by the system averages only about 54 per month and ranges from 45 to 62 on a month-to-month basis. It is clear that the variation in the number of applications completed per day is the cause of the discrepancy between the 70 incoming applications and the 54 completed applications.

Business process managers should find these results interesting. They illustrate a challenge faced, even by those managers who are cognizant that variation in outcomes can be expected. Many firms measure the output of their services, often on a monthly basis. Managers are held responsible for achieving certain targets while minimizing resource costs. Incentives may be built into their contracts, such as financial benefits (e.g., a bonus) when these targets are met. Rarely do these incentive systems account for the type of output variation we see in the simulated mortgage processing system. It appears that, when the system operates as expected, whether or not any target output level is met can be attributed to random chance. Hence, the manager will be rewarded or punished based on an outcome over which they have limited control. This phenomenon is known to affect morale of process managers and also affects workers who are sometimes held accountable by the manager for seemingly undesirable performance outcomes.

Summary & Key Takeaways

Service processes have more managerial challenges than manufacturing processes. This chapter described characteristics of service processes, discussed their challenges, and presented a simulation that illustrated their effects. Many of the concepts explored above will be addressed with detailed solution methodologies in future chapters. In summary, the key takeaways from Chapter 2 are:

1. With the exception of manufacturing personnel making tangible items, every working professional provides a service to customers. These jobs often have internal customers where benefits of especially good service may not be evident. At the same time, costs of poor or inefficient service are hidden from view of executives.
2. Service processes are diverse in nature, but they have common characteristics. With a few exceptions, a service process will consist of intangible inputs and outputs in the form of information. In addition, inventory cannot be used to ensure resource availability when demand is uncertain. Service activity durations are highly variable, which makes the application of many successful manufacturing practices infeasible.
3. The effective management of a service process requires process managers to overcome certain challenges. In many firms, service processes flow

across functional boundaries, leading to information handoff miscommunications. Departmental-based incentives may be inconsistent with the needs of customers. The hidden costs and benefits associated with service processes require strong leadership commitment.

4. With highly variable activity durations, coupled with uncertain demand and the inability to inventory a service, the output of a service process will vary significantly. This variation can result in mismanagement when administrators attribute performance changes to nonexistent causes.

Discussion Questions

1. For each process below, assume that you are the process manager for each process listed below. In each case, list the customers, inputs, outputs, flow units, and resources.

    (a) Uber X Ordering Process – Starting from you initiating the request and ending with the driver accepting the assignment.

    (b) Uber X Transportation Process – Starting from driver getting assignment and ending with delivery to your destination.

    (c) Uber X Billing Process – Starting with the ride ending and your payment; include process for contesting the charge.

    (d) Making a Sandwich at Subway – Starting from you placing an order and ending with bagging the sandwich.

    (e) Product Return at Retailer – Starting from you getting in line and ending with your money begin returned or your request being rejected.

    (f) Market Study for Retailer – Starting from you receiving instructions and ending with delivery of report.

    (g) Financial Analysis of Competitors for Consulting Firm – Starting from you determining the companies to include in the evaluation and ending with the completion of comparison report.

2. Choose a service process at your current or a previous workplace (be sure that it is a specific service process and not an entire service system). This process can be associated with any job you have held, even as a part time employee or volunteer. Start by briefly introducing the process. Then:

    (a) Indicate how the service process would be classified (gathering, analysis, etc.).

    (b) Indicate the type of transformation that takes place.

    (c) List its inputs, flow units, key activities, resources, and outputs.

    (d) List some complaints from customers and the challenges for managers of the process.

(e)   Discuss how information plays a role in the service process.

(f)   Choose one activity and estimate the average activity time and how much variation exists.

(g)   List the various functions or departments that played a role in the service process.

(h)   Discuss some of the hidden costs and benefits associated with the service process.

Reference

1 Maleyeff J. Analysis of service processes characteristics across a range of enterprises. *JSSM.* 2009; 2(1):29–35.

3

DEFINING VALUE

Typical Problems in a Business Process

Analysing a business process is fruitless without first identifying the problems that motivated the need for analysis. Performing an analysis without this specificity can make it difficult to define the scope and subsequent level of analytical detail. Problem identification is usually the event that motivates the need for the analysis. But, problems occurring during the operation of a business process may manifest in ways that are not clearly aligned with their root cause. This phenomenon presents a challenge and therefore an analyst should be aware of the need to focus on the identification of a problem's root cause rather than its symptoms.

A frequent problem encountered when operating a business process concerns processing time. Delays may be caused by a number of circumstances, including inadequate resource capacity, inconsistent worker training, waiting for information from other departments, correcting mistakes, or responding to confusion in customer-provided information. Any analysis focusing on the problem of long process durations needs to include all potential sources of delays.

Identifying problems in a business process is not always easy. Many problems are hidden in ways that compromise a manager's ability to notice their effect. For example, consider a firm's process used to update assembly instructions for do-it-yourself furniture assembly. When the time it takes to create accurate instructions is excessive, new product launches may be delayed. Although customers report satisfaction with the product and its ease of assembly, revenue may have been lost due to the launch delay.

The type of the work performed in many business processes also hinders problem identification. Often, a manager cannot determine the effectiveness of an office worker via casual observation. The worker may be working diligently to correct an earlier mistake, or they may be composing an e-mail to another department reminding them to send important information. In fact, worker idleness is not always the fault of the worker. They may be unable to complete a task due to process-related problems that they did not cause. In these cases, workers will often make themselves appear busy so as not to get noticed by their manager, which also contributes to the hidden nature of process problems.

Some typical business process problems are listed below. These problems exist in all firms – manufacturing and service, large and small, and for-profit and not-for-profit firms. They exist in processes with external customers as well as those with internal customers. Process analysts would be well served by appreciating the common problems, because they often have common solutions. The common problems that are frequently noted by service providers or their customers are:

1. Inconsistency in the quality of service delivery.
2. Long lead times to service customers.
3. Miscommunication with customers or other service providers.
4. Inaccurate data and other information.
5. Poor personnel planning and chaotic work requirements (e.g. a *fire-fighting* culture).
6. Inadequate worker training.
7. Inadequate support from other business functions.
8. Infrequent updating of procedures, terminology, systems, manuals, web sites, etc.
9. Gaming of requests by some customers (e.g., exaggerating importance to get jobs done quickly).
10. Repetition of activities (often because of earlier mistakes).

In this and subsequent chapters, four examples of business processes are used as illustration. They are somewhat simplified to make them more easily understood by all readers. However, many of the nuances that exist in business process analysis will be apparent. Each of four processes will be detailed below, including its classification, how the characteristics listed in Chapter 2 impact its operation, and typical problems that would be encountered.

Financial Audit Process

Audits are common in almost any industry, and therefore conducting an audit takes many forms. Here, the process associated with confirming a financial transaction is described. The process could be conducted by an outside firm or a department within a large firm. In either case, the process would commence after the client is identified, the audit team is assembled, and the client and audit team have met to schedule the audit.

This process would be classified as an *evaluation* process because it compares the way activities are performed to a specified standard. The flow unit is information. Although a letter is evaluated and mailed, it is the information on the letter that is critical. The activities in this process cross departmental lines – the audit department can only be effective if it receives support from the departments being audited and those who play a role in the transactions requiring evaluation. Activity durations will certainly vary due to the differences in complexity across transactions. Finally, many costs and benefits of this process are hidden. For example, neither the benefit of an auditor who is effective at explaining complicated rules to a client nor the cost of circling back to verify a messy transaction would be recorded in any record keeping system.

The typical problems encountered in an audit process of this type include: (a) inaccurate data and other information, (b) inconsistency in how flexibility is applied across audit team members, (c) miscommunication with customers due to the legal jargon that auditors employ, and (d) inadequate support from all involved departments. These root causes can all cause the auditing process to take longer than necessary, which is a waste of the firm's resources.

IT Change Request Process

In many firms, various approval processes are employed to determine preferred actions that consume the firm's resources. Consider an insurance firm that operates across regions (e.g., states or provinces) and is required to conform to the ever-changing regulations associated with each region it serves. In these cases, software used by insurance customers or their agents needs to be updated on a frequent basis. The process presented here is used by an insurance firm to evaluate how to correct information system software problems as reported by consumers to their insurance agent. The process starts with notification of the problem and ends with a decision whether or not to resolve the issue with an IT system change.

This process would be classified as an *analysis* process because it determines a course of action. Its flow unit is information and there are no physical manifestations of the information. It is transmitted both informally (e.g., verbally by the consumer to the agent) and formally (e.g., electronically by the agent to the operations department). Process flow crosses departmental boundaries because it includes the consumer, agent, operations department, and the IT department. Activity times are variable and it exhibits many hidden costs and benefits.

The typical problems encountered in an IT request process of this type include: (a) incomplete information from the customer because they are unaware of the underlying technological constructs, (b) inaccurate information from poorly trained agents, (c) exaggerated urgency from the agent so that their jobs get higher priority, and (d) simultaneous reporting of different problems having the same or similar root causes not identified until late in the process. These reasons all cause approval to take too long resulting in customers defecting to another firm.

Price Quoting Process

The quoting of prices is commonplace for many firms, including consulting, construction, and customized products and services. The price quoting process presented here would start with a member of the sales team asking for a price quote based on a customer request. The firm uses a system to create price quotes based on relevant information. Depending on the nature of the quote, detailed information is required from other departments before the price quoting system can be initiated. Process flow ends with successful input of all required data into the price quoting system.

This process would be classified as a *gathering* process because it requires collecting information from various sources. Once again, the flow unit is information. Customers initiate the process by providing information to the sales force, then many business functions provide information used to set the price, including marketing, IT, finance, operations, and design (i.e., innovation or R&D personnel). Its cross-functionality is a key characteristic of this service process. Activity times are variable, and many hidden costs and benefits exist. For example, a quote that takes too long may lose a customer while an especially accurate quote maximizes the profits of the firm.

Many problems encountered in processes of this type include: (a) attempts by certain sales personnel to inflate the importance of their customer's need, (b) chaotic work requirements due to the randomness of demand, (c) significant time wasted waiting for information from every functions, (d) verifying confusing or incomplete information, and (e) inaccurate estimates by other departments who do not possess the same urgency as others responsible for revenue generation.

Blood Testing Process

Many organizations operate testing processes, such as materials testing, heavy metal testing, or blood testing in medical settings. The process analysed here would take place in an emergency room or urgent care facility, where the testing of blood must be completed during a patient's evaluation. Process flow would start after the patient is evaluated and the test is ordered. The process includes drawing and testing the blood, then creating a report of the test results. A key customer of the process is the physician, who requires the test results to treat the patient.

This process would be classified as a *troubleshooting* process, especially if the laboratory personnel play a role in determining the test parameters. This process is interesting because there are two flow units: (a) the blood itself is a flow unit because it moves through the facility, and its physical and chemical characteristics are determined; and (b) information is a flow unit because it includes the patient's identity, type of test required, and description of results. The process involves more than one department because physicians, technicians, and the laboratory fall under different managerial structures. Hidden costs exist, such as when the testing process takes too long and the patient's symptoms become increasingly critical.

Typical problems with this process often concern: (a) the length of time it takes to get blood tested, (b) other patients who need to wait for a bed to become available, (c) when testing equipment is updated, terminology may change which can cause confusion or mistakes, (d) moving the blood requires personnel who may be busy with other tasks, (e) patients can be misidentified (although this is rare, the results can be catastrophic).

Definition of Value

A business process manager seeks to ensure that customers' needs are met at reasonable costs to the firm. *Value* is how the customer defines their needs. Many external (and some internal) customers pay for the service. These customers choose the service because they cannot or choose not to perform the activities themselves. Their satisfaction is based on the value they receive compared to the price they pay. Some external customers receive the service at no charge, because it supplements a core product or service offering (e.g., maintenance while on warranty). Most internal customers do not pay for the service but rather it is imposed upon them by the firm (e.g., software development). In all of these cases, it is important for the business process manager to understand how their customers define value.

Value is sometimes defined explicitly in formal contracts, especially in business-to-business relationships. More often, value is not defined in formal terms. In these cases, its definition can be nuanced and dynamic because customers have evolving needs and expectations. They tend to define value subjectively and they judge the service accordingly. The criteria used by service customers to define value are referred to as *dimensions of performance*. They are also called discriminators or differentiators. These dimensions are more precisely defined than the concepts of quality and reliability, which entail broad definitions of value.

Although performance dimensions are unique to each set of customers, they will typically be chosen as a subset of common dimensions. The analyst would focus on creating a list of dimensions representing how a typical customer defines value. Alternatively, customers can be segmented with performance dimensions defined for each segment. The list should include specific terms that everyone can understand (e.g., accuracy) rather than the general term that may be defined differently across individuals (e.g., quality). The list of dimensions should be kept short by choosing the single most relevant dimension in each category. The typical categories of performance dimensions are:

- Quality (e.g., conformance, accuracy, usefulness, completeness)
- Speed (e.g., promptness, responsiveness, timeliness, punctuality)
- Access (e.g., availability, convenience)
- Knowledge (e.g., competency, integrity, professionalism)
- Empathy (e.g., courtesy, friendliness, respectfulness, consideration)
- Communication (e.g., clarity, simplicity, conciseness, language)
- Security (e.g., privacy, physical safety, information protection, confidentiality)
- Credibility (e.g., trustworthiness, believability, honesty)
- Customization (e.g., flexibility, agility, recognition, special needs)
- Sensory judgement (e.g., taste, smell, cleanliness, appearance, atmosphere)

Cost is rarely listed as a performance dimension because customers judge a service based on the value they receive minus the cost (if any) they pay. It is important to reinforce that this definition of value applies only to customers. Business process managers should not let the firm's goals influence how their customers' value is defined. If a technician shows a customer how to fix a problem themselves without the need for future assistance, value is created for customers even if it results in less income to the firm. Below, the definition of value will be discussed for the four business processes described earlier.

Financial Audit Process

The main customer of the financial auditing process is the regulatory body (i.e., the legal department in a large firm and/or the government's regulatory agency). This customer requests the audit in order to ensure that financial transactions conform to their requirements, that it be done in a timely manner, that the report cover all necessary issues, and that the auditor quickly answer any questions they might have. For the regulatory body as customer, the main performance dimensions would likely be:

1. Accuracy – the auditor's work should be error-free
2. Conformance – the auditor's evaluation should be consistent with regulations
3. Timeliness – audit should complete their work quickly
4. Completeness – the audit should include evaluation of all necessary elements
5. Responsiveness – the auditor should answer questions quickly

The organization being audited is also a customer because they can obtain information about the quality of their financial reporting systems. This customer wants the audit to be fair, and special circumstances uniquely applicable to the client to be taken into consideration. They want the auditors to do their work quickly and be a positive presence when they are working within the firm. In most cases, they want to learn about new or revised regulations. For the client as customer, the main performance dimensions would likely be:

1. Timeliness – the audit should be done quickly
2. Competency – auditors should be cognizant of all regulations
3. Convenience – auditors should make it easy to interact with them
4. Courtesy – auditors should be polite and respectful while at the client location
5. Privacy – the auditor should not allow for others to obtain information about the client

IT Change Request Process

Because the IT change request process ensures that the firm's resources are properly allocated so that external customers receive superior service at reasonable cost, its main customer is the operations department. This department is responsible for designing and managing the operating system that consumers use to input information and that the firm uses to complete customer requests. These customers want the process to make the correct decisions and the reasons for these decisions to be justified. It is especially important for requests that are denied to include the reason, so that future deniable requests are less likely to be submitted. In fact, the intent of this type of process should be to eliminate its necessity. Decisions should also be made quickly because delays can affect external consumer satisfaction. Finally, service providers should be ready to answer questions about their decisions. For the operations department as customer, the main performance dimensions would likely be:

1. Timeliness – a decision should be made quickly
2. Agility – the evaluation should be flexible so that special circumstances are considered
3. Availability – process personnel should be ready to answer questions about the request
4. Competency – the evaluation should make use of state-of-the-art approaches
5. Clarity – any explanations about decisions should be easily understood

Price Quoting Process

One customer of the price quoting process is the external customer on whose behalf the request is made. This customer wants a fair quote to be provided quickly. They would like making the request to be easy, and their needs to be kept confidential. Finally, they would like to understand precisely what item the firm will create for them especially, in cases where their requests are somewhat innovative or unusual. For the external customer, the main performance dimensions would likely be:

1. Timeliness – a price quote should be provided quickly
2. Integrity – the firm should generate a fair price quote
3. Convenience – flexibility should exist in the information required to initiate a price quote
4. Privacy- the client's information should not be released to others
5. Clarity – any explanations accompanying the price quote should be easily understood

Another customer of this process is the firm's general manager (or other leader). This customer wants the quote to appropriately balance short and long term financial considerations, while keeping especially important customers engaged. They want the system to handle all types of requests, including those that are complex. Finally, they want the rationale imposed on the decision to be delineated in a useful and unambiguous manner. For the general manager as customer, the main performance dimensions would likely be:

1. Accuracy – the price quote should be effective at balancing revenue and costs
2. Flexibility – other relevant information about the customer should be considered
3. Timeliness – the quote should be completed quickly
4. Competency – details regarding the customized product should be appropriate
5. Conciseness – explanations should be short and clear

Blood Testing Process

Although the patient benefits from an effective blood testing process, its main customer in an emergency facility is the clinician (physician or another expert care provider), who needs to diagnose the patient's symptoms to determine the proper treatment. The clinician wants accurate results, and they want the laboratory staff to be competent so that they provide critical information even if not requested in the blood testing order. The test should be done quickly because the patient most likely is in pain or has a condition that will worsen over time. Finally, all regulatory requirements need to be met regarding the patient's privacy. For the clinician as customer, the main performance dimensions would likely be:

1. Accuracy – the tests should be error-free including information about the patient
2. Timeliness – the test should be done as quickly as needed
3. Competency – laboratory personnel should show a high skill level
4. Knowledge – laboratory personnel should contribute to testing decisions
5. Responsiveness – laboratory personnel should answer questions quickly

Determination of Performance Dimensions

A judicious approach should be used to determine performance dimensions that apply to customers. Care must be taken to avoid biasing the list of dimensions based on service providers' opinions. Service providers can be ignorant of customers, especially as customer needs evolve over time. Some organizations fall victim to *groupthink* because they make assumptions about customers (and the value they get from the service), which becomes consensus and discourages disagreement. Typically, customers are not explicitly cognizant of these dimensions and will not be familiar with the concept. Therefore, the list of performance dimensions must be created based on consultation with customers using mechanisms that customers can understand and contribute to.

Two approaches can be used to obtain the information required to determine customers' performance dimensions. Each approach is described below.

Customer Comments & Surveys

The first approach would entail analysing information voluntarily provided by customers. This information typically consists of comments or complaints. It is best to focus first on unsolicited comments rather than the answers to survey questions because the goal is to determine how customers judge value rather than their level of satisfaction in pre-conceived categories. For example, if some customers made comments similar to "Clerks are always readily available when I need them" and other customers made comments similar to "Sometimes the clerk is not there" these comments imply that customers value the availability of the service. The comments' positive or negative implications are less important than the realization that customers care about availability as a facet of their value definition.

When customer comments are not readily available, a questionnaire or in-depth interview should be employed. To avoid biasing results, questions should be made as open-ended as possible. For example, the scope of the business process should be presented in some detail, and the customer should be asked to list some likes, dislikes, and events that they especially remember. Although they are asked to list likes and dislikes, they should not be pressured to list some of each. They should also be reminded that their feedback should encompass their interaction before the process commences, during the process operation, and after the process is completed.

When in-depth interviews or open-ended questionnaires are used, results quickly converge on key issues even when the sample size is limited. For example, a legal department that reviews contracts may have an internal goal of reviewing each contract within two weeks of submission and achieve this goal reliably. However, it may become quickly apparent that customers are dissatisfied with this timeframe because they need the contracts reviewed on a timelier basis. This would be evident if responses were similar to: "I wait way too long for my lawyers to provide feedback to the draft contracts." In this case, the firm's attorneys may be the cause of lost business due to insufficient responsiveness during contract review.

Critical Incident Approach

The second approach to determine how customers define value is called a *critical incident* approach [1]. This approach shares features with in-depth interviewing, but it requires focusing on customers' examples of their experiences with the service, called satisfaction features. Satisfaction features are derived indirectly by asking customers to report all of the events that resulted in either satisfaction or dissatisfaction. For example, a group of customers may provide events that include "I waited too long before I was helped," "The lines were too long," "The service provider was able to handle my question quickly," "The lines are never long," and "I waited in line for a very long time." Although this list of events includes those that encompass both satisfaction and dissatisfaction, they are important. They imply that the performance dimension *timeliness* is important to customers.

Engaging customers using the critical incident approach needs to be undertaken after careful planning. If customers are local, one-on-one in-depth interviews are performed over focus groups [2]. Focus groups have pitfalls that could compromise the integrity of the information obtained. Some participants, who are shy or reticent, may not offer their true feelings because they fear ridicule. Others may understand the exercise as an attempt to achieve consensus and therefore may not be willing to oppose or challenge the group. In fact, often no consensus exists regarding process quality even though a consensus does exist regarding the dimensions. In-depth interviews offer greater flexibility on responses, work well with both extroverted and introverted customers, and will often yield unobvious results.

Many critical incidents are somewhat obvious, such as those events relating to the speed of the service. Other events can be less obvious even to an experienced business analyst. For example, internal customers of an environmental health and safety report may state: "The reports are great because they are easy to understand", "The reports contain some terminology that our staff have trouble understanding", "The consistent use of certain terms and phrases helps me understand the reports better," and "Perhaps a glossary could be included for technical terms." These critical incidents imply that the performance dimension clarity is important to customers.

As with the first method to determine performance dimensions, customers' criteria for judging value is more important than their level of satisfaction. The critical incident method should be done in an extremely open-ended manner because otherwise interviewers can bias results. For example, if asked specifically about privacy, customers may indicate importance. In reality, however, their evaluation of the service may not include privacy as an important consideration.

Summary & Key Takeaways

The analysis of a business process should be a systematic endeavor. It should recognize that business processes have unique problems that are inherent in their structures. The analyst must be focused on the problem and its root causes. In particular, the analysis should begin with understanding customers and determining how customers define value. In summary, the key takeaways from Chapter 3 are:

1. There are problems that are common across business processes due to their inherent structure; knowing what to look for is helpful.
2. Business process customers define value in unique ways that are subjective and multi-dimensional; any good analysis should start with identifying customers and determining how they define value.
3. Value should be evaluated with respect to each dimension of performance, which describe the specific ways in which customers will be satisfied or dissatisfied with process performance.
4. Performance dimensions need to be determined by customers rather than by service providers.
5. Customer performance dimensions can be determined using the critical incident technique, which is best implemented using one-on-one in-depth interviews.

Discussion Questions

1. Consider a manufacturing firm that outsources its distribution services. The business process being analysed is the planning of goods' shipments, which is the responsibility of the firm's logistics manager. The customers of the planning process are the regional warehouses, where products are stored upon receipt. The logistics manager indicates a desire that is very similar to the needs of a typical Amazon consumer. List 6 important performance dimension for these customers.

2. Consider a process conducted by a recruitment company, where the customers are both job-seekers and clients who need to hire talented workers. Job-seekers want to know information about the company and position, when they can have an interview, and feedback from the company. The client wants to be presented with ideal job candidates. They also would like to know more about the candidate pool and they want the recruitment company to ensure the validity of the information provided by applicants. Both types of customers want a fair process that is transparent, efficient, and flexible.

    a. List 6 important dimensions of performance for the client.
    b. List 6 important dimensions of performance for the job-seeker.

3. A convention center's event planning process has customers who are exhibitors and will be operating a booth at the trade show. To be successful, exhibitors would like the planning process to customize their booth (e.g., layout, shape, decorations), to be aware of the exhibitor's objectives, to ensure that exhibitors know the layout of the facility including important amenities, to take care of the exhibitor's property, and to answer questions promptly. List 6 important dimensions of performance for the exhibitor.

References

1   Gustafsson A, Johnson MD. *Competing in a service economy: how to create a competitive advantage through service development and innovation.* San Francisco: Jossey-Bass; 2003.
2   Stokes D, Bergin R. Methodology or "methodolatry"? An evaluation of focus groups and depth interviews. *QMR.* 2006; 9(1):26–37.

4

PROCESS MAPPING & ANALYSIS

Process Mapping

After the customer's definition of value is determined, the analysis should proceed to identifying those activities that the service provider employs when they deliver value for customers. This analysis would also determine how activities are connected, which is referred to as the *process flow*. A display (called a *process map*) would be created so that any interested party can understand how the process operates. Process maps should display all activities that take place and how a job proceeds through those activities. It can take many forms, including flowcharts, photographs, sketches, facility layouts, videos, or any other useful format. Various names have been given to a process display of this type, including process map, process flowchart, value stream map, current state map, and process blueprint.

A process map should show the business process as it currently operates. It is not a list of important process steps, and it should not display the process as it would ideally operate. A list of process activities would not suffice, because the process map should indicate the non-sequential flows that take place. The process map should motivate individuals to focus on an objectively-created display, in order to avoid degenerating into a "blame assignment" exercise. The intent of the process map is for all stakeholders (e.g., managers, employees, suppliers) to work together to solve a problem, not blame each other for the problem. By creating a pictorial representation of the current process, fingers will point to the display rather than to the project team members. To be effective, the display should be developed by a project team with individuals who collectively have knowledge of each process activity.

The format used to display the process should show the activities, how they are connected, where inputs are received, and the destination of outputs, with particular focus on where the process flow deviates from its ideal path (e.g., where errors are corrected, information is validated, or reminders are issued). It can include relevant numbers if data are readily available. The accuracy and intuitiveness of the display is more important than the particular format chosen. In most cases, the process map for a business process usually takes the form of a flowchart.

Because services tend to flow across departments, it is sometimes useful to include *swim lanes* representing different departments or functional entities. The swim lane structure is particularly important because many problems occur during the handoff of information across functional boundaries. In order to develop flowcharts with swim lanes, input should be provided by representatives of each function represented on the flow chart.

Other formats can be useful as well. For processes that include customers moving though a facility, it is sometimes useful to display the process map superimposed on the facility layout. In these cases, the process map would focus on the movement of customers through the process. These process maps often show the chaotic nature of customer movement, and are known as *spaghetti charts*. Similarly, a series of photographs can be used to show process activities, such as where customers stand while waiting for service. Videos can be useful to show movement of representative customers.

Process Map Development

Process maps can become unnecessarily complex when the business process is too broadly defined. It is usually best to narrow the project scope to focus on one aspect of the overall process or a specific problem. For example, a complete audit would consist of client recruitment, a team organization, audit planning, and auditor scheduling, even before the audit activities begin. Each of these components could be analysed as a separate business process. When a specific problem exists, such as incomplete customer information in a computerized customer interface, the process map should only encompass that portion of the process activities.

The main goal of a process map is to create a display that accurately depicts relevant process activities as they occur rather than as they are intended. The most important criteria for a successful process mapping effort are accuracy and clarity; they should be easily understood by all users, including those within the project team and those who may view the project report at a later time.

The creation of a service-oriented business process map should be internally consistent, but it is not necessary to follow any recommended formats. Some shapes are useful for certain purposes, such as using a diamond shape to show where the process flows in one of two or three potential directions. In these cases, the criterion for each direction should be listed next to each option. Rectangle shapes are useful for depicting a process activity, with the short name of the step written in the rectangle. When more than one type of process step exists, they can be distinguished using rounded (versus square) edges or dashed (versus solid) lines.

In the business process map, the flow of activities generally consists of information flows, although at times there may be both information flows and physical items (e.g., a materials testing process). Flows are depicted as solid lines with arrowheads showing their direction. When flows consist of both information and physical items, it may help to distinguish them by using dashed lines for tangible items and solid lines for information.

Although the start and end of the process map may be obvious for the developer, readers appreciate explicitly defined beginning and endpoints. An oval is often used for this purpose. To avoid showing lines that cross in confusing ways, sometimes circles with numbers are used to show the path of the flow. Although no standards exist, other shapes may be incorporated to show delays (or other forms of waiting), interaction with a computer system, or exchanges with other departments. Although the shapes may not be standard, users will quickly understand the meaning of most shapes and will appreciate consistency in their application. Adding labels to unusual aspects of the process map can help, as long as the labeling does not overcomplicate the display.

Identification of Waste

When analysing a business process map, the analyst should regard each unit of time as being spent on an *activity*. The analysis of each activity should be done according to the customer's value definition and their performance dimensions. Each activity can be categorized in two main ways: value-added (for the customer) or wasteful (from the customer's perspective). Some activities include work that directly contributes to increasing customer value – they are referred to as *value-added activities*. The total time required to perform all of the value-added activities would usually constitute the minimum (or theoretical) lead time for the process.

In almost every business process, the theoretical lead time will be much less than the actual lead times experienced by customers. For example, consider the blood testing process. Once the order is written, the process flow would include value-added activities of drawing the blood and testing the blood. The total time to perform these two activities may be 15–20 minutes. In reality, the total turnaround time can be 1–2 hours because of delays caused by: (a) waiting for the technician to draw the blood, (b) moving the blood to the ED outbox, (c) waiting for a volunteer to take the blood to the laboratory, (d) transporting the blood, (e) waiting for the laboratory technician to complete previous tests, (f) waiting for the testing equipment to be setup, (g) retesting the blood if a mistake is made or the test is not successful, (h) transporting the results to the ED, and (i) waiting for the physician to complete other activities before looking at the results.

The activities that consume time but do not add value for customers are referred to as non-value-added activities, or *wasteful activities*. The identification and removal of wasteful activities will minimize the gap between theoretical flow time and actual flow time. This categorization of activities applies to any process – manufacturing, service, healthcare, government, etc. Lean practitioners often use the Japanese term *muda* when referring to a wasteful activity. Muda is often categorized in two groups: (a) wasteful activities that are currently necessary (Type I muda) and (b) wasteful activities that are absolutely unnecessary (Type II muda). Type II muda would be the first type of waste addressed.

In the 1960's, then-Toyota engineer Shigeo Shingo developed a list of seven wastes that apply to manufacturing [1]. They are: (a) waiting for items in a queue waiting to be processed, (b) defects that do not meet quality standards resulting in remanufacturing or reworking the items, (c) inventory that is yet to be sold, (d) transportation of items between processes by cart, forklift, truck, boat, plane, etc., (e) motion of personnel or item movement within a process, (f) over-processing time spent finishing items due to inadequate capabilities (such as smoothing a hole after drilling), and (g) overproduction of extra items in an effort to create economies of scale.

Although interesting from a historical perspective, many of the wastes identified by Shingo do not apply to services or business processes. Although connections can be made between these categories of waste and those found in a service process, many of the categories would be irrelevant in a service. The terminology used in service systems would also be inconsistent with terms used in manufacturing. For example, although "defects" would certainly occur in service systems, they would typically be referred to as "mistakes" or "errors." Although "inventory" would be wasteful in any system, service processes typically cannot inventory their service, and they typically employ capacity buffers. Similarly, "overproduction" (analogous to providing a service above the immediate needs of a customer due to a need to create economies of scale) does not typically occur in a service system.

Properly identifying an activity as wasteful is more important than assigning each wasteful activity to a category. However, it is helpful to have a list of waste categories to assist in the analysis of a process map. The following seven categories were created for services and other non-manufacturing business processes [2]:

(1) *Delays* include time wasted waiting for a resource to become available. Delays would be manifested as an inbox (e.g., physical, electronic, etc.), a queue of customers (e.g., waiting in a line, holding for a call center representative, etc.), or any resource that is busy doing other tasks (e.g., people, machines, IT systems, etc.).

(2) *Mistakes* include errors or omissions that cause time to be spent correcting them. If found by customers, mistakes can result in loss of reputation or

customer defections (along with the time spent correcting the mistake). A secondary result of mistakes is the disruption of normal activities that cause delay in other work activities.

(3) *Movement* includes the physical transport of information, personnel, or equipment. In an ideal setting, this movement would be unnecessary. Examples include traveling to attend a meeting, going to a customer location to get information, or mailing reports to a customer.

(4) *Duplication* includes activities that are done elsewhere in the system or can be done more easily in another part of the system. Alternatively, a similar activity may be performed more than once. For example, duplication occurs when the same data are entered onto a form at two different locations in the system, or when data are recorded and later entered into a computer system.

(5) *Reviews* include activities that check completed or partially completed work for errors or omissions. Examples include confirming that standard accounting procedures are used, checking technical accuracy of an analysis, or creating a presentation to obtain management approval before proceeding to the next phase of a project.

(6) *Processing inefficiencies* include the ineffective use of a resource in performing a specific task. For example, generating reports without a standard template can cause personnel to spend extra time "reinventing the wheel" every time a report is generated. Idle time of workers is costly, but would not be included in this waste because this causes no delays and does not hamper the system's ability to add value for customers.

(7) *Resource inefficiencies* include the management of personnel, equipment, materials, or capital in ways that are below their level of competency. Examples would be time spent creating a work schedule, service personnel attending meetings, or skilled workers doing mundane tasks.

Some business processes themselves can be considered non value-added. For example, in an ideal situation, audits should not be necessary and therefore an audit process itself can sometimes be considered wasteful. However, customers of the audit process seek value from this process so it should be evaluated from their perspective. Therefore, each business process would be evaluated in a consistent way, regardless of the nature of the process.

In the following sections, the four business processes detailed in Chapter 3 are analysed. In each case, a process map is shown, and a list of value-added activities and some wasteful activities are listed.

Financial Audit Process

A process map for a portion of an audit process is shown in Figure 4.1, showing the activities that take place to verify the accuracy of financial transactions. The process map starts with the auditor extracting basic financial information

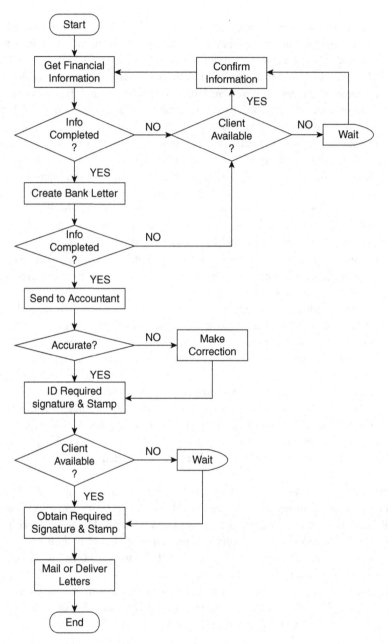

FIGURE 4.1 Financial Audit Process Map

from the client's financial management system, including financial statements, journal entries, and trial balances. For each transaction, the information is checked and information needed to make it valid is gathered from the client. Once the information is validated, a bank letter is drafted and sent to an accountant for verification of the required identification. Once the official stamp is added to each letter, they are mailed or hand-delivered to the bank for verification. The process includes many instances where the client needs to be involved, which can cause delays, as shown in several places in the process map.

This process was presented using a basic flowchart format. It contains several places where the process needs to *backtrack* to confirm accuracy, or change incomplete or inaccurate information. This process does not experience significant interaction between departments or functions in the client's firm. In fact, although the auditor may require interactions with multiple departments, the process is identical within each department, and therefore the specific departments need not be listed. The analysis of this process map would create the following list of value-added activities, and examples of wasteful activities:

Value-Added Activities: Bank letter creation, teaching client rules, exceptions to standard rulings, identification of regulatory violations

Wasteful Activities: Checking if the financial information is complete (review), waiting for client to confirm financial information (delay), client revising financial information (mistake, resource inefficiency), checking if bank letter is complete (review), accountant checking for accuracy (resource inefficiency, duplication), waiting for client to sign letter (delay), copying bank letters (duplication; processing inefficiency), delivering letters to bank (movement), delivering letters to accountant (movement), accountant delivering letters to superior for signature (movement), printing out bank letter (movement; processing inefficiency), superior signing the letter (resource inefficiency), generating bank letter in improper format (process inefficiency)

IT Change Request Process

The insurance firm's IT change request process map is shown as Figure 4.2. After discovering a software related issue or hearing from one or more customers, the insurance agent submits a request to the operations department. They document the request and determine if it requires a software change. If so, they forward the request to the IT function, where the request is validated. If validated, the operations manager creates a business case that is forwarded to executive management for approval.

This process was presented using swim lanes to highlight the interactions among the key stakeholders, starting with the insurance agent. By explicitly showing the functions, hand-offs of information across functional lines are

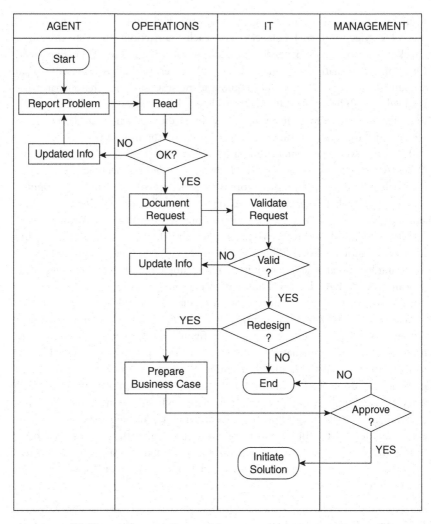

FIGURE 4.2 IT Change Request Process Map

highlight. These handoffs are often a source of problems in a service system due to various professional jargon used by personnel in different professions, such as operations professionals and IT professionals. In this case, the process map also highlights various approvals and places where incomplete information needs to be resubmitted. The analysis of this process map would create the following list of value-added activities, and examples of wasteful activities:

Value-Added Activities: Identification of a problem (Agent), preparation of business case (Operations), determining if re-design is necessary (IT)

Wasteful Activities: Agent contacting customer for clarification (processing inefficiency), operations checking request (review), waiting for agent to update information (delay), agent updating incomplete information (mistake), waiting for IT to validate the request (delay), IT validating request (review, duplication), waiting or operations to update invalid document (delay), operations updating document (mistake), waiting for operations to prepare business case (delay), management approval (review, resource inefficiency), generating a report in improper format (process inefficiency)

Price Quoting Process

A process map for the price quoting process is shown as Figure 4.3. It starts when the customer submits a request for a price quote to a member of the sales team. The information is reviewed before logging the request in the IT system. This system automatically checks for completeness of each required item, then submits the quote to a staff member who oversees collection of necessary information from various departments (only a sample of four departments is shown here). Once the information is gathered, it is entered into the sales quoting system and the quote is generated. If approved by management, it is presented to the customer.

This process was presented using a somewhat ad hoc flowchart, especially where information must be gathered from various departments. Double arrows are used to signify information potentially moving back and forth (i.e., when clarification is needed or additional information is sought). Backtracking in the case of incomplete information is also shown. The analysis of this process map would create the following list of value-added activities, and examples of wasteful activities:

Value-Added Activities: Sales assistance with customer, price quoting software analysis, obtaining information from other functions

Wasteful Activities: Waiting for sales to get updated customer information (delay), getting updated customer information when information is incomplete (mistake), salesforce re-logging a previously incomplete request (duplication; mistake), waiting for information from all other functions (delay), correcting errors in information from other functions (mistakes), entering information into price quoting system (duplication), management approval (review), revising request after rejection form management (mistake), waiting for management approval (delay), waiting for customer to get updated information (delay), all other functions providing information to sales (resource inefficiency), generating request in improper format (process inefficiency)

Blood Testing Process

The urgent care center's blood testing process is shown as Figure 4.4. The process starts with an order from the patient's physician. A technician is notified and, once available, they travel to the patient's bed to draw the

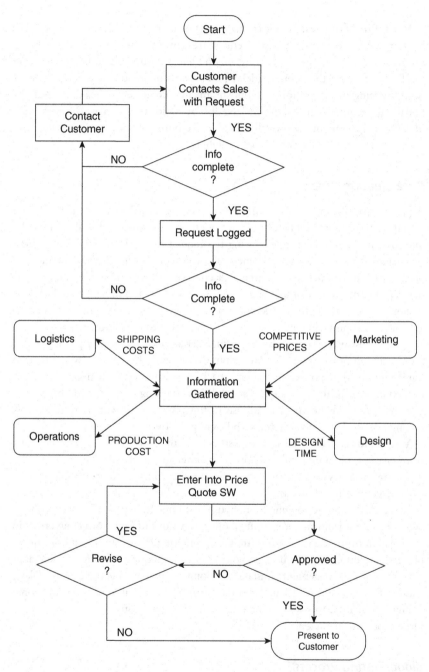

FIGURE 4.3 Price Quoting Process Map

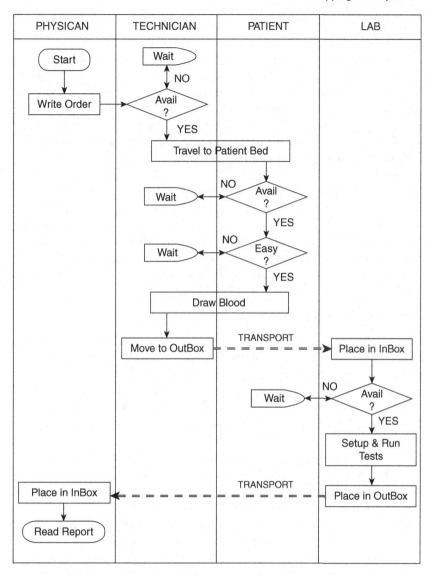

FIGURE 4.4 Blood Testing Process Map

blood. When the patient is ready, blood is drawn. In some cases, help is needed from a senior clinician if the blood is difficult to take, such as when a suitable blood vein is difficult to find. Once the blood is drawn, it is moved to the blood testing laboratory. When the necessary equipment becomes available, the equipment is setup, the blood is tested, a report is generated, and the report is sent to the patient's location for review by the attending physician.

This process is unique because it contains two critical flow units: (a) the patient's blood and (b) information about the types of tests and results of the testing procedure. It is prepared using a swim lane format to show the interaction between various parties involved in the process. Transporting the blood and the reports are shown using a double-line format. The various forms of delays are highlighted because any delay causes a patient to remain in a bed longer than necessary, preventing other patients from being treated promptly. The analysis of this process map would create the following list of value-added activities, and examples of wasteful activities:

Value-Added Activities: Drawing blood, testing blood

Wasteful Activities: Waiting for technician (delay), technician traveling to patient location (resource inefficiency; movement), waiting for patient to be ready for blood draw (delay), waiting for specialist to assist drawing blood (delay), moving blood to outbox (processing inefficiency), moving blood to the lab (movement), waiting for test equipment to become available (delay), setting up testing equipment (process inefficiency), moving written reports to the care facility (movement), redrawing blood (mistake; resource inefficiency)

Data Collection & Analysis

It is helpful to use data to supplement the analysis of a business process. Using data helps focus improvement efforts on problems that limit the ability of the process to provide value for customers. Data collection may be unnecessary when a problem's root cause is apparent. But, even in these cases, analysing data before and then after a process change can be useful to understand the effectiveness of counter-measures. In this section, some basic but powerful data collection and analysis methods are described.

The best way to collect data is first to think ahead to the analysis that is anticipated. The analysis will use displays and numerical calculations that are intuitive and have clear rules of interpretation. Unfortunately, even accurate displays can be confusing or misleading, correct calculations can be misunderstood, and interpretation can be inconsistent or ineffective. Many quality practitioners are trained to apply a standard set of methods, which are sometimes referred to as "Ishikawa's Basic Seven Tools of Quality" [3]. In fact, Kaoru Ishikawa (1915–1989) was a pioneer in the use of simple statistical tools in management that promote analysis and visualization. His seven tools are process maps (covered earlier in this chapter), check sheets, histograms, scatterplots, control charts (covered in a later chapter), cause-and-effect diagrams, and Pareto charts.

Check Sheets

A *check sheet* is used to collect data in a way that includes analysis without the need for additional graphical displays. Check sheets are effective when certain problems or issues are to be tabulated. They can be implemented in settings where little is known at the start of the data collection. Examples of effective application include tabulation of mistakes by type, problems by location, and complaints by category. They use tick marks to tabulate data, or symbols that represent alternatives within the data collection environment. They can be innovative and visually meaningful without the need for sophisticated computerized graphics.

Consider the price quoting process described earlier in this chapter. Delays are common when time needs to be spent correcting errors or waiting for information that is late in arriving. These wasteful activities cause quotes to take longer than necessary which affects the ability of the firm to give customers competitive quotations. A check sheet for collecting data on where in the process these instances are especially prevalent may start with a preliminary list: Customer, Salesperson, Marketing, Design, Logistics, and Operations. Then, using either past records or information from upcoming price quotes, errors and late submissions would be tabulated. This tabulation is done with the letter "L" for a late submission of information and an "E" for a submission containing an error (see Figure 4.5).

The check sheet shows at a glance that errors from the sales team and logistics department are the most likely source of errors, with more errors from the sales team and more late submissions by the logistics department. In addition, submissions from the marketing department have problems when they occur later in the week. These realities would motivate the development of methods to eliminate these particular sources of errors. Many of these methods are described in Chapter 5.

	Monday		Tuesday		Wednesday		Thursday		Friday	
	am	pm	am	pm	am	pm	am	pm	am	pm
Customer	L	L	E			E				
Salesperson	LEEEL EE	ELE	EEEL	EEE	ELEEL LEE	E	EEL		LEEE	
Marketing	E	EL		EEL		LL		LLEL	LLLEL LL	EELEE LLL
Design	E		L	E						
Logistics		LLEEL LLELL EL		LLLL		LLELL LL	LE	ELLLL LLEE		
Operations		EL	LE		LL	L	L	LEL	L	

FIGURE 4.5 Check Sheet: Source of Price Quoting Errors (L=Late, E=Error)

Cause-and-effect (Fishbone) Diagrams

A *cause-and-effect diagram* is also known as a fishbone diagram (due to its shape) or an Ishikawa diagram (due to its inventor). It is a convenient way to display a myriad of information that represents the combined knowledge of many stakeholders who are involved in the operation of the business process. The "head" of each diagram is an *effect*, such as a mistake or error. The "bone" is potential *causes* that are listed using a hierarchical structure that is similar to the bones of a fish. It can easily be updated as more becomes known about the process.

Consider the financial auditing process, where invalid transactions are common but their root cause has not been identified. By interviewing auditors, clients, client IT personnel, and bankers, a list of potential causes of invalid transactions was compiled. Figure 4.6 shows the cause-and-effect diagram, which helps all stakeholders understand potential causes in an intuitive manner. It is organized by 5 main categories of causes: method, client, outsiders, IT, and management.

Short descriptors are used to list each potential cause of an invalid transaction in order to keep the display from appearing too complex. For example, under the management branch, "Dept. Barriers" refers to all problem associated with how the variation departments and functions interact. It would likely include different types of miscommunications (such as terms used) or differences in priorities causing some departments to lack the urgency necessary to provide accurate information quickly.

Pareto Charts

A *Pareto chart* is a well-established mechanism for focusing an analyst's attention on the issues that have the greatest impact on the business process. It is based on the so-called 80/20 principle proposed by Vilfredo Pareto (1848–1923).

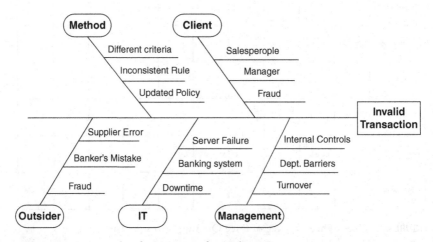

FIGURE 4.6 Cause-and-Effect Diagram for Auditing Process

Pareto noticed that 20% of Italians owned 80% of the land in Italy. In business, a similar disproportion exists when one compares causes to effects. For example, if mistakes are tabulated, a few types of mistakes will likely be responsible for the majority of mistakes made in the firm. When used as a tool to analyse data from a business process, the Pareto chart is designed to focus attention on those causes that have the most impact on performance.

Consider an apartment broker located in a University town that assists students in finding suitable apartments. The company uses the messaging platform WeChat to interact with its customers. It includes a website with apartment lists and an on-line application. It also arranges visits to apartments for students, develops lease contracts, and arranges for rental payments. The support group of the company responds to questions sent using WeChat. The subject of each message is categorized and tabulated every quarter. A Pareto chart for the least three months is shown in Figure 4.7, which lists the subjects according to their frequency. Its left vertical axis shows the number of messages while the right vertical axis shows the cumulative percentage.

The Pareto chart shows that the top 2 of the 12 categories of questions (17% of the categories) accounted for about 60% of the messages. The largest number of WeChat messages concerns the on-line application. This result should motivate the firm to give highest priority to improving this aspect of the service, which could contain confusing entries or terms that many students do not understand. It is notable that the second most popular category is the "other" category. This result is unfortunate because nothing can be done to reduce these questions without collecting more data on their specifics. It is not uncommon for data collection systems to lack the types of updates necessary to keep the information highly relevant.

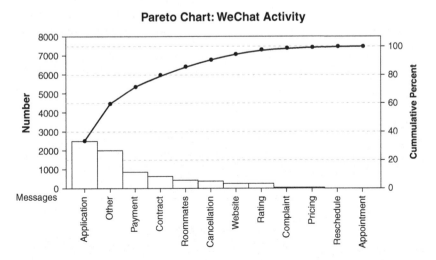

FIGURE 4.7 Pareto Chart Example

Histograms

When the data are measurements that fall on a continuous scale, a *histogram* is useful to display their variation. In a business process providing a service, these data most often consist of time to complete certain tasks. Other examples include customer characteristics (e.g., age, income, etc.), billing amounts, and characteristics of tangible items that accompany the service (e.g., temperature of food). For example, consider data collected from the IT update approval process described earlier in this chapter. The time to either approve or deny an IT change is shown in Figure 4.8. In the histogram, the frequency (number of occurrences) is shown for ranges of data, where the midpoint of the range is used to label the horizontal axis. For example, there were 7 occurrences when the processing time was between 10 and 16 data (this is the bar centered at 13 days).

An analyst would note that the histogram shows a wide range of potential processing times. Most of the processing times fall somewhere between 10 days and 40 days. A statistically sophisticated reader may be interested in the average (24.7 days) and the standard deviation (7.8 days). We also see that the pattern of variation follows the well known bell shape, referred to as the normal distribution of data. It should be emphasized that the histogram does not account for timing. Hence, it is only accurate when a process generating the data is operating in a stable (i.e., unchanging) manner. Stability can be confirmed with control chart, which is discussed in Chapter 11.

Scatterplots

In a quest to diagnose the cause of a problem, a quality analyst often compares data sets. A scatterplot is a well-known display for determining if a relationship exists between two data sets. For example, the scatter plot in Figure 4.9 shows the relationship between the age of an admitted patient and their length of stay (LOS, in days) at a hospital. Each of the points plotted represents one patient.

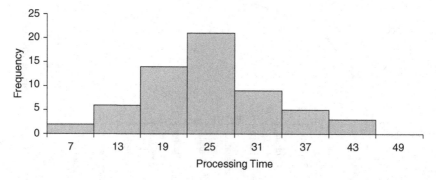

FIGURE 4.8 Processing Time in Days

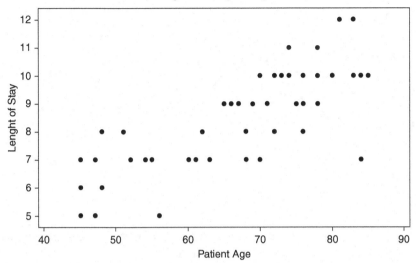

FIGURE 4.9 Scatter Plot for Hospital LOS Data

The display should be scaled to "zoom in" on the points. When data sets contain many sets of multiple points having the same values (e.g., several 60-year-old patients who all stay in the hospital exactly 7 days), the display can be somewhat misleading. In these cases, more sophisticated software packages will show the multiple points by optionally placing the points very close to (but not exactly on) the correct location.

When there appears to be a relationship between the two outcomes, Excel can quantify (and/or display) a number of possible mathematical relationships. These relationships include linear, polynomial, exponential, as well as others. In the case above, an analyst may wish to determine the mathematical relationship between age and LOS. This can be accomplished by showing a trend (in this case, a linear trend appear to be accurate) and associated equation. The trend line equation does take into account repeated pairs of data.

When no relationship exists (or the analyst is unsure that a relationship exists), a trend line should <u>not</u> be added to the scatter plot. For example, consider the relationship between billing amount and days to receipt of the bill shown in Figure 4.10. The scatter plot shows that no relationship exists – as the billing amount increases, there is no change in the days to receipt (by this conclusion, we literally mean that no important relation exists – there may be a very small but unimportant relationship). In a case like this, where the analyst concludes that no relationship exists, it is best not to include a trend line. A trend line will necessarily

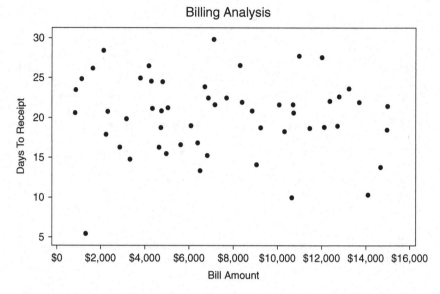

FIGURE 4.10 Scatter Plot for Billing Department

show an up or down movement, due to the randomness of the data. By including the line on the chart, a viewer may be misinformed and react inappropriately. Trend lines can also be misleading when a true, but nonlinear, relationship exists.

Summary & Key Takeaways

A process cannot be improved without first being well-understood. By displaying the activities that occur during the operation of a business process, an analyst or project team will set the stage for effective analysis. Process maps can change the focus of an analysis from assessing blame to finding solutions due to their objective and impersonal nature. By identifying the activities that deliver value and uncovering activities that are wasteful, the project team can effectively make changes that improve its ability to satisfy customers. In summary, the key takeaways from Chapter 4 are:

(1) A process map takes many forms; its usefulness is enhanced when the format highlights the types of problems that typically exist.
(2) The analysis of a process map should focus on the activities that add value as well as the activities that are wasteful.
(3) Wasteful activities fall into categories; knowing these categories is helpful for determining those activities that do not add value for customers.
(4) To supplement the analysis of business process activities, the use of data can help focus attention on where problems have the largest effect.

(5) Basic "tools of quality" can be used to visualize process performance without the need for sophisticated data analysis routines.

Discussion Questions

An executive job-placement service helps companies find qualified candidates for high-level positions. An important process is job specification, consisting of the following activities: (a) answering call from client and discussing appropriateness of position, (b) scheduling a meeting with the client, (c) rescheduling the meeting because of an illness, (d) preparing introductory presentation for client, (d) driving to client location, (e) waiting for a late client, (f) meeting with client to discuss job requirements, (g) driving back to the office, (h) calling a client to confirm confusing information, (i) preparing job specifications, (j) sending job specifications to a client for review, (k) revising job specifications based on client feedback, (l) sending job specifications to the client for review, (m) client leaves voice mail indicating satisfaction with job specifications.

(1) Classify each of the activities as value-added or wasteful.
(2) Assume that the placement process is taking too long. How can a cause-and-effect diagram be used to help the business process manager? Provide an example with at least 12 entries that could be found in a fishbone diagram.
(3) After identifying the possible cause through a cause-and-effect diagram, which tool should the business process manager use to collect performance data and find out the priority of the cause needing to be solved? What is the reason you chose this tool?
(4) After collecting the data, which tool would you recommend the business process manager to use for confirming the positive relationship between effect and cause? What is the reason you recommend this tool?

References

1 Shingo S. *A study of the Toyota production system*. Milwaukee, WI: Productivity Press; 1989.
2 Maleyeff J. Exploration of internal service systems using lean principles. *Management Decision*. 2006; 44(5):674–89.
3 Ishikawa K. *Guide to quality control*. 2nd ed.. White Plains, NY: Quality Resources; 1986.

5

WASTE REMOVAL

The Five Whys and Finding Root Cause

The analysis of a process map identifies activities that are wasteful. That being stated, their elimination should not consist of a quick solution that offers only a temporary respite. For example, consider an architectural firm where young architects make errors in proposals at disproportionate rates compared to their more senior colleagues. Errors will be reduced by requiring that each proposal by first-year architects be reviewed by a senior architect before submission to clients. However, the time to write and deliver the proposal will be increased and resource inefficiencies will be created by using senior architects to act, in effect, as inspectors. The best approach is to find ways to eliminate the possibility of the mistake happening, or at least reducing its likelihood. Alternative approaches to removing wasteful activities associated with errors in proposals are discussed below.

Care must also be taken to avoid addressing problem symptoms rather than problem causes. For these reasons, a structured root cause analysis (RCA) should be followed. Root causes of problems in a business process can be attributed to humans, technologies, workplaces, or systems. System causes would encompass the organizational structure, employee inventive systems, management practices, procedures, policies, and work methods. The quality leader W. Edwards Deming (1900–1993) famously stated "I should estimate that in my experience most troubles and most possibilities for improvement add up to the proportions something like this: 94% belongs to the system (responsibility of management) ..." Even if one is inclined to disagree with Deming, it is clear that a RCA should not start with assuming that a worker is to blame for a problem.

A popular approach to finding root cause is referred to as the *five whys*. This method is iterative in that it uncovers root causes by successively asking "why" until a root cause is identified. This method, in effect, explores cause-and-effect relationships in a step-by-step manner. For example, consider a firm where employee attendance at certain optional training courses has decreased in recent months. A typical solution would be to send out reminders, but this action would make the process include more non-value-added activities. The five whys may proceed as follows:

1. Why are many employees not attending a training class for which they registered? Because of conflicts in employees' work schedules.
2. Why? Because their schedule changes after they register for the course.
3. Why? Because they are required to register far in advance.
4. Why? Because the training department wants to optimize trainers' time and cost.
5. Why? Because the firm requires that the training company needs to fill classes to make a suitable profit.

At this point, it would be clear that any solution should involve evaluating the training company and its practices in light of the requirements imposed by the firm. The intent would be to shorten the lead time between course registration and course delivery.

Applying the five whys also helps prevent members of a project team from implementing solutions in a biased manner. The answers need to be based on facts, not opinions. At Toyota, a method known as *genchi genbutsu* (typically translated as *go and see*) is employed [1]. Project team members would go to the source. In the case of a business process it would mean to go to the department that operates the process and directly observe its operation. Below, additional examples are provided corresponding to each business process described in Chapters 3 and 4.

Financial Audit Process

In a financial auditing process, data show that the time to issue bank letters is longer than expected. The five whys may proceed as follows:

1. Why does it take so long to issue a bank letter? Because many of the initial bank letter drafts are incomplete.
2. Why? Because they do not contain the type of account in question.
3. Why? Because the financial transaction system lists the account number but not the account type.
4. Why? Because it is not a necessary item in their system.

At this point, we see that the root cause is due to important information not being included in the financial transaction system. If the system cannot be readily updated to include this information, auditors should take action to have this information readily available at the beginning of future audits.

IT Change Request Process

In an IT change request process, data show that change requests take a very long time to complete. The five whys may proceed as follows:

1. Why does it take so long to complete many requests? Because it takes a long time for IT personnel to evaluate the business case submitted by operations.
2. Why? Because there are inconsistencies in how the business cases are written.
3. Why? Because many different operating personnel create business cases.
4. Why? Because it is not a frequent activity and it is often assigned to new workers, including interns.

At this point, we see the root cause is the lack of urgency at the operations department. Leadership should get involved to incentivize the operations department to give priority to change requests, or methods should be employed to make development of business cases significantly easier.

Price Quoting Process

In a price quoting process, data shows that many quotes are rejected early in the process. The five whys may proceed as follows:

1. Why are so many quotes rejected early? Because customers' input include incorrect information.
2. Why? Because they do not know the meaning of certain terms.
3. Why? Because we use jargon unique to our business.

At this point, we see the root cause involves terminology used to convey information from the firm to its customers. Changing the terminology used by the firm when requesting information from customers should be considered.

Blood Testing Process

In a blood testing process, data shows that patients occupy a bed for a very long time, limiting the capacity of the ED for other patients. The five whys may proceed as follows:

1. Why are beds occupied when no treatment is taking place? Because the blood testing process take a long time.
2. Why? Because in many cases physicians do not know that lab test results are available for review.
3. Why? Because they need to log into the system to see if the report is there and they do not take this action very frequently.
4. Why? Because they are busy treating other patients.

At this point, we see the root cause is the requirement that the physicians take specific and potentially unnecessary action to check if test results are available. A mechanism should be implemented to notify physicians in more appropriate ways.

Waste Removal: Achieving BCF by Being Smarter

The *better, cheaper, faster* (BCF) mantra has traditionally been used to guide operations. It seeks to optimize three distinctly different performance categories: better quality, cheaper costs, and faster service. Over the years, many managers have taken action to improve one of the three categories while trying not to sacrifice performance in the other two categories. But these cases often became a "pick two" exercise, whereby one goal is sacrificed to improve the others. For example, an emphasis on improving the "better" category may be approached by instituting more detailed inspections that make the process take longer to complete. The emphasis in this chapter will be making *smart* decisions that would improve all three categories or, at a minimum, improve one or two categories without decreasing effectiveness in another category.

The best example may be the reaction to a business process that generates too many mistakes. An unwise approach would be to assign a senior manager to review each report before it is published. Although this approach may reduce errors in published reports, it will add considerably to the time it takes to complete the process. By using one of the methods discussed below, a smarter approach would be to eliminate the root cause of the mistakes.

When removing wasteful activities, many (especially younger) workers may offer suggestions to automate certain activities, which would require an IT application. Although IT solutions may be effective, they will generally require many changes to the process to accommodate the new technology. These ideas should not be discounted, but their development should include redesign of the entire process flow to ensure that no new problems are introduced (i.e., unintended consequences).

Smarter approaches to reducing waste in a business process take many forms. In the remainder of this section, three general approaches are discussed – those that adapt ideas that work well in services that share common traits, those that adapt ideas that work well in manufacturing, and those that make use of Lean methods.

Learning from Similar Processes

In Chapter 2, business processes were classified according to their transformation (physical, physiological, exchange, informational, locational, and storage). Business processes that have transformations in common may also have problems and solutions in common, even if the process is seemingly different. For example, the storage transformation can be found in each of the following services: hotels (keeping housed customers comfortable), hospitals (keeping admitted patients healthy), freight (keeping stored merchandise undamaged), and a pre-school (keeping children safe). For this transformation, hotel managers likely have the most expertise because it represents the primary focus of their business. Accordingly, many hospital administrators have adapted ideas from hotels to make patient stays more pleasant. Owners of pre-schools would have little or no expertise with respect to this transformation. Hence, they would benefit from learning more about other processes whose transformation is location-related.

Another form of classification discussed in Chapter 2 concerned business process types: troubleshooting, gathering, evaluation, analysis, planning, and consultation. Consider these business processes that are all classified as troubleshooting: an internal help desk (for diagnosing and solving IT problems), a hospital's emergency room (for diagnosing and treating patients), and a third-party call center (for helping customers solve billing problems). In each of these cases, quick and accurate diagnosis is important. Hospitals use electronic health records (EHR) to record each patient's symptoms and treatment plan, which also assist in developing better health care solutions for all patients. Help desks and call centers would be well served by studying how implementing EHR can improve their firm's operations and inform designers of customer likes and dislikes.

Understanding common traits of seemingly dissimilar business processes can also be done less formally. In these cases, the analyst should focus on activities, rather than the overall process, in order to avoid limiting their set of solutions. For example, a hospital's trauma team copied the choreographed pit stops of Italy's Formula One racing team. This team understood that the process followed by a pit crew, involving a group of up to 20 specialists descending on a racecar, in which each member performs a specific task quickly while not interfering with other members, requires strong planning and communication. This process is not unlike an accident victim arriving by ambulance to an emergency room, where teams of physicians, nurses, and technicians work together to diagnose and stabilize a patient.

Mistakes are also common when workers become distracted. Solutions to this problem can be found in a policy required by the U.S. Federal Airline Administration, known as the "sterile cockpit" rule. This requirement states that during critical times such as takeoff and landing of aircraft, crew members may only perform the duties required for this task with no other activities, conversations, or other forms of distraction. A requirement similar to the sterile cockpit would hold promise in other processes where distractions cause problems, such as product inspections, copy-editing, or security screening.

Lessons from Manufacturing

Some experts suggest that applying Lean methods to services should start by applying methods to those services that are similar to a manufacturing process, such as the processing of an invoice. This approach is flawed. To understand why, a few Lean production methods will be explained. In a Lean production setting, the creation of a production line based on *takt time* is often performed [1]. Here, production lines are designed as a series of activities (like the original Ford assembly line) so that their output rate matches the expected demand rate. During each unit of takt, one item is made at each activity. The ability to operate a takt time production system requires highly reliable processes and constant activity times. Because constant activity times are rare in a service process, there is no need to teach this method to workers outside of manufacturing environments. The simulation in Chapter 2 illustrates the poor results obtained if this approach is attempted in a service process.

Many other Lean production methods are used to carefully control inventory. The most popular method in this regard is *kanban* [2]. Here, ordering of parts is initiated when they need to replenish parts that are delivered to customers rather than based on a forecast of projected needs. Because businesses rarely have inventory as an important element of the service they provide, kanban need not be taught to service workers or business process managers. But, some services include tangible items (such as food, literature, or supplies) and kanban can be used to control these items.

Some service processes, such as a blood testing process, include *setup activities* and would benefit from a Lean production method designed to reduce resource downtime called *Single-Minute Exchange of Die* [3]. Consider a blood testing process where testing machines need to be prepared by first cleaning, then entering patient information and testing parameters. SMED concepts can be employed by starting the setup while previous tests are running – for example, the laboratory could be notified when the blood order is written, which is sooner than they are currently notified. With this information, the laboratory manager can more intelligently manage their devices, lowering costs (by combining patient tests that use similar setups), and speeding up the service by starting setups before the blood arrives.

Using Lean Methods

Many of the methods discussed above can be described as ad hoc methods because they rely on process managers to think "outside the box." Creative or innovative thinking can enhance this exercise. In most cases, it would be better for a project team to apply a group of methods that are well known to reduce waste. Lean practitioners apply a number of approaches in this regard. In the sections below, typical Lean methods are described, with examples that apply to the four business process examples that have been covered in this and previous chapters. The Lean methods discussed below are well known to practitioners, and they have been presented in a variety of popular books [1, 4, 5].

Standard Work

Unless special circumstances exist, there will be a singular best way to perform a task within a business function, called *standard work*. It differs somewhat from *best practice*, which is often applied to an entire process instead of a particular task. A standard work method helps to ensure good quality and consistent task durations for similar tasks. Developing standard work methods should be the joint responsibility of managers and workers. Workers have first-hand knowledge of the job and its customers, and resistance to change is less likely when the workers play a role in developing new or revised procedures.

Standard work in a business process can take many forms, including a template, checklist, consistent training, customer segmentation, reservations, guided customer flow, and a common customer request form. Consider the operation of a call center that responds to customer inquiries. Standard work can help make the call center more effective by enforcing a script that the operator follows to ensure consistency and completeness of service. In addition, standard work can maximize the call center's value to the organization by setting up a standard procedure to tabulate, categorize, and periodically report information gathered from customers.

Templates are an effective tool to implement standard work for the creation of proposals, business cases, reports, and other documents. They are especially useful when customers seek consistency in the format and content of the documents they receive. Standard approaches are very helpful when the documents are written by a variety of workers within an organization. Finally, communicating the results of quantitative analyses can be improved by standard approaches, such as posters that follow similar formats.

Standard Work for the IT Change Request Process

The earlier application of the five whys discovered that the prevalence of new and inexperienced writers led to inconsistencies in business case documents. This root cause resulted in many business cases being returned from the IT department to the operations department for revision. This infrequent task is done by new workers in a rotational program as a way to familiarize them with the operations of the firm. But, the combination of an infrequent task and inexperienced workers causes many inconsistencies in the report's content, format, and accuracy.

A standard template can simplify the development of a business case, while creating consistency from one case to another and across various workers. A template includes requirements that certain sections be completed with instructions of how to populate each section of the business case document. It would include, for example, an executive summary section with important authors, stakeholders, contact information, and summaries of scope and justification. Quantitative estimates of customers impacted, the nature of the impact, and potential benefits would be calculated using a consistent algorithm, with little chance of bias or subjectivity. Customers (i.e., IT personnel) will appreciate their consistency, and templates are not costly to implement.

The 5S Method

The Lean method called *5S* consists of principles that ensure an organized workplace, where paperwork, tools and other items necessary to perform an activity are readily available. With this approach, no time is wasted finding what is needed to perform an activity and mistakes are reduced. The names of the 5S's have Japanese origins, but a set of similar English words has been suggested. The Japanese (and near-equivalent English terms) are:

Seiri (sort): Collect the items needed to do the work and remove everything else.

Seiton (straighten): Identify the best location for each required item.

Seiso (shine): Keep the workplace clean and clear of clutter.

Seiketsu (standardize): Create a procedure for making use of each required item.

Shitsuke (sustain): Familiarize each worker with the procedure for using each item, and ensure anything that compromises the procedure is quickly identified.

An example of the application of 5S's is a "shadow box," where the location of each tool is embedded in a container using foam cutouts. Other examples include organizing tools in the order they will be used (e.g., during a repair operation or during surgery in a hospital), sorting trash at its origin (to eliminate the need to sort later), using different colored slips in a bank for deposits and withdrawals, and creating an easy to navigate web site.

5S for the Financial Audit Process

The earlier application of the five whys discovered that financial transaction confirmation was delayed because the type of account was not included in the financial ledgers. Each year, auditors were forced to make inquiries with clients and others to gather this information, which was required on the bank letters. This situation, in isolation, might be considered absurd. Why is it that, year after year, auditors waste time with this task? It is because of the tendency of an individual worker to consider certain non-value-added activities to be a necessary part of their job. They may not be aware that other auditors waste time in a similar manner or that, in previous years, precisely the same wasteful tasks were performed. In addition, supervisors observing the auditor at work easily cannot distinguish time spent on wasteful instead of value-added activities.

As a result of implementing the 5S method, auditors would know where to find the account types quickly. An application is described below:

Seiri (sort): Identify all of the accounts and, for each account, where their type would be located. Ensure that the workplace is free of materials not needed for auditing tasks.

Seiton (straighten): Determine where the list of accounts with their types will be kept, perhaps using a color coded list to separate account types to make them easier to find.

Seiso (shine): Keep the work area clean and clear of clutter, so that the standard list can be found quickly.

Seiketsu (standardize): Create and document a standard approach for each worker to find the account types. Place an instruction sheet in each auditor's workplace. If the list needs to be moved, be sure to have a way to ensure that it is replaced in its proper location.

Shitsuke (sustain): Ensure that each new auditor is aware of the 5S system, and create a mechanism for identifying problems that may occur in the future. For example, workers may be instructed to write a post-it note for new accounts that are not included in the standard list.

Although some time would be spent setting up the 5S method, little or no costs would be added on an ongoing basis. Its benefits include improved timeliness of the business process, fewer mistakes, and reduced auditor frustration.

Poka-yoke

Poka-yoke, a Japanese term meaning *mistake proofing*, is a way to ensure that an activity cannot be performed incorrectly. Although poka-yoke can be thought of as an element of standard work development, it generally requires a physical mechanism. When implementing poka-yoke, a practitioner may start by developing ways to reduce the likelihood of a mistake. A better, but more challenging, approach would be to develop a capability that prevents the mistakes from happening. Ideally, poka-yoke would guarantee that a mistake cannot be made.

Often, common sense approaches can form the basis of poka-yoke. Some everyday examples of poka-yoke are filing cabinets in which only one drawer can be opened at a time (to prevent topping of the cabinet), placing your car's key with an item so you do not forget to take it with you, tethering a gasoline cap to the car frame (to prevent leaving the cap at the pump), and egg cartons (to prevent miscounting or damage). Although information technology can be helpful, it should be carefully implemented so that all mistakes are avoided. For example, the use of an identification barcode on a customer's request form can reduce the occurrence of misidentifying customers. However, this system should also ensure that misidentifications are not possible before the barcode is created.

Poka-yoke for the Price Quoting Process

The earlier application of the five whys discovered that differences in terminology caused delays due to mistakes and call-backs for clarification. The price quoting process is dominated by the gathering of information from various business functions, and each function consists of a group of professionals with diverse knowledge and terminology. For example, consider the following functions and some terms that may confuse others: engineering design (heuristics, algorithm), logistics (waybill, fill rate), marketing (bounce rate, lead), and operations (yield, nonconformance). Acronyms commonly known to one group may not be known to others, such as: engineering design (FEA, ANN, BOM), logistics (BOL, WMS, VMI), marketing (CRM, CTA, CTR), and operations (JIT, SPC, ISO).

A number of poka-yoke approaches can be implemented to reduce delays caused by terminology that is communicated across functions. Due to the intangible nature of the information being transmitted across functions, an IT-based solution could reduce or eliminate these delays. For example, the design of an IT interface that automatically targets certain terms, acronyms, or abbreviations may autocorrect to an established word or phrase.

Poka-yoke can also be incorporated as an element of other Lean methods. For example, standard templates could be developed for responding to price quote information requests. Within these templates, only jargon familiar with all functions would be used. Personnel would be trained to avoid certain terms, acronyms, or abbreviations. For example, the Joint Commission (that accredits healthcare organizations) maintains a "do not use" list of abbreviations, such as "u" for unit, because it can be mistaken for the numbers zero or four when hand-written quickly.

Visual Controls

Visual controls, also called the visual workplace, involves the communication of important information in a shared and commonly understood format. They enhance inter-process communication so that everyone has a common focus on doing the highest priority work properly. A typical example is the display of all current open tickets in a help desk service, with the status of each job or project using a color code to signify its status. Visual controls work best when processes are co-located, although IT systems can be developed to provide visual controls to processes that are geographically dispersed.

Other common examples of visual controls are clearly delineated locations for tools and equipment, as well as clearly labelled walking paths to assist workers or visitors in a facility. An interesting application of visual workplace principles is the use of poster presentations to show improvement projects, which can motivate employee participation in future projects. Another application of visual controls is posting a cause-and-effect diagram to communicate potential problem causes. The incorporation of post-it notes can enhance the updating of information, list problems as they are encountered, or show real time information flow through a process.

Visual Controls in the Blood Testing Process

The earlier application of the five whys discovered that delays in the blood testing process occurred because of the ineffective way in which physicians were notified about the availability of lab results. Each physician was required to log into a medical record system to check if blood test results were ready for review. A better mechanism needs to be implemented whereby the availability of completed blood test results is made more explicit to each attending physician.

Various options of the visual controls concept can be implemented in an urgent care center. One option is to employ a method similar to that used in a restaurant to notify servers that food is ready to deliver to customers. If test results are delivered electronically from the blood testing laboratory, laboratory personnel could trigger the notification. Finally, a simple light-coded display can be set up in the treatment area, where a light (for the designated physician) is turned on when they have test results available. In fact, creation of an audio signal and the light code together could be considered. This system could be expanded to include test results generated from images (MRI, X-rays, etc.) or other diagnostic tests.

Summary & Key Takeaways

Reducing the time spent on non-value-added activities will have a positive effect on the ability of a business process to satisfy customers. This chapter detailed various approaches used to remove or reduce the number of wasteful activities. Business process managers and workers should be cognizant of the presence of wasteful activities, even though they appear to be a normal aspect of their jobs. In summary, the key takeaways from Chapter 5 are:

1. The root cause of problems should be found using methods such as the five whys, and improvements should be focused on root causes rather than visible symptoms.
2. Achieving better, cheaper, faster (BCF) should be considered one goal, rather than three separate goals. Improving BCF is accomplished by being smarter about reducing waste in the business process.
3. The ability to make improvements in a business process by identifying similar processes (even those in dissimilar firms) is helpful because others may have already solved the problem at hand.
4. Lean methods can be used to reduce wasteful activities in a business process, including standard work, 5S, poka-yoke, and visual controls.
5. When applying Lean methods, the intent should be to guarantee that the process provides effective solutions for customers in as short a time as possible.

Discussion Questions

1. Consider a process where many internal reports that tabulate environmental records written by the firm's Environmental Health & Safety (EH&S) department are returned due to errors found after publication. The five whys were derived as follows:

   - Why do the reports contain many errors? Because the writers tend to make errors concerning current regulations.
   - Why? Because the writers are unaware of changes in regulations.
   - Why? Because their training does not include coverage of relevant regulations for each department.
   - Why? Because regulations change frequently and content training would quickly become obsolete.

   What is the root cause? Which employees (writers, trainers, readers, etc.), if any, should be held responsible for the problem?
2. If a service manager wants his service providers to be flexible when satisfying customer needs, is it always a bad idea to implement standard work?
3. You work for an Italian restaurant and your job is to deliver pizzas to local homes and apartments. Your boss asks you to implement poka-yoke by calling each customer before you arrive to confirm their address. Why is this <u>not</u> a good example of an effective Lean method?

References

1 Liker JK. *The Toyota way*. New York: McGraw-Hill; 2004.
2 Japan management association. *Kanban: just-in-time at Toyota*. Revised. Portland, Oregon, USA: Productivity Press; 1989.

3 Shingo S. *A study of the Toyota production system*. Milwaukee, WI: Productivity Press; 1989.

4 Protzman C, Whiton F, Kerpchar J, Lewandowski C, Stenberg S, Grounds P. *The lean practitioner's field book*. New York: CRC Press; 2016. 15 pp.

5 Womack JP, Jones DT. *Lean thinking*. New York: Simon and Schuster; 1996.

6

CONSUMPTION MAPPING

Service Providers & Customers

Every service provider appreciates the importance of customer satisfaction. However, it is common for service providers to lack a fundamental understanding of their customers' expealerience. There can also be major differences in the background of service providers and their customers as it relates to the service offering. After all, the customer requests the service because they lack the ability or inclination to perform the service themselves. This situation can lead to significant disconnects between service providers' performance and customers' expectations. This effect is often customer confusion and frustration, along with potential for a less than satisfactory service outcome.

The customer experience is addressed in this chapter. A form of analysis is presented that, although similar to process mapping, is designed to focus solely on the actions and reactions of customers. Such an analysis helps find ways to increase value for customers. For example, by understanding jet engine customers' needs, many manufacturers now provide maintenance and repair services to supplement their product offerings. Some automobile insurance companies add value by offering free quotes to customers, including their competitor's prices.

Service providers often lack an appreciation for the actions that customers take just prior to contacting the service, including confusion when informing the service provider of their needs. For example, before contacting a troubleshooting service, the customer may need to diagnose the problem, attempt simple solutions, find the service's contact information, and explain the problem to the service provider. What customers do after the service is completed can also be unknown to the service provider. Consider the following vignette:

> After completing her first full year in the accounting department of the Sterling Equipment Corporation, Ellen became eligible for her employers' education benefit. She applied to a local business school, where she was accepted as a part-time MBA student. During the first week of the service operations management course, her professor introduced the semester-long assignment. It required each student to choose a service they provide as part of their normal workload. The project consisted of a critical evaluation of the service and a set of improvement recommendations. Ellen chose the standard "third day" monthly accounting reports that she helped to complete (their name stems from their deadline, which is the third day of each month after the month being reported).
>
> The first phase of the project required each student to meet with a customer of the service to ascertain their needs, and to inquire about what pleased and displeased them about the current service. Ellen met with Dave, the senior vice president of operations, who began by telling Ellen, "I have been in this position 11 years and you are the first person from accounting ever to ask me about the accounting statements." This surprised Ellen because she was under the assumption that she was trained in accordance with the needs of her internal customers.
>
> Dave explained that he was happy with the accuracy of the statements and that her department rarely missed the "third day" deadline. He was also pleased that her department responded quickly when he had questions. While not entirely displeased, he did explain that getting the statements a day earlier would suit him because his assistant needs about a day to run some special calculations. He went on to explain the nature of the additional calculations. Ellen realized that, given her access to raw data, she could easily make the additional calculations as part of the routine reporting system without delaying report delivery.

The vignette illustrates that understanding how customers interact with a service can motivate service providers to find ways that will add value for their customers. Additional value can be provided to customers by modifying the service offered, in this case based on what customers do after the service is completed. In some cases, this change would require a new process which customers have not yet requested, such as when an automobile insurance company provides its customers with repairs or a replacement vehicle. Potential for adding value also occurs before and during the service process when uncertainty, confusion, and frustration are an unfortunate aspect of the customer experience.

The Customer Experience

To fully understand the customer experience when using a product or interacting with a service provider, a deep immersion is necessary. Deep immersion goes beyond satisfaction surveys and focus groups, which require a degree of familiarity that biases the information obtained. For example, when all laundry detergents came in powder form, customers learned to dissolve a certain amount of detergent in water before loading clothes. This activity was expected by consumers and therefore they did not complain of its necessity. Today, laundry detergent is most often sold in liquid form, precluding the need for pre-dissolving the detergent. Directly observing consumers using this product was vital to obtaining this detailed understanding of their experience.

Economists appreciate that consumer decision making consists of a combination of rational (i.e., analytical) and behavioral (i.e., emotional) elements. Rational decisions are based on measureable benefits that can often be expressed as a mathematical or other objective principle. In reality, however, most consumers include emotional elements, such as risk avoidance, when making decisions. A similar concept applies to customers of a business process. Their experience encompasses both a rational component and an emotional element.

Service providers should appreciate that each customer evaluates service value using both a rational and an emotional lens. They should realize that the emotional aspect will likely vary from customer to customer. For example, one customer using an IT interface to provide inputs may be confused by certain terminology while another customer may be comfortable with the interface. These differences are also based on expectations. In most cases, common emotions will likely exist across most customers.

According to Barlow and Maul [1] customers are rarely neutral about the service they receive because an emotional response dominates their satisfaction level. Berry et al [2] stated that "Companies must manage the emotional component of experiences with the same rigor they bring to the management of products and service functionality." Service providers who create positive emotional experiences will maintain goodwill with customers that can help overcome service deficiencies. Consider the following four scenarios:

- A customer has a **bad** rational and **bad** emotional experience (e.g., getting bad advice from an unfriendly call center representative). This scenario is obviously the worst-case outcome for the business process manager. Service providers can expect external customers to defect and internal customers to pressure the firm's leaders to consider outsourcing this service.
- A customer has a **bad** rational and **good** emotional experience (e.g., a courteous IT programmer who makes mistakes): This scenario often results in empathy expressed by customers towards service providers. They will often remain customers in the short term in hopes that the service will improve.

- A customer has a **good** rational and **bad** emotional experience (e.g., waiting all day for a technician to effectively repair a cable TV problem): This scenario can pose future problems for business process managers because customers will be apathetic about the future state of the service. It is especially risky when customers are external because competitive service providers will be considered. Because internal customers are apathetic, there will be no resistance within the firm when outsourcing the business process is under consideration.
- A customer has a **good** rational and **good** emotional experience (e.g., accurate accountant with great professional attitude): This scenario is obviously the best-case outcome for customers. External customers will recommend the service to others. Internal customers will speak positively about the service to others within the firm, improving the reputation and visibility of service managers and providers.

In order to add value for customers, a map that represents the customer experience is useful. A process map is not helpful when studying customers' experiences because it focuses on the activities of service providers rather than actions (and especially the emotions) of customers. Several methods have been proposed to evaluate the customer experience. Shostack [3] (and many others) proposed a *service blueprint* that includes "fail points" (e.g., where the service can fall short of meeting customer needs) and timeframe (e.g., how long it takes to correct the mistake).

A similar approach is referred to as *customer journey mapping*. Service blueprints and customer journey maps typically include three sections: showing the steps followed by customers, showing the "touch points" where customers interact directly with service providers, and the back office operations that are also detailed in process maps. Many of these efforts, however, capture the rational actions but fall short of capturing customers' emotional response. For example, a display showing a customer receiving an invoice needs to indicate potential confusion due to the terminology or organization of the invoice. The actions that can occur if information, such as payment terms, are misunderstood should also be indicated.

The term consumption has also been applied to the customer experience (i.e., the customer *consumes* the service) and *consumption mapping* is used to display the actions and emotions of customers as they consume the service [4]. Whether the display is created in the form of a service blueprint, customer journey map, or consumption map, its effectiveness depends on the accuracy at which it shows customers' emotions. Spraragen and Chan [5] argue convincingly that a service blueprint needs to capture "emotional qualities that the customer experiences during key moments of the service." They add textual annotations to service blueprints that list emotionally-related issues at key locations. Their method can be somewhat limited, such as when many possible emotional reactions exist at many locations in the consumption process. Other potentially useful methods for mapping consumption include photographs, videotapes, and audio interviews with customers as they consume the service. For example, a photo showing a busy person sorting through mail or a video (or audio) of a person interacting with a help desk can be used to analyse consumption.

Consumption Mapping

The best consumption maps will: (a) accurately depict the experience of a typical customer, (b) include "visible wastes" in the consumption process, (c) include frustrations and other forms of "hidden wastes" in the consumption process, and (d) include a format that enables process managers to intuitively understand their customers. Without all of the above, the focus of improvements tends to be on: (a) what is easy to fix, (b) what is already considered important by service providers, (c) what is easiest to measure, or (d) where complaints are focused.

The emotions indicated on a consumption map should be comprehensive but not too complex for viewers to understand. Although many approaches can be developed, the approach described below uses icons to represent specific categories of emotions and other issues affecting the customer experience. The icons would also encompass potential for improving satisfaction by indicating those places where adding value can most likely be accomplished. In the consumption maps presented below, standard icons are used to represent the following:

- Potential satisfaction
- Waiting
- Frustration or other forms of dissatisfaction
- Confusion or uncertainty
- Traveling or moving
- Other emotional aspects specific to the service being mapped (customized icons may be used here)

Consumption appears to a customer as a linear set of steps, because they are the only concerned party and they can only perform one action at a time. Therefore, the basic construction of a consumption map is less complex than a typical process map. It is the displaying of customers' emotional elements that makes the consumption map especially meaningful. The format used below will consist of showing each step using a rectangle with two adjacent sections. The left section will describe the actions taken by the customer and the right section will list icons illustrating the customer's emotions.

Before proceeding, it should be clear to the reader that consumption maps concern the customer. The customer experience will likely begin with the service request, and therefore this aspect of consumption should be included on the consumption map. What the customer does on the output side of the process should also be included. Finally, any situations where the customer interacts with the service provider should be included on the consumption map. In these cases, it makes sense to indicate where in the business process flow these interactions occur.

Financial Audit Consumption Map

A consumption map for a portion of the audit process is shown in Figure 6.1, where the customer is the client. The portion being displayed includes the client's experience after receiving each day's list of questions from auditors. These questions deal with financial transactions about which an auditor has uncertainty or needs additional information. The client will review the list from that day as well as the unaddressed questions from previous days. The consumption map shows other key actions: clarifying some of the questions with auditors, documenting answers to the questions whose answers are readily apparent, creating a subsequent list of complicated questions then meeting with a supervisor, and finally documenting the answers to the remainder of these questions.

Throughout the consumption map, the potential for time delays are dominant (e.g., the time it takes to document the answers to questions or waiting for the meeting with the supervisor). There are several actions where confusion will occur (e.g., due to terminology with which the client is unfamiliar). Dissatisfaction occurs because the client cannot perform their primary responsibilities when addressing auditors' questions. Finally, the time spent travelling to the supervisor's location is also shown.

One opportunity for adding value is noted on the consumption map (shown using the satisfaction icon). During interactions with auditors to clarify questions, the client can gain valuable knowledge about relevant financial regulations. This knowledge should help them in the future. With this characteristic in mind, it would be wise for a service provider to find other opportunities to teach clients more about the regulations.

IT Change Request Consumption Map

A consumption map for the insurance firm's IT change process is shown in Figure 6.2. It concerns the experience of the customer, either a policy holder or a new customer, who identifies what appears to be a problem while navigating the firm's website. The customer contacts their agent or the call center. They describe the problem, and later respond to questions from the agent or other representative of the firm. After the issue is routed to the operations department, they may need to respond to other questions from a service

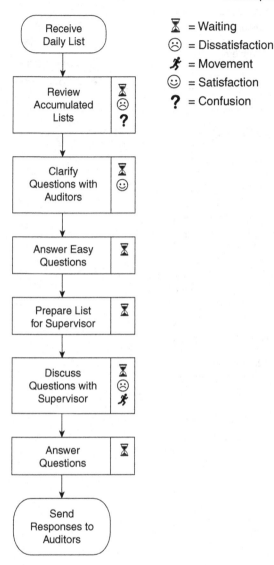

FIGURE 6.1 Financial Audit Consumption Map

provider who needs to develop the business case for creating a solution. The customer may or may not be informed regarding how the issue was resolved.

The process map shows that confusion is the dominant emotion experienced by customers. Confusion begins when the customer needs to determine who needs to be contacted about the problem. Confusion can also exist when they determine how to present the problem to either the agent or the call center.

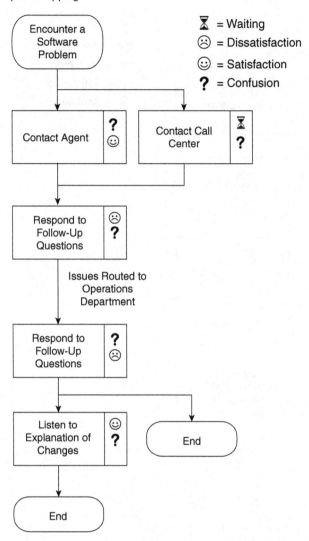

FIGURE 6.2 IT Change Request Consumption Map

They may also be confused during conversations or written communications for someone from the firm, because of the jargon used by either operations personnel (i.e., insurance jargon) or IT staff (i.e., computer jargon). Because the customer is able to continue with other tasks, after reporting the problem, they likely will not consider waiting to be especially troublesome (with the exception of the call center).

The process manager should ensure that those workers interacting with customers are aware of the challenges in talking to someone who is inexperienced with IT in general and with their IT system. The manager can also ensure that customers can quickly determine how to call the agent or call center (perhaps a special telephone number can be provided for reporting software problems). It is noted in the consumption map that the customer may or may not be contacted regarding the solution of the problem. Because this is a potential area for increased satisfaction, the system should have ways to ensure that each customer reporting a software problem is contacted with its reconciliation information, and given thanks for their help.

Price Quoting Consumption Map

A consumption map for the price quoting process is shown in Figure 6.3. Here, the customer is a consumer who seeks to receive pricing information for a customized product. The consumption map begins when the quote is initiated. The consumer starts by identifying a company to make the product. Once one or more potential producers are identified, the consumer contacts the company and provides them with the information they think is required. At that point, or sometime later, they respond to questions from a representative of the manufacturer. This activity may involve clarifications or obtaining additional information (e.g., special material requirements). Then, after a period of time, the consumer receives the price quote and takes appropriate action.

This consumption map shows that the actions of the customer at the beginning of the process are an important predictor of its overall success – the customer needs to select the producer, find their contact information, then present the required inputs. The producer should be aware that they may lose business if they are not identified as a potential producer. This activity may also result in confusion if the jargon is not clearly understood. It may also result in a customer contacting the firm with a request for a product that the firm cannot produce. As the consumption map proceeds, there are many places where the customer needs to wait. The customer's desire for speed should translate as a sense of urgency for all departments involved in delivering the service.

There is also potential to frustrate the customer when answering questions about the product if the service provider does not account for the consumer's ignorance about the firm's business. Finally, there are opportunities to especially please the consumer when, for example, the price quote document includes other information that would be useful to the customer. This information can help the customer understand how to improve their approach to requesting a future quote.

Blood Testing Consumption Map

A consumption map for the urgent care center's blood testing process is shown as Figure 6.4. In this case, the customer is the patient whose blood needs to be

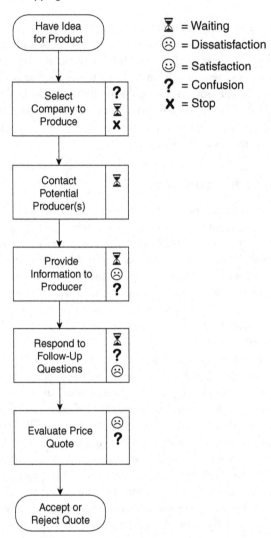

FIGURE 6.3 Price Quoting Consumption Map

tested. The actions of the patient appear relatively straightforward. The patient starts by explaining their symptoms to the physician. After the blood testing order is written, a technician draws blood from the patient. After the test is complete, the physician discusses results with the patient and the treatment plan is explained.

There are aspects of the patient's experience that would be important for the care provider to understand. There are two main potentials for delay – both can add anxiety for a patient who is concerned about their health. There

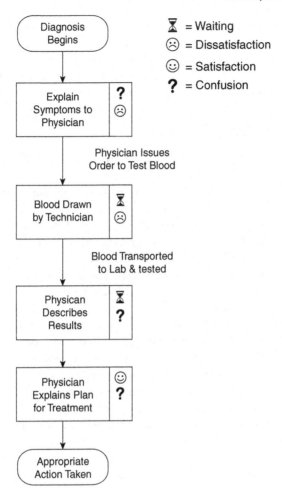

Diagnosis
Begins

⧗ = Waiting
☹ = Dissatisfaction
☺ = Satisfaction
? = Confusion

| Explain Symptoms to Physician | ? ☹ |

Physician Issues
Order to Test Blood

| Blood Drawn by Technician | ⧗ ☹ |

Blood Transported
to Lab & tested

| Physican Describes Results | ⧗ ? |

| Physician Explains Plan for Treatment | ☺ ? |

Appropriate
Action Taken

FIGURE 6.4 Blood Testing Consumption Map

are also activities that can be confusing for the patient, such as when they explain symptoms to the physician or when they are discussing the results and treatment plan. Potential for dissatisfaction exists during the drawing of blood, because this activity can be painful and stressful. Finally, potential for considerable satisfaction can occur during the treatment plan discussion, especially if the physician combines empathy with factual information delivery.

It is worth noting why confusion can exist early in the consumption map. The physician will be processing factual information from a patient through a decision algorithm that is designed to determine the potential for certain diseases or illnesses. However, although the physician may consider the information factual, in fact the patient may not be understanding the questions or be able to estimate important parameters. For example, physicians often ask about the duration of symptoms while patients may not be able to recall precisely when the symptoms started. Physicians should be careful to account for this uncertainty and not give the impression that a patient is less than helpful if they cannot recall certain facts.

Consumption Analysis

Value can be added for customers in several ways, such as making interactions more satisfying, reducing delays, and decreasing the amount of uncertainty, confusion, or frustration. To this end, every service should be thought of as a means to solve a customer's problem. Sometimes the problem-based assumption is clear – such as when a customer approaches a help desk or arrives at an urgent care center. At other times, the problem-based assumption is less obvious. For example, taking a taxi to a sporting event is solving the problem "I need to get to the event." The problem solved by an HR manager identifying suitable job candidates is that "The manufacturing department needs skilled workers." Writing a proposal in response to a request from a funding agency is solving a problem that can be stated as "We need to ensure that the capital we provide is used in appropriate ways that are consistent with our mission."

Womack and Jones [4] refer to waiting and other customer actions while consuming the service as *unpaid work*. Examples of unpaid work are often found at the beginning of the service. In the price quoting system, a customer is required to do the unpaid work of identifying the producer, then finding contact information for the producer's sales representative. Unpaid work also occurs at the end of the service, such as when an executive's assistant spends one day analysing accounting statements to support their department's decisions.

By thinking of the business process's customer as having a problem needing to be solved, the following becomes clear: *The customer wants their specific problem solved completely and quickly, and they don't want to feel confused or frustrated.* Each of these goals is discussed in more detail below.

Solve the Customer's Problem Completely

The effects of not solving a customer's problem completely can often be found at the end of the service. In the vignette presented above, the customer of the monthly accounting reports was required to employ an assistant to manipulate and analyse accounting information gleamed from each monthly report. This is a clear example of not solving a customer's problem completely.

Womack and Jones [4] present an interesting example of a firm that provides IT solutions, Fujitsu Services, who used a unique approach to hire a help-desk provider. Traditionally, providers who offered the lowest cost per call would be the preferred vendor, although other factors would be considered before a final decision was made. Fujitsu's alternative approach was motivated by the desire to solve the customer's problem completely. That is, along with solving the current problem, call center representatives would be encouraged to provide information to educate callers thereby reducing the likelihood of future calls. The traditional cost per call approach would not incentivize this behavior because calls would take longer and, if successful, the number of future calls would be reduced. Fujitsu Services' approach was to ask bidders for a fixed aggregate bid based on a projected call volume. By moving from a variable to a fixed revenue model, the bidder would be incentivized to reduce the number of calls.

Solve the Customer's Problem Quickly

Queues are the main physical manifestation of customers not getting their problem solved quickly. Examples include long lines at checkout, long hold times at a call center, and longer lead time estimates. In effect, anytime a customer is waiting for a service to be completed, they are in a queue. A customer waiting for their product quote is in a queue, even if they are able to perform other tasks. Long queue times translate to long and often erratic lead times for the service. When the total time from start to finish is unpredictable, customers will be frustrated both by the length of time, as well as the inability of the service provider to accurately estimate when the service will be completed.

Service providers often account for long lead times by requiring customers to make requests with significant lead time declarations. For example, if the duration of a training department's scheduling process is excessive, employees may be required to enrol in courses long before their delivery. These circumstances can result in additional problems for customers and service providers, such as many absentees to training courses due to employees' erratic work requirements, which preclude long term commitments for training. A faster scheduling process will allow employees to enrol in training on a more effective just-in-time basis.

Business process managers need to be aware that asking workers to perform tasks faster is usually not the answer to long lead times. Often, the root causes of the excessive duration are non-value-added activities whose removal would shorten process durations. Asking workers to work faster may result in more mistakes made by "cutting corners." For example, if a significant portion of the lead time is consumed by waiting for customers or other departments to provide information, service providers may resort to making educated guesses that are often inaccurate.

Don't Frustrate or Confuse the Customer

Customers of a business process can often be dissatisfied when they are required to perform tasks associated with the service. Usually, this form of dissatisfaction becomes especially noticeable when tasks cause emotional reactions such as frustration or confusion. Eliminating the need for customers to perform these tasks adds value to the customer experience.

Consider when the customer needs to make an appointment with a service provider. This task can be frustrating because of a business's inconvenient hours of operation or when contact information is difficult to find. It can be confusing if the service provider asks for details using terminology not well understood by customers (e.g., when making an appointment for repair). Internal customers have similar frustrations when they need to find information on employee benefits using an ineffective self-service system at their firm.

Customers are especially frustrated when they experience wasted time performing a task that should be unnecessary. This occurs, for example, when customers contacting a bank's call center may be asked to verify their identity multiple times if transferred to more than one department. A classic example occurs when a customer is required to wait at home for a long portion of a workday for a delivery or repair.

A more hidden form of customer frustration exists when the service process is designed to solve a problem that should have never occurred. Waiting for needed repairs would not be necessary if the firm's products functioned properly for its intended lifespan. Internally, many processes are designed to give approval. A process that approves business expense reports is needed only because employees are not trusted to create accurate expense reports.

Summary & Key Takeaways

Business process managers should be well aware of the experience of their customers, both internal and external. They should understand the actions required by their customers before, during and after the service is completed, from both a rational and emotional standpoint. Giving the customer exactly what they need without frustrating or confusing the customers should be a priority. In summary, the key takeaways from Chapter 6 are:

1. Understanding the customer experience requires detailed immersion into how a customer interacts with the business process.
2. Customer interaction with the business process can occur before the process begins, during the process operation, and after the process is completed.
3. A consumption map showing the customer actions and their emotions during these actions should be developed.
4. The analysis of a consumption map should focus on the hidden frustrations and confusions that customers experience, along with more obvious delays and where additional satisfaction can be addressed.
5. The customer wants their specific problem solved completely and quickly, and they don't want to feel confused or frustrated.

Discussion Questions

Consider a process where you are served as a customer. It could be as an internal customer in your workplace or as an external customer to any firm.

1. Create a consumption map.
2. Use icons on the consumption map to illustrate visible wastes (e.g., delays, travel, early termination) and hidden wastes (e.g., confusion, dissatisfaction, frustration).
3. Use an icon to show where value is or can be added, and list a few ideas on how value can be added.

References

1 Barlow J, Maul D. *Emotional value: creating strong bonds with your customers.* Oakland, California, USA: Berrett-Koehler Publishers; 2000.
2 Berry LL, Carbone LP, Haeckel SH. Managing the total customer experience. *MIT Sloan Management Review.* 2002; 43(3):85–89.
3 Shostack G. Designing services that deliver. *Harv Bus Rev.* 1984; 62(1):133.
4 Womack JP, Jones DT. *Lean solutions.* New York: Free Press; 2005.
5 Spraragen SL, Chan C. Service blueprinting: when customer satisfaction numbers are not enough. *International DMI Education Conference.* 2008 Apr; Cergy-Pointoise, France: ESSEC Business School.

7

ADDING VALUE

Adding Value

Many examples can be found of firms that have become more competitive by offering supplemental services to their customers. Disney provides a complete vacation experience, including making travel arrangements, providing local transportation to and from the airport, and setting up hotel accommodations. Progressive Insurance offer their concierge service where, along with processing an accident claim, they will take care of the repairs for the customer and provide them with a rental car. Many banks will provide budgeting assistance to customers by sending detailed end-of-year statements that categorize spending on checking or credit card accounts. And some real estate companies take charge of renting a client's property while it is on the sales market.

Adding value to customers of internal services is also possible. Many firms offer their employees shuttle buses to and from major transportation hubs to reduce their commutes and save them parking fees. A call center can tabulate the comments and complaints pertaining to each internal department, and use statistical methods to highlight abnormalities so that the producers keep abreast of consumer satisfaction in a timely manner. Human resource departments can add value for internal clients looking to hire qualified workers by keeping them informed of salary expectations and where qualified job seekers can be located.

In this chapter, two approaches for adding value are presented. The first approach seeks to make it easier for the customer to consume the service, often by employing Lean methods. These methods are easy for customers to understand and for service providers to apply. They can often be implemented without costly new processes or technologies. The second approach adds value by innovation. These approaches add new services to those already provided, or extend the service beyond its current boundaries. They are especially effective because they can increase revenue without the need to recruit new customers. For internal services, they can significantly improve customer satisfaction so that the reputation of the business process is improved and outsourcing becomes less likely.

As discussed in Chapter 6, the service provider should intend to solve the customer's problem quickly and completely, while minimizing the customer's frustration and confusion. Consider a financial auditing process. Value can be added by the auditors in many ways including: (a) educating clients about financial regulations during the routine procedures associated with the audit – although this activity may not save time during the question-and-answer session, it will solve the customer's problem more quickly in future audits; (b) organizing several informal social events with client personnel during or just before their visit – these events provide an opportunity to create dialog and to foster more comfortable relationships that can lead to more effective interactions; (c) arranging customized educational opportunities, where questions that apply to the firm are discussed – these sessions could include a list of the most frequently asked questions from past audits; and (d) creating a series of short podcasts or videos – their content can include important updates of relevant laws and regulatory changes.

Adding Value Using Lean Methods

Although typically used to minimize waste in the business process, many Lean methods can be used to create a better experience for customers. The most appropriate methods include standard work, 5S, poka-yoke, and visual controls. Some new challenges will be encountered when implementing even simple Lean methods with the participation of customers. Customers' level of expertise is more diverse than that of workers and therefore care must be taken to implement methods that do not require a specific background or expertise. In addition, the firm is not likely to have the opportunity to train customers on the use of a specific method.

Lean methods that are applied to improve the customer experience will tend to be more limited in scope than the same method applied within the business process. When technology is used to implement the method, care must be taken to create a process that avoids automating previous frustrations or adding confusion. For example, if a set of customer inputs are automated, care should be taken to ensure that confusing terminology is not included in the automated version of the input form. In fact, automation can limit flexibility so using well understood terms is vitally important.

Consider a facilities department that is responsible for the buildings and rooms that are used during training programs. This department can make effective use of 5S by creating a container with places for each device or material required for classes (e.g., markers, eraser, slide advancer, cables, etc.). Not only would this method make it easier for the training staff to find the necessary teaching materials, but the facilities department can quickly determine when additional materials are needed. Another interesting application of 5S exists in this department concerning their website. Having a well organized section that includes classroom location, size, equipment, layout, and photos, can limit last-minute problems by informing instructors of the classroom's capabilities, and by informing students of the classroom location, parking, etc.

In the sections that follow, examples illustrating the use of Lean methods to improve the customer experience are presented. The examples are provided for each of the processes described and evaluated in earlier chapters.

Financial Audit Process

Analysis of the financial audit consumption map showed potential for confusion and dissatisfaction when customers review the list of daily questions. They may be confused about the questions and eventually act in a passive aggressive manner by ignoring accumulated lists. Frustration can increase as questions accumulate. Clients may take substantial time to answer questions, such as when they need to travel or they are working from a home office. More questions accumulate during these delays. Customer dissatisfaction increases when multiple instances of the same questions appear on the list or when different auditors submit questions already answered for other auditors.

A method that includes elements of 5S, standard work, and visual controls can be implemented to improve this portion of the consumption process. One approach is for auditors to place shared files in a common location for clients to access. These files would be organized according to the type of account and the nature of the transaction. They would replace disorganized and redundant lists that were previously issued to clients on a daily basis. The files could have a standard color-coded format to distinguish questions that have been answered from those that are unanswered, and to highlight high-priority questions. Customers will be less frustrated and confused because only one list would exist with clearly delineated status information.

IT Change Request Process

The analysis of the IT change request consumption map showed the potential for dissatisfaction when customers need to respond to follow-up questions. These questions are a consequence of customer confusion that causes incomplete information or other mistakes in problem descriptions. The specialized terminology used by IT personnel can cause problems during subsequent question-and-answer sessions, especially when IT personnel are not trained to deal with the non-technical public effectively.

Various Lean methods could be used to improve the customer experience. Standard work could be applied in the call center when customers report the software problem, whereby a standard format would be followed to pinpoint the problem very specifically while using terms that a typical customer would understand. Poka-yoke can also be used to ensure that key contents of an information form are completed. If the information is not complete, customers would be unable to submit the request. The incorporation of 5S can ensure that customers spend less time determining who to call about the problem, by placing contact information in an obvious position on the website.

Price Quoting Process

The analysis of the price quoting consumption map shows the potential for confusion and dissatisfaction when customers are asked to provide information to the producer. Customers encounter similar emotions when they are required to respond to follow-up questions. These actions would be considered a waste of time by customers. The customer experience can be improved by implementing several approaches based on Lean methods.

A standard work process can be developed whereby clear and unambiguous explanations are used to request each bit of information about the product requested. The explanations would use terms that a typical customer would understand. The firm could also build trust by making their pricing policies visible and transparent. They may consider providing a self-service mechanism to screen for obvious challenges associated with the customer request. In this way, products that the company cannot customize effectively would stop the process at early stages. Because the price quoting process requires the collection of information across several divisions, a clearly defined requirement could shorten the waiting time and avoid follow-up questions. Visual controls can also be used to improve the transparency within each division so that actions are more coordinated.

Blood Testing Process

The analysis of the blood testing consumption map shows potential for dissatisfaction during the drawing of blood. Patient dissatisfaction can manifest in dread of minor pain, potential fainting, and more extreme anxiety by those patients with past experiences of significant pain. Healthcare providers use various forms of cognitive behavioral therapy (CBT) to help patients deal with chronic pain. Although not designed for temporary pain, these methods can help reduce unhelpful thoughts and replace them with more helpful thoughts by replacing emotional feeling with rational judgements. A method called applied tension treatment (ATT) can temporarily increase blood pressure, thereby reducing the risk of fainting.

The visual controls approach of Lean can be applied in the blood testing system to reduce pain using CBT that the patient can view while waiting for the technician. For patients prone to fainting, the ATT method could be also described in the visual display. The technician can have a checklist for each patient that quickly ascertains any potential issues for the blood draw, then shows the procedure recommended for a particular case.

Adding Value by Innovation

Value can also be added for customers by implementing new approaches in ways that may appear unprecedented. These innovative approaches can be incremental (requiring small changes to implement) or radical (requiring more substantial changes to implement). Incremental innovations tend to be those that create additional value by means of an improvement to, or extension of, the existing service offering. An example of an incremental innovation would be a self-service database that allows a division manager to retrieve health and safety information as-needed, where previously the information was provided quarterly as a generic report. New value would be added because of the increased ability of the manager to address problems on a more timely basis. The need to wait for new reports or use information from old reports would be eliminated.

Radical innovations would be those that create additional value by means of a new offering that looks substantially different from what customers expect. Radical innovation can be evolutionary or revolutionary, although distinguishing between the two is not important. An example of an evolutionary radical innovation is the creation of customized financial reports that includes new metrics specifically designed for each customer, where previous reports were sent to a variety of customers in a generic form. An example of revolutionary radical innovation could be a self-service machine for dispensing tools in a manufacturing facility using the employee's ID card to associate the equipment needed with the jobs performed. The new value added would be improved availability of the tools, as well as providing management with the ability to charge relevant departments accordingly.

To increase the chance that an innovation will be implemented, a three-step verification is necessary: (a) the organizational verification evaluates the consistency of the new offering against the short and long term strategic vision of the firm, (b) the customer verification evaluates the skills and motivation of customers relative to the new offering especially if new technologies are required, and (c) the culture verification evaluates both customers and the firm to ensure that they are comfortable with the new offering. Ideally, customers will become more engaged and service providers' excitement will increase.

Random Word Approach

A common misconception is that only certain creative individuals have the innate ability to develop innovations. Innovations, even those that seem radical, are created by making connections between seemingly dissimilar phenomena. Franz Johansson provides many examples of innovation when "you step into an intersection of fields, disciplines, or cultures" [1]. Although there are many examples where this intersection occurred naturally (e.g., in fifteenth century Italy), it can be artificially created through methodologies that help a project team *unlearn* what they already know about the business process.

The *random word* approach helps team members unlearn and make new connections they would otherwise not make. The method will be described in the context of an example. A major electronics retailer in North America sells many brands including its own private brand, with products made by an original equipment manufacturer. The retailer takes advantage of its interactions with consumers by soliciting feedback, which it uses to improve designs of these products. In fact, some of its store brand products account for the highest market share in its category. At the time of the project, the retailer had started to open stores internationally. It found that consumers in some markets were reluctant to provide feedback as readily as North American consumers. A project team was created to find ways to solicit information from a consumer who would not be inclined to voluntarily provide feedback.

The random word method would proceed as follows:

1. The problem to be solved is specified.
2. A word is created using a *random word generator* (numerous free random word generators can be found on the Internet).
3. Project team members engage in word association by quickly listing other words or phrases that are connected in some way to the original word, or to those words or phrases proposed by other team members. Importantly, this step will help solve the problem by getting team members to forget about the problem at hand, so they should not be engaged in solving the problem during this step.
4. The project team reverts back to the problem at hand and relates the information generated in step 3 to the original problem, taking only about 5–10 minutes.
5. The methodology returns to Step 2 until the meeting time has expired or until a suitable number of ideas are suggested. The number of ideas should be large at this point. Later, they will be paired down based on cost, implementation concerns, or other criteria.

A team of interns engaged in a brainstorming arranged by a consultant to generate ideas for solving the problem at the retailer. The first random word, snow, generated terms and phrases such as "rain," "ice," "Rainey" (the name of a fellow intern), and "Snow White" (from the Disney movie *Snow White and the 7 Dwarfs*). The last phrase generated the word cartoon, then dress up, then disguise. Soon thereafter, an idea (the first listed below) was generated. Other random words followed and many ideas were created. Some of the ideas and the random word that initiated the associated discussion are listed below:

- **Snow**: Disguise store workers to resemble customers, who would then informally engage actual customers who are shopping in the store while asking them about experiences with products sold there.
- **Flashlight**: Based on someone mentioning "spotlight", an idea was generated to rent space in a neutral area (e.g., street corner or mall) to showcase one product while eliciting feedback from people who are not normally customers of the retailer.
- **Doorbell**: Display a product on a board with buttons representing features and ask customers to press the button for the features they use.
- **Mouse**: Because mice can be hard to find, place retail workers in locations that are more convenient for customers.
- **Kangaroo**: Based on someone mentioning "hopping", place examples around the store showing where customer feedback improved products.
- **Editor**: Create formal or informal relationships with technical magazine or website editors to exchange product-related information.

When implementing the random word method, no ideas are rejected out of hand. This method promotes out-of-the-box thinking and innovative idea generation. Consider a brainstorming session for ways to improve the customer experience for customers of an HR recruiting process. In this case, customers would be located in the various departments of the firm. A random word exercise was performed with a group of participants who were learning the technique of random word generation for innovative idea generation. The following random words were generated and sample ideas are shown with each word.

- **Era** – Ask department managers to give the HR staff a list of employees who have adapted well to change so that the HR staff can evaluate their backgrounds.
- **Testing** – Ask department managers to give the HR staff a set of questions that closely reflect recent challenges in their department so that they can be embedded in upcoming interviews.
- **Musician** – When specific skills are in short supply, consider recruiting musicians because they possess analytical skills and tend to be self-disciplined.

- **Crazy** – Work with HR to list irrational questions to gauge an applicant's ability to think creatively but empathetically.
- **Trailing** – Based on someone stating "look back to move forward" – find correlations between employees that have experienced rapid advancement and their backgrounds.
- **Geology** – Ask questions of candidates that gauge their ability to show enthusiasm for their profession – because geologists can get very excited about topics that many others find boring.

As a final example, consider a software development firm located in India that other firms use to outsource software development services. With many clients in North America, Europe, and other countries in Asia, the firm has had difficulty scheduling meetings with customers due to the various time zone differences. Specially, 80% of customers are located in either San Diego, Boston, Rome, or Shanghai. With the rapid changes in the market, customers frequently have new requirements and the firm needs to constantly add new features to the software. To ensure that the firm can make these changes in an effective and timely manner, a daily meeting can be essential to communicate with customers. However, the time zone differences make it very difficult to arrange these meetings at times that are convenient to all stakeholders.

An exercise was created using the random word techniques that were generated. The ideas (and the random word that spawned the idea) were: (a) create a convenient way for customers to accumulate lists of questions (receipt); (b) travel to customer locations early in each project to develop better relationships (move); (c) record the meetings and add time stamps for important information that concerns specific customers (live); and (d) create meeting times that are equally inconvenient for all parties (consensus).

Required Innovation Infrastructure

Taking risks in many organizations is either implicitly or explicitly discouraged. Because innovation takes time and is not always successful, it is difficult for innovative thinking to take root in these cases. Nurturing a culture that prevents problems from occurring is also difficult to cultivate due to organizational dynamics [2]. Innovative thinking involves risks of failure, and therefore the organization should let the rewards for success more than offset the punishment for failure. If punishment can be minimized or removed, then workers and managers can nurture the excitement associated with creating new ideas that improve customers' experience. In fact, this excitement has been shown to translate to more job satisfaction even when it is not accompanied by monetary rewards [3].

Firms that are known for innovation have long recognized that learning is enhanced through failure, although this realization should be viewed with some trepidation. Customers can be lost and reputation can be harmed when unintended consequences create more harm than good for customers. Hence, an innovative work culture needs to include a structure for highlighting problems, generating ideas, and evaluating those ideas in ways that appropriately balance risks and benefits. For example, rather than hiding failures, they should be shared within the organization so that they are not repeated and the organization as a whole learns from these failures.

Barriers to innovation should be removed before an organization attempts to create a culture of innovation. Some important barriers include: a belief that innovation is too risky, a lack of systematic innovation processes, and little or no reward for innovation [4]. The firm's resources should be devoted to innovation in a visible way, such as encouraging participation in projects seeking to find new approaches to serving customers. For example, management can impose an expectation that employees spend a certain portion of each work week engaging with creative endeavors, either through formal projects or less formal individual approaches. These workers would be encouraged to create and test innovative ideas, but also to base these ideas on data-driven criteria.

Finally, knowledge sharing has positive influence on innovation capacity. Implementing ways to share knowledge will create the higher potential for success [5]. Innovative thinking and acting applies to individuals, teams, projects, and the firm [6]. For example, the results of previous innovation projects can be documented in the form of posters that are displayed in lobbies, cafeterias, and other high traffic locations in a facility. The communities of interest consist of workers and managers across the entire firm who may be motivated to take part in similar innovation projects.

Application of Self Service

Many business processes have created self-service mechanisms in order to give customers exactly what they need when they need it. The approach of self-service originated with retail food stores. Originally, the customer requested each item from the shopkeeper, who retrieved the item for them. Today, customers choose the items they want, then proceed to a checkout counter. Over the years, self-service has become commonplace for many services, such as buying fuel at an automobile service station, withdrawing money at an ATM, washing clothes at a laundromat, and disposing of dishes at a fast-food restaurant.

Along with giving the customer exactly the service they seek, self-service has many advantages for the service provider. By sharing the responsibility of providing the service with the customer, self-service creates capacity at precisely the time it is needed. This flexible capacity is free to the producer. The result will be lower costs and more predictable capacity requirements for the service provider. Some hidden benefits of self service also exist, such as the reduction of errors when handing off information from customer to service provider.

Self-service has secondary advantages for customers and service providers. Customers can access information when it is convenient for them rather than for the service provider. There is little or no delay between when the service is desired and when it is delivered. Many tasks that service providers find repetitive, such as the collection of routine information, are transferred to the customer. This change can make employees' jobs more enjoyable.

The biggest challenge associated with self-service is ensuring that customers have the capability to perform the service without assistance. New technologies are often employed, such as the Internet (with or without artificial intelligence) or machinery (e.g., an ATM or checkout line). Risks are increased when the technology is not well understood by customers. Service availability can become dependent on new external factors, such as wifi availability and affordability. Because one-on-one human interaction is extremely flexible, eliminating these interactions can cause either customers or service providers to become frustrated if their needs do not align. Finally, long term risks for the service provider exist if customers lose their loyalty to the firm or to the department that is offering the service.

Self-service has become commonplace in internal services within larger firms. Many HR functions, such as benefits administration, tax statement delivery, and vacation monitoring are performed by employees. Customer relationship databases are shared so that many departments can analyse their contents to serve their purposes. Technology assistance is also available via self-service, such as detailed installation instructions, supplies ordering, and frequently-asked questions.

Consider the price quoting process, a portion of whose consumption map is displayed in Chapter 6. The consumption map shows that customers experience significant time waiting for the service to be completed. Waiting is frustrating for customers and can cause the service provider to lose sales opportunities if another producer provides a quote sooner, or if the customer seeks new producers in the future. A self-service mechanism can be considered whereby the customer-provided inputs initiate obtaining information directly from the various departments (i.e., bypassing the sales team member). For this system to operate effectively, each department would need to specify the standard information they need from the customer. With this revision to the process, impractical quotes would be identified quickly, so that the information can be modified or the project abandoned in short order. Even when the news is not good for either party, prompt information exchange will enhance the emotional experience of the customer and create empathy towards the service provider.

Summary & Key Takeaways

Service providers should find ways to add value to the customer experience. Giving the customer exactly what they need without wasting their time should be a priority. In summary, the key takeaways from Chapter 7 are:

1. Adding value should focus on solving a customer's problem completely and not wasting their time in the process of delivering the service.
2. Adding value can be done using Lean methods such as mistake proofing and standard work.
3. More innovative approaches can be leveraged to add value using a random word generator to create innovative ideas.
4. Self-service can be used effectively to add value for customers, but should be undertaken with caution, especially if it involves new technologies with which customers may not be familiar.

Discussion Questions

Consider a business process that forecasts demand for the supply chain planners to use to create production plans. To plan production effectively, weekly forecasts need to be created for about 450 final products for the next 6 months (i.e., 26 weeks). Forecasters use advertising and other planned promotional events to help with forecast development. Assume that currently, marketing and sales departments do not effectively communicate these events to forecasters, which causes inaccuracies in the forecasted demand.

1. Create ideas for improvement using Lean methods of standard work, poka-yoke, visual controls, 5S, and other methods.
2. Create innovative ideas for improvement with the following random words: zipper, convince, zealous, and memory.

References

1 Johansson F. *The Medici effect: what elephants & epidemics can teach us about innovation.* Cambridge, MA: Harvard Business School Press; 2006.
2 Repenning NP, Sterman JD. Nobody ever gets credit for fixing problems that never happened: creating and sustaining process improvement. *California Management Review.* 2001; 43(4):64–88.
3 O'Connor G, Euchner J. The people side of breakthrough innovation: an interview with Gina O'Connor. *Research-Technology Management.* 2017; 60(4):12–18.
4 Loewe P, Dominiquini J. Overcoming the barriers to effective innovation. *Strategy & Leadership.* 2006; 34(1):24–31.
5 Oliver S, Kandadi K. How to develop knowledge culture in organizations? A multiple case study of large distributed organizations. *JKM.* 2006; 10(4):6–24.
6 Wenger E, Mcdermott R, Snyder W, Lakomski G. *Cultivating communities of practice: a guide to managing knowledge.* Boston, MA: Harvard Business Review Press; 2004. 89p.

8

DETERMINING CAPACITY LEVELS

Business Process Capacity Planning

Capacity planning involves determining resource needs that would optimize resource costs in light of customer demand forecasts. The focus of capacity planning for services is usually on workforce planning and workforce scheduling. Services cannot use inventory to buffer against demand fluctuations over time and demand uncertainties within a time period. Therefore, service process capacity planning uses careful capacity allocations and capacity buffering to deal with demand uncertainty. When performed effectively, servers are available when demand exists and labor costs are minimized. Achieving these goals is a challenge when customer demand is not easy to forecast or when service times vary from customer to customer.

Capacity planning for a business process is usually done informally, especially for those processes that serve internal customers. Capacity-related decisions can affect business process performance in both visible and hidden ways. Long queues at a call center is a visible manifestation of poor capacity planning. It is visible because performance data would quantify the waiting times and some customers will register complaints. A hidden manifestation of poor capacity planning is the quoting of long project lead times. In these cases, the service provider may consistently meet deadlines even though customers would consider these lead times excessive. But, it is unlikely that a customer will register a complaint unless specifically prompted.

Structured capacity planning requires a forecast, but a firm's forecasting department will rarely be devoted to forecasting requirements for internal services. Often, last year's demand is simply projected forward with an assumed increase or decrease based on business conditions or management desires. The demand for many business processes can be erratic, in particular those that respond to the needs of other departments, such as troubleshooting, repair, or legal services. In other cases, a fairly predictable set of activities is required and a capacity plan can be created without complications.

Example: Audit Department

Consider an auditing department within a large firm, where the business process performs financial audits for internal departments in preparation for the annual submission of pro-forma financial statements. These financial statements must be accurate and adhere to strict regulatory requirements. Management of the auditing department, which consists of senior auditors, associate auditors, and interns, is concerned about planning workforce requirements that are consistent with the needs of internal customers and the skills (and associated cost) of workers.

The heaviest and fairly predictable demand for audits occurs in the 3–4 months before financial statements are submitted to regulators (which occurs in late March). During the rest of the year, the department performs other services. They include periodic follow-up audits required because of deficiencies found by regulators, answering questions from internal departments, and training that the department performs to support other departments – this includes formal courses and one-on-one consultation. The demand for these activities would be less predictable.

The department's manager wishes to determine a monthly workforce plan for senior auditors, associate auditors, and interns. Their deployment would be determined based on projected demand for various audit-related services. The monthly workforce plan would take account of the current number of workers and the options (and costs) for adding worker capacity. For example, new workers can be hired, overtime can be planned, or some work can be performed by temporary contract workers. Each of these options would have associated costs that the planner would need to consider.

When creating the workforce plan, the audit department managers need to have estimates for the amount of time required to perform the various jobs performed by their department. Worker assignments each month would account for other worker tasks (e.g., senior auditors attending leadership meetings, associate auditors being allocated time to prepare for professional certification examinations) and for flexible workers' availability (e.g., interns main availability is in the summer and during other University breaks). The efficiency of each type of worker would also be considered (e.g. interns would be less efficient than full-time associate auditors).

Finally, the planner would need to reserve some time in the workforce plan to account for the uncertainty associated with demand for its services and variation in activity times. For example, the time to develop a 3-day training course would vary depending on the amount of consistency in the older course materials with changes in legal requirements. Demand for troubleshooting processes varies greatly in the same way that demand for emergency services cannot be predicted precisely.

Dealing with Uncertainty

When planning capacity, uncertainty is accounted for in two ways. For normal demand and operational uncertainty, a capacity buffer is planned. The buffer size, usually expressed as a percentage, represents the extra capacity that is planned to ensure that effective service is provided. Operating a service process without a capacity buffer will result in an inability to complete jobs at the same pace as demand. This phenomenon was illustrated with a simulation in Chapter 2. Readers may recall that his loan approval process averaged 70 applications per month. With no buffering of capacity, the applications completed averaged only 54 per month. To better match output rates to input rates in the presence of uncertainty, a suitable capacity buffer typically ranges from 5% to 15%. They can be customized for specific environments (see Chapter 9), or standard buffer percentages can be employed (described below).

The other main approach to accounting for uncertainty when planning capacity is by implementing risk management methods. This approach is used to account for extraordinary differences between the forecast and the actual demand that is caused by external factors. These approaches would typically involve the identification of risks that can disrupt the business process and the quantification of their impacts. This analysis would be followed by plans for avoiding disruptions, reducing their likelihood, or mitigating effects of the disruption. For example, a flu epidemic that affects many auditors simultaneously during the key auditing periods could cause great disruption. Strategies to mitigate this risk may include ensuring that all employees receive flu shots, or contracting with companies so that auditors can be hired quickly on a temporary basis. Risk management of a business process is covered in Chapter 14.

Key Definitions

Capacity planning should ensure that future resource availability exists when needed. If done effectively, an appropriate balance is maintained between the needs of the customer (to be serviced promptly) and the needs of the firm (to provide service at reasonable costs). The capacity planning process should be done in a structured manner to ensure that this balance is maintained. Planning is itself a business process that requires the planner to manipulate resources (mainly workforce) to best meet the needs of customers by being available when and where the demand for the resource exists.

A few formal definitions are required:

- *Resource efficiency* is the percentage of time that a resource would be expected to operate after any unplanned disruptions, such as power (or network) outages, washroom breaks, equipment downtime (e.g., replacing a laser printer's ink cartridge), etc. The disruptions would typically not include meals or other scheduled breaks.
- *Capacity* is the amount of work a resource can do, usually expressed in jobs per time interval, such as customers per hour. Capacity may or may not be adjusted based on resource efficiency. In the remainder of this chapter, capacity will include an adjustment for resource efficiency.
- *Capacity buffer* is the percentage of time the planner reserves due to uncertainty in customer demand and/or activity time variation. It will increase in proportion to the magnitude of the variations (e.g., processes where customers arrive randomly would require larger capacity buffers than those where customers make appointments).
- *Demand* is the amount of work anticipated, expressed as a rate using the same units as capacity. This value is typically the forecast of customer needs.
- *Resource utilization* is the ratio of demand to capacity. This value represents the average percentage of time that a resource will be serving customers during the planning period by category of service.

A capacity plan is *feasible* when resource utilization shows that it can get the work accomplished after adjusting for efficiency and the capacity buffer. For example, assuming that capacity is adjusted based on the resource's efficiency and the capacity buffer is 10%, then the planned resource utilization is feasible if it does not exceed 90%. The 90% goal can be referred to as the target resource utilization. When the planned resource utilization is more than the target resource utilization (i.e., it is infeasible), then the resource cannot keep pace with customer demand to the level desired by the planner. A feasible capacity plan is *optimal* when it is the best possible plan based on the criteria used to evaluate its effectiveness (usually cost or a similar financial metric).

Capacity Buffering

The cost of capacity buffering is directly proportional to the cost of the resource. For example, processes using skilled labor will have higher capacity buffer costs than those with unskilled labor. Professional services, such as those found in legal or medical settings, would tend to have high capacity buffer costs. Their financial impact can be mitigated if service providers can be placed on standby status. For example, emergency room physicians are often assigned on-call status, whereby they would quickly travel to the hospital when needed. In other cases, flexible workers primarily assigned to other activities may be called upon to assist with a service process experiencing an excessive customer queue.

Planners should exercise caution when on-call or flexible workers are used for capacity buffering. To be effective, managers must assure that these workers will: (a) quickly and easily move from their primary activity to the service needing assistance, and (b) resume their primary activity without excessive delay (e.g., they can "pick up where they left off") once they are no longer needed.

Precise capacity buffers can be determined using a mathematical approach based on queuing theory or using a simulation of the system under study. The mathematical modeling of queues is described in Chapter 9. An important phenomenon associated with queuing systems is proven mathematically and also confirmed in practice. This phenomenon concerns the relationship between resource utilization and customer wait times. For service processes with uncertain activity times, waiting times increase in proportion to increases in resource utilization according to a *hockey-stick* function that is shown in Figure 8.1.

The capacity planner should target the server (i.e., resource) utilization just before the curve begins its steep ascent. This target value is referred to as the *knee* of the curve. The precise location of the knee depends on two main

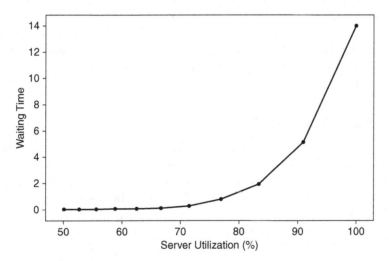

FIGURE 8.1 Relationship of Utilization to Waiting Times (Example)

factors: (a) the demand pattern, and (b) the service time variation. Demand is either scheduled (e.g., by appointment) or they arrive randomly. Service time variation is typically measured by collecting data on service times, then calculating the ratio of the standard deviation of the service times and the average service time (called the coefficient of variation, or CV).

A set of standard capacity buffer levels is recommended based on research performed on various business processes having uncertain activity times. The suggested buffer level depends on the amount of service time variation and the nature of customer demand. Low-medium service time variation would have a CV of 10-30%, which will typically include routine activities. High service time variation would have a CV above 40%, and typically include activities such as troubleshooting, analysis, and consultation. The recommended capacity buffer levels are:

- 5% for scheduled demand with low-medium service time variation
- 10% for scheduled demand with high service time variation
- 10% for random demand with low-medium service time variation
- 15% for random demand with high service time variation

Referring to the financial auditing department described earlier, the capacity buffer would vary depending on the month being planned. In months consisting of routine audits that are known in advance, a buffer level of 5% makes sense because jobs are scheduled and the amount of time to perform audit tasks should not vary substantially. In the months during which demand consists primarily of troubleshooting, a capacity buffer of 15% is recommended because demand is random and the duration of this work is highly variable. A capacity buffer of 10% is appropriate for months when demand includes a combination of scheduled and random, and service times include those that exhibit different levels of variation.

Calculating Resource Utilization

An Excel-based *Capacity Planning Template* is included in this book's eResources, along with a video describing its use. It determines the utilization of a group of resources performing a common set of tasks, such as three associate auditors assigned to troubleshooting. Prior to using the template, the average time required to service a customer (not including queue time) needs to be determined by observing a business process and collecting data on each customer's service time. Based on these data, the average service time is calculated, expressed in minutes per customer. The expected demand is also input in the template. Demand would be expressed in customers per hour. The template converts average service time to capacity then compares capacity with expected demand to calculate the projected resource utilization.

For example, if the average time to serve a customer is 4 minutes per customer, then the capacity of each resource unit is 15 customers per hour. The easiest way to make the conversion from average service time (in minutes) to capacity (in hours) is to divide 60 (minutes/hour) by the average service time (minutes). If multiple resources are available, the capacity of the resource group would be the product of the number of resources and the capacity of each resource unit. For example, if the average service time is 4 minutes per customer and 5 workers are available, then the capacity of the resource group is 75 customers per hour.

A step-by-step procedure for calculating resource utilization (assuming that service time includes adjustment for efficiency) is described here:

1. The service time (e.g., minutes per customer) for the resource is determined (via direct observation or using electronic records); it is adjusted according to the resource's efficiency.
2. The capacity for each resource unit (e.g., customers per hour) is calculated.
3. The number of available resources is determined (either the existing number or a planned number).
4. The capacity of the resource group is determined by multiplying the capacity of each resource unit (Step 2) by the number of resource units (Step 3).
5. The demand forecast (customers per hour) is determined.
6. The planned resource utilization is the ratio of demand (Step 5) and capacity (Step 4).

Consider a new facility that provides services of investment customers on a walk-in basis, where planned resource utilizations are to be determined. Forecasts, based on locations with similar demographics, indicate that during the 10:00–3:00 timeframe, an average of 86 customers will arrive. The forecast indicates that 30% of customers will seek investment advice and they are each served by one of 3 advisors. Sixty percent of customers will seek to complete a simple transaction, like deposit a check, and these transactions are handled by 3 service agents. One receptionist speaks to every customer to determine their needs. Ten percent of customers will leave the facility after consulting with the receptionist. Because the advisors will also perform any necessary simple transactions, no customers require both a service agent and an investment advisor. The data analysis showed the average service times are 3 minutes for the receptionist (with low-medium variation), 24 minutes for an advisor (with high variation), and 9 minutes for a service agent (with low-medium variation).

The resource utilization for the receptionist is shown in Figure 8.2 using the capacity planning template:

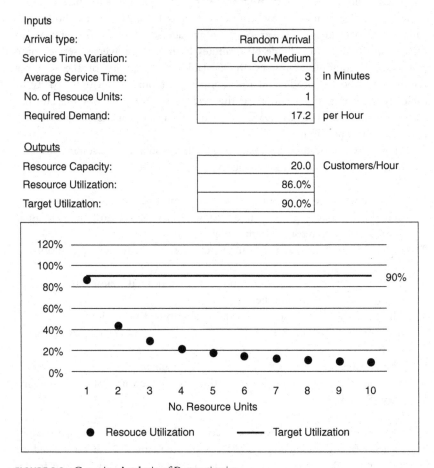

Capacity Planning Analysis

Inputs

Arrival type:	Random Arrival
Service Time Variation:	Low-Medium
Average Service Time:	3
No. of Resouce Units:	1
Required Demand:	17.2

in Minutes

per Hour

Outputs

Resource Capacity:	20.0
Resource Utilization:	86.0%
Target Utilization:	90.0%

Customers/Hour

FIGURE 8.2 Capacity Analysis of Receptionist

Demand is random because appointments are not made. The capacity buffer for random demand and low–medium service time variation is 10%, and therefore the target resource utilization is 90%. The demand is forecasted to be 17.2 customers per hour because the forecast is for 86 customers to arrive during a 5 hour interval. Resource utilization will be 86.0%, which falls below the target utilization. Therefore, this plan is feasible.

The resource utilization for the investment advisors is shown in Figure 8.3.

Demand is random because appointments are not made. The capacity buffer for random demand and high service time variation is 15%, and therefore the target resource utilization is 85%. The demand is forecasted to be 6.9 customers per hour because 30% of the 17.2 customers per hour seek investment

Capacity Planning Analysis

Inputs

Arrival type:	Random Arrival
Service Time Variation:	High
Average Service Time:	24	in Minutes
No. of Resouce Units:	3
Required Demand:	6.9	per Hour

Outputs

Resource Capacity:	7.5	Customers/Hour
Resource Utilization:	92.0%
Target Utilization:	85.0%

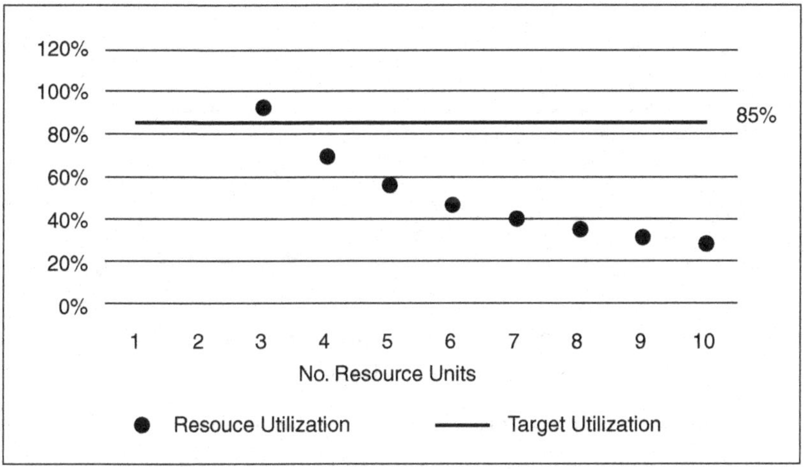

FIGURE 8.3 Capacity Analysis of Investment Advisors

advice. Resource utilization will be 92.0%, which falls above the target utilization. Therefore, to make this plan feasible, one more investment advisor would be required (as shown in the graph).

The resource utilization for the service agents is shown in Figure 8.4. Demand is random because appointments are not made. The capacity buffer for random demand and low-medium service time variation is 10%, and therefore the target resource utilization is 90%. The demand is forecasted to be 10.3 customers per hour because 60% of the 17.2 customers per hour seek this service. Resource utilization will be 51.5%, which falls well below the target utilization. In fact, the number of service agents can be reduced from 3 to 2 because (as shown in the graph) the resource utilization for 2 service agents would be less than 90%.

Capacity Planning Analysis

Inputs

Arrival type:	Random Arrival
Service Time Variation:	Low-Medium
Average Service Time:	9	in Minutes
No. of Resouce Units:	3
Required Demand:	10.3	per Hour

Outputs

Resource Capacity:	20.0	Customers/Hour
Resource Utilization:	51.5%
Target Utilization:	90.0%

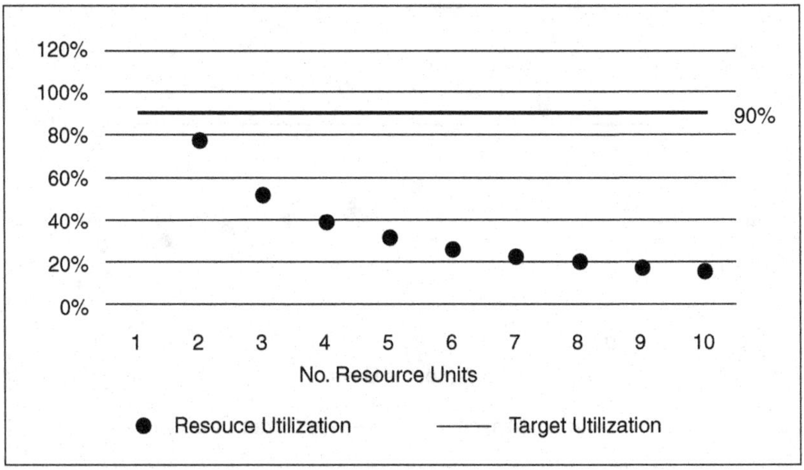

FIGURE 8.4 Capacity Analysis of Service Agents

Workforce Scheduling

Workforce planning determines worker allocations based on expected customer demand and is generally performed on a weekly or monthly basis. Each plan looks forward up to one year. Workforce scheduling determines more detailed work schedules for service providers. If effective, workforce scheduling ensures that customers' needs are met when and where demand for the service exists. Ineffective workforce scheduling results in either idle time for workers (i.e., higher than necessary costs for the firm), or long waits for customers (when the process is congested due to an overload of work for service providers).

In an ideal setting, data would be available on each type of service provided and the average service time for each type of service. These data would typically be available in a call center, where the system typically records the category of each call (e.g., hardware Product A, software product C, etc.) and their durations. This situation is unique because most business processes do not include this level of detail. However, the example is informative because it illustrates the type of data that need to be estimated by the workforce scheduler, and it informs future data collection efforts. Most business processes do have records on total time worked and number of customers served, and therefore at a minimum they estimate the service time per customer per worker.

Typically, workforce scheduling focuses on assigning each worker to a "shift." Typical shift configurations are 5 consecutive days of 8 hours per day (followed by 2 days off), or 3 consecutive days of 12 hours per day (followed by 3 days off). More flexibility can exist when part-time shifts of 2–6 hours are possible, or when so-called "split shifts" can be created (e.g., two 4 hour periods during a day with some unpaid time off between work periods). Scheduling workers to this level of detail requires that managers use forecasts of demand by day and hour.

Each scheduling scenario includes different and potentially unique factors that make workforce scheduling difficult to perform using a standard approach. Readers familiar with advanced optimization methods may be able to create mathematically optimal schedules using these methods. In most cases, however, an experience-based trial-and-error approach will yield effective results. This approach requires the planner to experiment with various shift configurations so that capacity best matches demand requirements. This approach is used in the example presented below.

Workforce Scheduling for Contact Center

In the auditing department, a virtual contact center is setup whereby internal customers can call with questions or problems pertaining to financial regulations. It is referred to as a virtual contact center because associate auditors are assigned to answer calls while sitting at their desks, and the IT system routes calls to associate auditors based on a work schedule. Each associate auditor sends 4 hours per day performing this task. In order to avoid confusion, the 4 hours can be separated into two 2-hour periods, or one 4-hour period.

Associate auditors who staff the contact center are located in Germany. With internal customers located in North America, Europe, and Asia, the hourly demand for the contact center varies significantly based on time zone differences. The contact center is available between the hours of 9:00 am to 4:00 pm in Germany. Although European customers call throughout this timeframe, Asian customers tend to call during earlier hours while North American customers tend to call during later hours.

After adjusting for efficiencies and adding a suitable capacity buffer, the number of associate auditors required at 9 AM, 10 AM, etc., is 7, 6, 5, 4, 3, 4, 5, and 6, for each of the eight contact center hours. These hourly demand forecasts correspond to a daily demand of 40 hours and therefore 10 associate auditors will be assigned (because each of them works 4 hours per week at the virtual call center). When scheduling auditors, all requests from customers will be completed by day's end, but not necessarily during the hour they called. A suitable schedule is shown in Table 8.1, where the 10 auditors are shown in one row with a letter X used to indicate their 4-hour work schedule. Notice that the over/under row shows a deficit in the number of auditors during two hours (9 AM and 11 AM), but those customers would be served with the excess capacity in the hours 1 PM and 3 PM.

Managing Customer Expectations

The field of operations research originated much of the mathematical foundations of waiting line analysis using methods associated with *queuing theory*. These practical methods, covered in Chapter 9, are used to predict queue lengths and waiting times for a variety of settings that include both manufacturing and service processes. They are usually, but not always, relevant to internal services. For example, executives who receive accounting statements on the third day of each month would not be considered as waiting in a queue for the service to be completed. But many other internal customers, including those who seek troubleshooting, approvals, legal advice, and market analysis results, will join a queue while they wait for the service to be completed.

TABLE 8.1 Contact Center Workforce Schedule

	3 PM	*10 PM*	*11 AM*	*12 PM*	*1 PM*	*2 PM*	*3 PM*	*4 PM*
Auditor 1	x	x	x	x				
Auditor 2	x	x	x	x				
Auditor 3	x	x	x	x				
Auditor 4	x	x	x	x				
Auditor 5					x	x	x	x
Auditor 6					x	x	x	x
Auditor 7					x	x	x	x
Auditor 8					x	x	x	x
Auditor 9	x	x					x	x
Auditor 10	x	x					x	x
Capacity	6	6	4	4	4	4	6	6
Demand	7	6	5	4	3	4	5	6
Over/Under	−1	0	−1	0	1	0	1	0

The field of operations research also included less analytical approaches to improve customer satisfaction. Pioneering work in the psychology of queuing was performed by Larson. [1] This work has extended to specific methods for making waiting more bearable, using methods that "entertain, enlighten, and engage" customers. [2] This section summarizes some of these methods and other approaches to managing customers' expectations while they wait for a service to be completed.

Unfortunately, some service providers resort to quoting long lead times to customers. When they provide results on or before their self-proclaimed due dates, they assume that customers are satisfied. However, customers cannot be fooled. They may not have a strong emotional response to on-time service completion, but they will have an emotional response to the initial long lead time quote. This approach by service providers can have long term detrimental effects on their department. For example, if an IT department quotes a 6 month completion time for a relatively simple software update, outsourcing options may be considered by the firm even if this deadline is met in 100% of projects.

It is difficult to quantify the impact of customer wait times for a number of reasons. For example, differences between customers' perception of the wait could cause some customers to be unhappy with a certain wait time, and others satisfied or neutral. Waiting in line can also seem longer for some customers when certain factors are present, such as uncertainty (of the wait duration), unfairness (if other customers appear to be given higher priority or if the queue is disorganized), and boredom (because waiting feels longer for customers without distractions such as reading or listening material). Therefore, in conjunction with configuring queues to have reasonable wait times, firms should use other means to mitigate the effect of waiting. Some well-known ideas are listed below:

Occupy Customers

Waiting is especially noticeable to customers when they are not able to use this time in other ways. Therefore, a service provider should find ways to distract customers while they are in queue. For example, it has been found that replacing the doors of an elevator with mirrors, although it has no effect on waiting times, decreases the number of complaints. The mirrors distract customers so that they become less aware of delays. A method like this will only be effective if the waiting times are reasonable; it is designed to make customers less aware of the passage of time.

Many services have traditionally entertained waiting customers by providing magazines in a waiting area, placing a monitor in a workplace lobby, or playing music for telephone callers while holding. These methods are also used by grocery stores, who often place magazines in checkout lines and play music over loudspeakers. Specializing the content is very helpful, such as showing cartoons or anime on a television when children will be accompanying waiting parents. A hardware troubleshooting service that requires customers to wait for repairs could show videos of new products or peripherals that make them aware of new technologies and their application.

Another approach to occupying customers is to make the customer an active participant by asking them to complete a form or other mechanism that will increase the speed of the service. For example, some restaurants allow waiting customers to record their food orders while they wait for a table, while others provide them with a pager so they can walk away from the waiting area. Occupying customers by educating them on topics likely to be important in the service provided minimizes perceived wait time and also speeds the service. Customer feedback can also be elicited during their wait.

Reduce Anxiety & Exude Fairness

The negative effects of waiting are amplified when customers perceive that they are not being treated fairly. This emotion can be present whether or not the service provider intends to create circumstances that cause this emotion. For example, the lack of well-defined rules or places to queue can cause some customers to "cut the line" due to confusion or their wilful ignorance of societal rules. Therefore, service providers need to inform customers of the queue priorities then create systems to implement rules fairly. One method would be to segment customers so that those with "common" or short duration needs will not wait with other customers (such as the express line in a grocery store).

Creating empathy by greeting customers as soon as they arrive also helps to improve the perceived customer experience. However, customers can become frustrated when personnel are visible but are not engaged in servicing customers. These circumstances give customers the impression that the firm is indifferent to their plight. For example, customers waiting for a flu shot perceive nurses negatively when some of them are chatting while on break. It is recommended that these nurses move to an area not be seen by customers.

For an internal service such as R&D, analytics, IT, or troubleshooting, it is common for jobs needed by some customers to be given higher priorities than other jobs. Most internal customers would understand that business-related reasons would exist, but when priorities appear to be arbitrary dissatisfaction can occur. Therefore, business process managers need to create fair policies for prioritizing work, and they should make the prioritizing procedure as transparent as possible. This effort could include using visual controls so that all customers can see the set of priorities assigned to every customer.

Keep Customers Informed

A common approach that customers appreciate is providing them with information about the status of their service request or the expected waiting time for service. Call centers routinely inform customers of the expected wait time, which allows customers to decide whether or not to wait, or allows them to take part in other activities during the duration of the wait. Technology can also help by posting average wait times during various time periods. Examples are highway displays showing wait times at various border crossings or website displays showing the wait times at various motor vehicle locations.

By using the same mechanisms to inform customers of potential wait times, service providers can encourage demand during non-peak periods. This approach generally consists of changing prices and is common in restaurants, hotels, and airlines (it has increasingly been accomplished in real time). A self-service version of this method would be the use of several Internet applications that show the number of customers by hour who visit various stores and restaurants. The information provided can be used by customers when planning their visits.

Summary & Key Takeaways

Capacity planning is important for any business process because it determines the most effective allocation of resources to meet customer service needs. It is especially challenging in business processes because service times almost always vary, and often customers arrive in random patterns. In summary, the key takeaways from Chapter 8 are:

1. Capacity planning for services requires consideration of the expected demand, capacity available, and a capacity buffer.
2. Capacity buffers are required for services, which will be larger when customers arrive at random or when service times exhibit higher levels of variation.
3. Resource utilizations should be calculated for each time interval, and resources (especially workforces) should be planned to best match demand with server ability to satisfy demand.
4. Worker schedules, by hour or by shift, can be created by reconciling demand with the restrictions inherent in shift or hourly schedules.
5. There are ways to make customers less aware of the time spent waiting, although that should not be considered preferable to shorter wait times.

Problems Set

1. Consider a sandwich shop, where customers will arrive randomly at a rate of 150 per hour. The process map shows the following flow (and average processing time per customer): (a) customer marks the selection on a form (average 45 seconds); (b) sandwich is prepared by a sandwich maker (average 90 seconds); (c) customer chooses additional items (average 60 seconds); (d) payment

processing at cashier (average 40 seconds); and (e) customer picks up sandwich at a designated location (average 20 seconds). The shop employs 2 cashiers, 6 sandwich makers, and 1 person at the pickup station. The variation of service process is moderate. Calculate the resource utilization of the cashiers (customers/minute), the sandwich makers (customers/minute), and the pickup station worker (customers/minute).

2.   Consider a non-profit organization, where grant proposals are written by the business development director. The proposals will be required randomly. The director devotes 6 hours per day to the proposals, with each proposal averaging 31 hours of effort. Each month consists of 12 working days (the director works other days, but not on proposals). The variation of the proposal writing process is moderate. For this proposal writing process, is the capacity of the director sufficient during a month where two proposals are required?

3.   Consider an insurance agent who files residential insurance claims. On average, the agent spends 12 minutes per claim and two agents work in the facility. During a certain time period, demand is forecasted to be 10.5 claims per hour, and arrives randomly. The random variation of the time it takes to complete a claim is high. How many agents are needed?

References

1   Larson R. Perspectives on queues: social justice and the psychology of queues. *Operations Research*. 1987; 35(6):895.

2   Katz K, Larson B, Larson R. Prescription for the waiting-in-line blues: entertain, enlighten, and engage. *Sloan Management Review*. 1991; 32(2):44.

9

MODELING BUSINESS PROCESS QUEUES

A Queuing System and its Analysis

Chapter 8 discussed the challenges associated with determining capacity for a business process. Recommendations were made regarding standard capacity buffers (i.e., target resource utilizations) and ways to account for behavioral characteristics of customers. In this chapter, the use of analytical queuing models is described. These models predict performance characteristics for business processes, but can only be used when certain assumptions apply. An analytical model is described that operates on a fairly robust set of assumptions. This model can be useful to predict waiting times and to compare alterative process configurations.

The analysis of a *queuing system* is performed with either an analytical *queuing model* or a *Monte Carlo simulation*. Queuing models tend to be mathematical abstractions that are useful when the real system adheres to the assumptions of the model. They are easy to use as long as a tool is provided to perform the somewhat complex calculations. Monte Carlo simulations are computer programs that mimic the business system, similar to the mortgage application processing simulation in Chapter 2. They are useful when the system is too complex for analytical modeling. Simulation modeling requires development capability, including technical expertise and software. "Monte Carlo" refers to the use of random number generators to mimic uncertainty within the simulation logic.

Figure 9.1: Illustrates the basic structure of all queuing systems. Specific configurations differ depending on the nature of each key component of the system. Properly characterizing a queuing system is important because it informs the method of analysis. In addition, it provides a convenient mechanism for communicating information to others without delving into specific details.

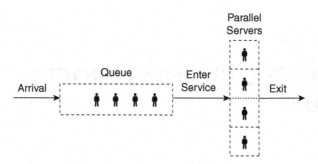

FIGURE 9.1 Structure of a Queuing System

A queuing system includes the following components:

(a) The *arrival* pattern is how customers enter the system following either a pre-determined pattern (e.g., scheduled appointments) or a random pattern. When arrivals are random, their time between arrivals (i.e., the interval from the arrival of one customer to the arrival of the next customer) can be determined based on theory or analysed statistically. Some arrival patterns include the possibility of customers arriving in batches (e.g., at airport customs after a plane lands).

(b) The *queue* is a set of waiting customers that occurs when all servers are busy assisting other customers. Some queues are physical (e.g., when a banking customer waits for an ATM) and others are virtual (e.g., when a customer continues to work while they wait for a service provider to return a call). Some queues have a finite length, whereby customers encountering a full queue will not enter the system (e.g., when a telephone system has a limit on holds). A queue discipline also exists, which dictates the priority given to each customer. Typically, queue disciples are first-come first-served or priority-based.

(c) One or more parallel *servers* will assist customers. Service times may be deterministic (i.e., not subject to uncertainty) or random. When service times are random, a data set of service times needs to be analysed to determine the nature of its random variation. Examples include the normal (bell shaped) pattern of variation and various patterns that are right-skewed.

(d) Customers *exit* the system after service is complete. In some queuing systems, customers flow back into the queue (where they become new arrivals). For example, a certain percentage of customers will call back to a call center because their problem continued after the recommended solution was implemented.

Wherever a resource exists, a queuing system will be present. At a retail establishment's checkout counter, customers wait in a common line on a first-come first-served basis until one of the cashiers becomes available. At a R&D facility, each project is assigned a priority and waits (virtually) for a scientist to become available. At a restaurant, customers arrive in randomly-sized batches. A hospital has a variety of queuing systems, which would be found wherever patients wait for a doctor, nurse, technician, or device. Even a bank's parking lot is a queuing system, where each parking location acts as a server.

When managing queues with multiple servers, two options will typically exist: (a) deploying a single queue regardless of the number of servers, or (b) deploying one queue for each server. For example, many grocery stores require each customer to choose a checkout line with a single dedicated server. On the other hand, many self-service checkout lines employ multiple devices (i.e., servers) and customers wait in a common queue for one of the devices to become available. In general, multi-server single queue systems perform better than a set of single server independent queues.

Measures of Effectiveness

The effectiveness of a queuing system is generally measured according to two perspectives. Both perspectives are important to a decision maker. They are described below:

(a) From the customer's perspective, effectiveness is generally measured by either *waiting time in queue* or *total time in system*. The latter timeframe includes both the queue time and the service time, and is also referred to as turnaround time. These measures will have an average level and they will vary over time. An analyst may also be interested in predicting the percentage of customers who will wait more than a threshold standard.
(b) From the service provider's perspective, effectiveness is generally measured by predicting *server utilization* (or similarly, service provider's idle time, which is the *capacity buffer* size). Queue length is another important measure of effectiveness because it has implications for the design of the service facility (or the size of virtual systems such as a telephone network capacity). For example, an analyst may want to determine how often the queue length will exceed the unacceptable queue size.

Reconciling these two perspectives – the customers' need for quick service and the firm's need for lower costs – is necessary. The decision concerning how many servers to deploy is challenging because one perspective (i.e., server cost) is financially quantifiable while the other perspective (i.e., customer service) is rarely financially quantifiable. We know the cost difference between 3 and 4 servers, but we don't know the financial impact of 5 and 25 minutes for a waiting customer. It is obviously important, however, because waiting time is correlated with customer satisfaction, which is correlated with revenue. In fact, dissatisfied customers will likely impact goodwill of the business process and increase the number of customer defections.

Quantifying Uncertainty

Various uncertainties will affect the performance of a business process in which customers wait for service. When analysing a queuing system, the two most important sets of uncertainties are those that affect customer arrivals and service times. In some cases, certain underlying phenomena will determine the nature of these variations. In other cases, a data collection effort would be required to quantify the uncertainty. When data are analysed, a probability model that best represents the system's random behavior would be identified.

In conjunction with understanding the random variation associated with arrivals and service, knowledge of the various analytical queuing models is also helpful. The simplest queuing models assume that the arrivals and service times are *Markovian*. When this assumption is valid, the arrival pattern and/or service times are said to conform with a *Poisson process*, as described below. An analyst would use data to seek confirmation that the system's uncertainty is consistent with this assumption.

Arrival Uncertainty

When customer arrivals are not scheduled, their arrival pattern will be subject to uncertainty. When customers arrive independently of one another, their arrival pattern will be consistent with a Poisson process. In these cases, the *time between arrivals* (TBA) of customers varies according to the exponential probability model. A Poisson process can be explained using a physical simulation. The simulation makes use of a standard six-sided die. Each roll of the die represents a one-minute duration. If a "6" is rolled, a customer arrived during that minute (otherwise, no arrival took place). For example, if the roll sequence was 3, 4, 1, 6, then the TBA = 4 because the first "6" occurred on the 4th roll. The likelihood that the TBA = 1 is 1/6 (the chance of rolling a 6), while the likelihood that the TBA = 2 would be 5/32 (the product of 5/6 and 1/6). Because 5/32 is less than 1/6, and it follows that likelihoods associated with each possible TBA will decrease as TBA increases. In addition, the average TBA would be 6 minutes.

The exponential model with average TBA equal to 6 is shown in Figure 9.2. Here, the discrete time scale used in the die roll simulation is replaced with a more accurate continuous time scale. A reader can think of the area under the curve as equal to the likelihood that the TBA will fall in the range chosen. The total area equals 100%. For example, the probability that the TBA is less than 2 is the area under the curve between TBA = 0 and TBA = 2. The next customer will arrive, on average, in 6 minutes. But the most likely next arrival is

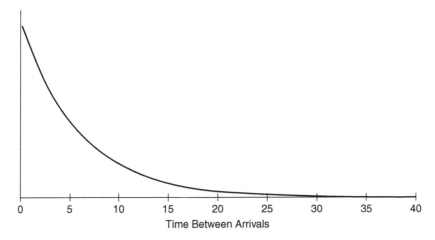

FIGURE 9.2 Exponential Distribution with Average TBA of 6.0

sooner, rather than later. It may not be likely that the next arrival occurs in the next minute, it is more likely that the next arrival will occur in the next minute than it is that the next arrival will be two minutes from now. When the TBA is exponentially distributed, customers arrive at a constant rate. For this example, because the average TBA is 6, the average rate of customer arrivals is 10 customers per hour. This rate will not change as long as the Poisson Process exists.

Service Time Uncertainty

Service time variation is usually similar to the exponential distribution because service time variation tends to be skewed "right." This is quite natural for the duration of a service because most unusual service requests take longer than average to complete. Although the exponential model often applies to service times, other potential models exhibit less skewness (these alternative models include the beta, the log normal, and the gamma). In all cases, the analytical or simulation modeling approach must start with the analysis of service time data to determine its distribution.

Consider an example where data are collected on the amount of time it takes to validate a customer's membership status at a service center. The following service times data were recorded for 50 customers (all in minutes): 5.7, 19.5, 22.7, 11.6, 13.8, 1.6, 5.7, 1.4, 3.5, 2.4, 5.4, 1.7, 32.8, 4.2, 10.0, 0.4, 19.9, 1.1, 10.7, 1.6, 0.7, 0.4, 2.1, 21.8, 4.4, 2.7, 14.7, 0.3, 3.9, 3.1, 18.4, 3.2, 12.4, 4.8, 0.1, 10.1, 8.7, 4.7, 1.3, 18.5, 6.4, 2.1, 9.2, 6.9, 6.4, 30.4, 9.2, 1.0, 4.6 and 5.5 minutes. Figure 9.3 is a histogram of this service time data. Note that the height of the bars, which decrease from left to right, exhibit a shape consistent with the exponential model.

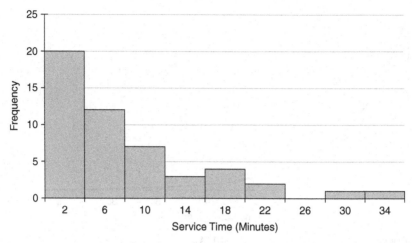

FIGURE 9.3 Histogram for Service Times

The 50 service times had an average of 7.87 minutes, and therefore we can conclude that the service times follow an exponential distribution with an average of about 7.87 minutes. Analysts should be aware that the histogram is based on a sample of data, and therefore the size of each bar is subject to random variations. Hence, an analyst would not expect its shape to precisely duplicate the exponential curve, especially when the sample size is less than 100 customers.

The M/M/s Queuing Model

Many analytical queuing models exist. Each model can analyse a specified set of queuing systems depending on the consistency between the assumptions of the model and the real system. A standard coding system was developed by Kendall [1] to assist analysts in understanding the assumptions and communicating with other analysts. The code is as follows: A/B/s/D/N/K, where:

- A is the arrival time model
- B is the service time model
- s is the number of parallel servers
- D is the queue discipline
- N is the system capacity (number of customers allowed)
- K is the size of the customer population

Each component of the code has a standard one or two letter abbreviation. In this module, the M/M/s model will be discussed and its use will be illustrated. The M/M/s assumes:

- Poisson arrivals with rate λ (lambda), expressed as arrivals per time interval (the M is an abbreviation of Markovian).
- Exponential service with rate μ (mu) expressed as service completions per time interval.
- s parallel servers.
- Any queue discipline (i.e., results do not depend on the discipline).
- Infinite queue size (i.e., there is no maximum queue size).
- Infinite customer population (i.e., the population of customers is not limited).

The model is only useful when: $\frac{\lambda}{\mu s} < 1$ (if this condition is not valid, the queue size would continually increase over time). Users of the model must ensure that the rates λ and μ are stated correctly and consistently – both in terms of rates (customers per time interval) and the time interval (minutes, hours, etc.). For example, it would be equivalent to express λ as: 0.05 arrivals/ second, 3 arrivals/minute, or 180 arrivals/hour. For service times, the specification of μ is counter-intuitive. Services durations are usually expressed as time per customer (e.g., 15 minutes per customer). But, the value of μ needs to be expressed as number of customers served per time interval (e.g., if the average service time is 15 minutes, μ = 4 customers/hour).

Consider the operation of a new walk-in financial center with one consultant on duty. Customers arrive independently of one another and the anticipated arrival rate is 14 customers per hour. The anticipated average service time is 3.6 minutes, which will be assumed to be exponentially distributed. Here, the M/M/1 model applies because both arrivals and service times are Markovian, and there is one server. The values for λ (arrival rate) and μ (service rate) are 14 customers/hour and 16.7 customers/hour, respectively. Note that the service rate of 16.7 customers/hour is obtained by conversion of the average service time (i.e., 60 minutes/hour divided by 3.6 minutes/customer).

An Excel-based *Queue Model Template* has been created that implements the M/M/s model. It is included in the book's eResources, along with a video describing its use. This template can be used for any M/M/s analysis, as long as the number of servers does not exceed 10. For the walk-in financial center, Figure 9.4 shows the analysis for one server. The template provides several measures of effectiveness, including server utilization, average queue length, average time in queue, and average time in system. A graphical display shows how the server utilization changes when more or less servers are employed. The template also shows the percentage of customers who wait, along with probabilities corresponding to the number of customers in the queue and in the system. The probabilities associated with the number of customers in the queue is also shown graphically.

The results of the analysis indicate that the server utilization is 83.8% (i.e., the server will be idle 16.2% of the time, which constitutes the size of the

M/M/s Queueing System Analysis

Arrival Rate (λ)	14	Average Number of Arrivals Per Time Interval
Service Rate (μ)	16.7	Average Number of Customers Servered Per Time Interval
No. Servers (s)	1	Number of Servers (10 or less)

Number of Customers		
In System	In Queue	Probability
0	0	0.162
1	0	0.136
2	1	0.114
3	2	0.095
4	3	0.080
5	4	0.067
6	5	0.056
7	6	0.047
8	7	0.039
9	8	0.033
10	9	0.028
11	10	0.023
12	11	0.019
13	12	0.016
14	13	0.014
15	14	0.011
16	15	0.010
17	16	0.008
18	17	0.007
19	18	0.006
20	19	0.005
21	20	0.004
22	21	0.003
23	22	0.003
24	23	0.002
25	24	0.012

Summaries:

Server Utilization:	83.8%
Average Queue Length	4.3
Average Number in System	5.2
Average Time in Queue	0.31
Average Time in System	0.37
Percentage Who Wait	83.8%

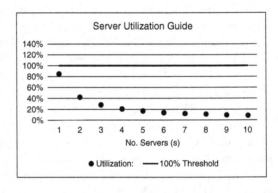

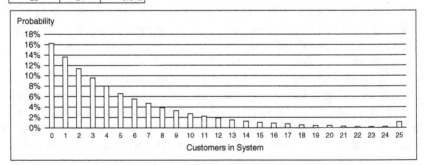

FIGURE 9.4 M/M/1 Example with Excel Template

capacity buffer). There will be one customer in the system 13.6% of the time (this customer would be at the server and the queue would be empty). There will be two customers in the system 11.4% of the time (one being served and one in the queue). The average queue length would be 4.35 customers, and average time in queue will be 0.31 hours and the average time in system will be 0.37 hours. The graph of probabilities shows that, often, there will be many customers in the system. This graph helps analysts gauge the customer experience and to determine the required size of a service facility.

Note that the time units associated with average time in queue and average time in system are consistent with λ and μ (in this case, hours). At times, it is convenient to translate fractional time units into smaller intervals. Therefore, the inputs could have been entered in customers per minute. In this case, λ would be entered as 0.2333 (14 divided by 60) and μ would be entered as 0.2783 (16.7 divided by 60). If this were done, all results would be the same, except the average time in queue (now 18.6 minutes) and the average time in system (now 22.2 minutes).

The Excel template is very helpful for determining how the queuing system would perform with less or more servers. Although the template is not shown here, by changing the number of servers from 1 to 2, the following important changes would be evident. The average waiting time in queue will be reduced to 0.0128 hours (0.77 minutes). The average queue size is reduced to 0.18 customers (almost zero). Server utilization will decrease to 41.9%. That is, the server will be idle over half of the time. The business process manger would need to determine the best option. One server results in an average waiting time of over 18 minutes, while two severs reduces the average wait time to less than a minute but doubles the cost of servers.

Comprehensive Example

A coffee shop is considering a drive-up window, with the intent to improve customer service. The increased revenue should more than offset the fixed installation and variable labor costs. The coffee shop employs a combination of full-time and part-time workers. A previous project included information on current arrival and service times. Arrival rates vary according to time of day, but follow a Poisson process within each time period. Service time data were also collected. Currently 4 servers are on duty during the peak morning period. No other information is available regarding the staffing of servers. For other time periods, labor assignments have been inconsistent and therefore no suitable "benchmark" service level is available.

A study was undertaken in cooperation with other similar shops that use a drive-up window. This study concluded that, once a drive-up window is installed, customers with simpler service requests will tend to use the window in higher proportion than those entering the shop. Specifically, with installation of the drive-up window, current service times in the store would be increased an average of 25% and the service times at the window would average about half of the current service times.

A market study, using a focus group and an informal survey, estimated that demand would be affected by installing the drive-up window. Specifically,

30% of current customers will use the window. A new group of customers, about 20% above the current customer base, will also use the window. A consultant is asked to do a preliminary analysis with queuing models to determine if the installation of the window should be considered.

The current arrival rates to the coffee shop are 105 customers/hour (morning), 90 customers/hour (mid-day), and 75 customers/hour (late afternoon). The coffee shop is closed during evening hours. For the proposed system that includes the drive-up window, the rates will change based on the market study data. For the morning timeframe, 20% of current customers (21/hour) and 30% more new customers (31.5/hour) results in an overall arrival rate of 52.5 customers/hour at the window during the morning period. Similarly, the rate of arrivals at the window will be 45 customers/hour (mid-day) and 37.5 customers/hour (late afternoon). Seventy percent of current customers will come into the store. Therefore, the arrival rates will be 73.5 customers/hour (morning), 63 customers/hour (mid-day), and 52.5 customers/hour (late afternoon). The study also concluded that the arrival process is Markovian because customers arrive independently of one another. The arrival rates for each alternative configuration is shown in Table 9.1.

A data analysis of service times for the current system was performed showing that service times follow an exponential distribution. The average service time was 2.02 minutes, which was rounded to 2.0 minutes per customer. Hence, for the current system, the service rate is 30 customers/hour, regardless of the timeframe. The service rates for the current and new configurations were calculated based on the analysis performed at similar businesses. The service rate is 60 customers/hour at the window (a decrease of 50% from the current system because average service time is reduced to 1.0 minutes). Finally, the service rate is 24 customers/hour in the store (because the average service time in the store will increase by 25% to 2.5 minutes/customer). The service rates for each alterative configuration is shown in Table 9.1.

Now that all of the information is available and the appropriateness of the M/M/s model has been confirmed, the queuing analysis will commence. First, the current system will be analysed. The only precise information known is

TABLE 9.1 Queuing Model Parameters (Rates are Expressed per Hour)

| | Current System | | Proposed System | | | |
| | In Shop Only | | Window | | In Shop | |
	λ	μ	λ	μ	λ	μ
Morning	105	30	52.5	60	73.5	24
Mid-Day	90	30	45	60	63	24
Late Afternoon	75	30	37.5	60	52.5	24

that 4 servers are employed during the peak morning period. When inputs are entered for the morning peak period ($\lambda = 105$, $\mu = 30$, $s = 4$), the average waiting time is 3.0 minutes and the server utilization is 87.5%. Management agrees that these waiting times appear to be consistent with their experience. Therefore, an average waiting time of 3.0 minutes will be a benchmark for determining server needs for other periods in the current system. Using the M/M/s queuing model, the results below would be obtained:

- Morning (4 servers): 87.5% server utilization, 3.0 minute average wait in queue
- Mid-Day (4 servers): 75.0% server utilization, 1.0 minute average wait in queue
- Late Afternoon (3 servers): 83.3% server utilization, 2.8 minute average wait in queue

Second, the new configuration (with the drive-up window) will be evaluated. Management agrees that the 3-minute average wait would be the threshold against which to evaluate service for any alternative configurations. That is, management would prefer new configurations that have average wait time of 3 minutes or less.

For the window, which can only accommodate 1 server, applying the M/M/1 model yields the following results:

- Morning (1 server): 87.5% server utilization, 7.0 minute average wait in queue
- Mid-Day (1 server): 75.0% server utilization, 3.0 minute average wait in queue
- Late Afternoon (1 server): 62.5% server utilization, 1.7 minute average wait in queue

For the peak morning period, one server results in 7 min of waiting, which is above benchmark, but 2 servers at the window are not feasible. However, we know that if the line is long, some customers will go into store and therefore a certain proportion of revenue would be retained (assuming that the lines in the store are not too long), but some revenue will not be realized.

In the store, which can accommodate any number of servers, applying the M/M/s model yields the following results assuming a 3-minute maximum average waiting time:

- Morning (4 servers): 76.6% server utilization, 1.4 minute average wait in queue
- Mid-Day (4 servers): 65.6% server utilization, 0.7 minute average wait in queue
- Late Afternoon (3 servers): 72.9% server utilization, 1.6 minute average wait in queue

TABLE 9.2 Comparison (Workers with Utilization and Average Wait Time)

	Current System	Proposed System		
Period	In Store	Window	In Store	Total
Morning	4 (87.5% 3.0 min)	1 (87.5% 7.0 min)	4(76.6% 1.4 min)	5
Mid-Day	4 (75.0% 1.0 min)	1 (75.0% 3.0 min)	4(65.6% 0.7 min)	5
Late Aft	3 (83.3%, 2.8 min)	1 (62.5% 1.7 min)	3 (72.9% 1.6 min)	4

For the morning, 4 servers results in an average of only 1.4 min of waiting, but carryover from the window will be expected that will likely add to this wait time. For the mid-day period, 3 servers result in 5.2 min of waiting, which is above benchmark, so management should consider use 4 servers during those times. For the late afternoon, 3 servers will provide an acceptable result.

The final recommendation should be informed by the model, but not dictated by the model. Based on the 3-minute average wait standard specified by management, the number of servers for these two options are summarized in Table 9.2 (the 7.0 minute average wait at the Window is left as-is because no workers can be added).

For the proposed system with the drive-up window, one additional server would be required. The labor cost associated with the two optional configurations should be calculated. Management would need to determine if the 20% increase in customers (with an adjustment based on those who will not wait at the window and not enter the store) would offset the installation cost of the window and the additional server.

Standard Capacity Buffer Levels

Some general rules for capacity buffering have been developed that eliminate the need for every business process manager to analyse their process operation using an analytical model. The key to this effort is the appreciation that, when arrivals and/or service times are random, a non-linear relationship will exist between resource utilization and customer waiting time. In these cases, once a certain threshold of utilization is reached, waiting times will increase dramatically.

As an illustration, consider a call center where customer calls arrive at a rate of 40 per hour. Because customers arrive independently of one another, we can assume that the arrivals follow a Poisson process. Studies have shown that service time is exponential, averaging 15 minutes per customer and therefore we can apply the M/M/s model. Figure 9.5 shows the waiting times with servers ranging from 20 to 11 (e.g., when s=13, the server utilization will be 77% and the average wait time will be about 1.5 minutes). As servers are decreased from 20 through 13 servers, utilization increases from 50% to 77%, and waiting

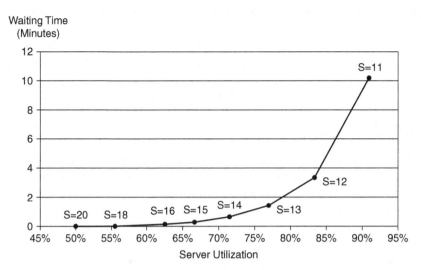

FIGURE 9.5 Call Center: Server Utilization Vs. Average Wait Time

times increase in an approximately linear fashion. However, the change from 13 to 12 servers (77% to 83% utilization) results in a larger waiting line increase than the previous trend, as does the waiting time increase resulting from a change from 12 to 11 servers (83% to 91% utilization). This unique mathematical relationship is known as a *hockey-stick* function. In this example, a server utilization of 85% appears to be an appropriate threshold that is suitable for a decision.

The precise point on the hockey-stick function where waiting times begin to increase dramatically depends on the variation in service times and the nature of customer arrivals. Standard capacity buffers can, however, be established. These capacity buffer levels depend on whether the customers arrive randomly or they are scheduled, and the level of service time variation from customer to customer. To determine the level of service time variation, an analyst would collect service time data (not including queue time), and calculate the average and standard deviation of the resulting data set. Then, the ratio of the standard deviation and the average, called the coefficient of variation (CV) would be calculated. According to probability theory, a CV near 100% is consistent with an exponential distribution.

The following standard capacity buffer rules are recommended. The recommendations are based on the arrival pattern and amount of service time variation. High service time variation would occur when the CV is above 40% and low-medium service time variation occurs when the CV is between 10% and 30%. The standard capacity buffer sizes are:

- Scheduled Arrivals, Low-Medium Service Time Variation: 5% Capacity Buffer
- Scheduled Arrivals, High Service Time Variation: 10% Capacity Buffer
- Random Arrivals, Low-Medium Service Time Variation: 10% Capacity Buffer
- Random Arrivals, High Service Time Variation: 15% Capacity Buffer

The Impact of Reducing Waste

Capacity buffers can be very effective at controlling customer wait times. But they can be very costly, especially when server costs are high. High costs can be attributed to labor (e.g., professional workers, medical professionals, or consultants), or equipment (e.g., testing centers or medical technologies). A 15% capacity buffer would mean that each worker would be idle during about one of seven working hours.

Capacity buffers can also be increased without adding workers, because existing service times will often consist of non-value-added activities. This wasted time occurs when inefficiencies exist in many processes. For example, a human resource worker's ability to obtain required information from internal customers takes longer than should be necessary. It especially occurs when the service is made up of interconnected activities that cross functional lines and require cooperation across departments.

Given the hockey-stick functional relationship between server utilization and waiting times, decreasing service times by a small amount can have disproportionate benefits for customers. Returning to the previous call center example, the average service time was 15 minutes and customers arrived at the rate of 40 - per hour. With 11 servers, the server utilization is 90.9% and the average wait time for callers is 10.2 minutes (see Figure 9.5). Let's assume that the 15 minute average service time can be reduced by 45 seconds to 14.25 minutes. Because 11 servers can now serve an average of 46.3 customers in one hour, server unitization with 11 servers is reduced to 86.4%. In the hockey-stick function, we see that the average waiting time for this server utilization is about 5 minutes (it is exactly 5.2 minutes based on the M/M/s model).

To summarize this example, service times were reduced by an average of 45 seconds (0.75 minutes). This change reduced the average waiting time for customers from 10.2 minutes to 5.2 minutes. By removing 45 seconds from the average service time, customers' waiting time decreased by an average of 5 minutes. This result may seem counter-intuitive, but it is a direct result of the hockey-stick phenomenon in queuing systems.

Over time, services can become more complex or the amount of wasteful activities may slowly increase. As a result, the resource utilization increase may go unnoticed. But, this increase will eventually reach a critical threshold, after which customer queues (and wait times) will increase dramatically. Long queues are also erratic queues. Managers may experience "good days" and "bad days" in terms of customer service when server utilizations are very high. However, the root causes of the bad days are not due to special causes present that day – they are due to the unnoticed increase in service times.

Lean methods can help business processes achieve better results without the need for high-cost capacity buffers. The methods discussed earlier in this book, such as standard work, 5S's, and poka-yoke can reduce service times so that queue times can be managed in a cost effective manner. Other methods for achieving similar results include implementing self-service mechanisms so that some of the service burden is removed from the service provider's responsibility. Finally, the use of technology can assist, but only where waste is not automated.

Summary & Key Takeaways

Balancing the financial needs of the firm with the responsiveness needs of customers requires that queues be actively managed. The use of an analytical queuing model can evaluate queuing systems that will be found wherever critical resources are needed to serve customers. Managing queues for services is complex because service times almost always vary, usually varying significantly. And, customers often arrive in random patterns. In summary, the key takeaways from Chapter 9 are:

1. Random customer arrivals and service times can be represented by a probability model.
2. A queuing model can be used to determine the most effective number of servers in a business process that balances the customer desire for fast service and service provider desire for low resource costs.
3. The M/M/s queuing model applies in many practical settings; it is easily implemented using an Excel template.
4. A standard threshold for capacity buffering can be developed based on the nature of demand variation and service time variation.
5. Lean methods can lower queue times dramatically by reducing service activity times which can have dramatic effects on customer service.

Problems Set

1. In an IT call center, it is estimated that 30% of the customers will have serious problems which require an average of 20 minutes to solve, 60% will have troubleshooting problems which require an average of 10 minutes to solve, and 10% will have non-complicated problems which require

an average of 12 minutes to solve. In total, 40 customers need the call center during each hour and they arrive independently of one another. All service times are exponentially distributed.

a. What would be the average waiting times if 3 employees are hired for serious problems, 6 employees for troubleshooting problems, and 1 for non-complicated problems?

b. If the number of arrivals increased by 15%, how many servers are needed in each category to keep the average time less than 15 minutes?

2. At a law firm, 24 customers arrive per hour and 25% of them need a space to park their car. The service time for consultation averages 45 minutes. How many parking spaces does the law firm need to rent so that the percentage of people who cannot access a free parking space is less than 5%? Assume that arrivals are independent of one another and that the service times are exponentially distributed.

3. Customer waiting time is to be analysed for a new mobile phone store layout, where customers are segmented into three categories: new purchase, troubleshooting, and billing inquires. The store's layout will not allow sharing of servers across the three categories. It is estimated that 20% of customers will be interested in a new purchase, 50% will arrive for troubleshooting, and 30% will be there for billing inquires. Average service times will be 16 minutes for new purchases, 9 minutes for trouble-shooting, and 6 minutes for billing inquiries. In total, 50 customers arrive at the store during each hour. Customers arrive independently of one another and service times are exponentially distributed.

a. What would be the average waiting times (in minutes) if the following number of servers were employed: 3 for new purchases, 5 for troubleshooting, and 2 for billing inquiries?

b. If all average waiting times are targeted at under 5 minutes, how many servers would be needed in each category?

Reference

1 Kendall DG. Some problems in the theory of queues. *Journal of the Royal Statistical Society: Series B (Methodological)*. 1951; 13(2):151–73.

10

MEASURING BUSINESS PROCESS PERFORMANCE

Determining Performance Metrics

Practitioners are well aware of *better, cheaper, faster* (BCF) as three important high-level goals in any business. These three dimensions are certainly important – all customers want high quality (i.e., better), and they want it as quickly as possible (i.e., faster) and at the lowest cost (i.e., cheaper). However, the definition of "better" can itself be multi-dimensional, especially when it pertains to customers of a service. In Chapter 3, the definition of value as defined by customers formed the basis of a business process analysis. These dimensions informed development of process maps and the identification of value-added and wasteful activities. Once wasteful practices are removed and effective capacity levels are determined, the process should be able to deliver an effective service.

Performance of the business process needs to be measured on an ongoing basis. Many firms employ a quality (or performance) management system that collects and analyses performance data. These systems evaluate performance relative to the goals set by the firm. They also show when performance degrades so a root cause investigation can be initiated. Performance management for a business process offers unique challenges due to the multi-dimensionality of customer desires. In addition, many firms do not devote suitable attention to creating and maintaining a performance management system, especially for processes that serve internal customers.

The appreciation of performance dimensions is integral to delivering value that is measured by customers' needs rather than by cost-effectiveness and other service providers' desires. For services, performance dimensions vary based on the nature of the service. In a bank, for example, the performance dimensions are typically accuracy, transaction timeliness, convenience, courtesy, and information security. In manufacturing, dimensions tend to be more narrowly focused on conformance to design specifications and timely delivery, although rarely does a manufacturer provide only products. For example, if maintenance instructions are created by the manufacturer, performance dimensions would include the accuracy and clarity of instructions.

Performance metrics are used to measure how the process is operating. There should be one or more metrics associated with each performance dimension. Well-known metrics are common in many business processes. They include the percentage of jobs completed, the average customer turnaround time, the number of complaints, and the percentage of customers returning because their problem was not solved. In certain industries, standard metrics are used to facilitate comparison across firms. Standard metrics are common for call centers, hospitals, education, and insurance firms.

When metrics already exist, the business process manager should align each performance dimension with at least one appropriate metric. There are often cases where new metrics are required or when the bulk of existing metrics concern only a subset of dimensions. Often, metrics concern the cost it takes to deliver the service. These metrics, although critically important, are not used to gauge the ability to meet customer needs. Therefore, they are not discussed in this chapter.

At times, one or more performance dimensions require the creation of new performance metrics. In these cases, it is best to find a standard metric that is easily understood. Metrics need to be created when none exist. In all cases, each metric should be the simplest way to measure performance. For the four business processes detailed earlier in the book, examples of performance metrics are listed below. Readers may recall that the list of performance metrics is consistent with the performance dimensions developed in Chapter 3.

Financial Audit Process Metrics

The financial auditing process has two main customers. For the client as customer, key performance dimensions and example performance metrics could be:

Timeliness: Proportions of proposals delivered on or before due date.

Competency: Number of return visits to correct problems with audits.

Convenience: Average time required for participation by client.

Courtesy: Number of protocol violations during unscheduled visits to observe auditors.

Privacy: Number of privacy violations reported by the bank.

For the government (i.e., regulator) as customer, key performance dimensions and example performance metrics could be:

Accuracy: Number of revisions made per proposal.

Timeliness: Proportion of audits completed on time.

Conformance: Number of errors found during regulator quality review.

Completeness: Number of additions made to audit reports.

Responsiveness: Turnaround time to answer an e-mail message.

IT Change Approval Process Metrics

The IT change approval process has two main customers. For the insurance firm's operations department as customer, key performance dimensions and example performance metrics could be:

Timeliness: Average time to complete evaluation.

Agility: Number of IT changes rejected.

Availability: Proportion of attendance at scheduled meetings.

Competency: Number of revisions required during programming activities.

Clarity: Number of questions asked by programmers.

For the policy holder as customer, key performance dimensions and example performance metrics could be:

Simplicity: Length of communication required to inform customer.

Usefulness: Customer retention rate.

Availability: Proportion of telephone calls answered by voice-mail.

Courtesy: Nonconforming results of periodic audits of customer communications.

Responsiveness: Proportion of e-mail messages not answered within 4 working hours.

Price Quoting Process Metrics

The price quoting process has two main customers. For the external customer making the request, key performance dimensions and example performance metrics could be:

Timeliness: Total turnaround time.

Integrity: Offered price versus market average price.

Convenience: Number of separate interactions made by customer to submit information.

Privacy: Results of periodic inspection of records.

Clarity: Number of follow-up questions asked by customers.

For the firm's business manager as customer, key performance dimensions and example performance metrics could be:

Accuracy: Number of follow-up questions asked by customers.

Flexibility: Number of new customers with accepted quotes.

Timeliness: Average time to complete quote.

Competency: Number of issues reported by manufacturing.

Conciseness: Proportion of accepted quotes with low profit margins.

Blood Testing Process Metrics

The blood testing process has two main customers. For the patient as customer, key performance dimensions and example performance metrics could be:

Clarity: Number of follow-up questions from patients.

Timeliness: Average time from order to consultation with physician.

Competency: Proportion of samples that need to be retaken.

Painlessness: Number of attempts to draw blood per patient.

Privacy: Number of violations of HIPAA rules.

For the physician as customer, key performance dimensions and example performance metrics could be:

Accuracy: Number of retakes due to incorrect test being done.

Timeliness: Average time from order to consultation with physician.

Competency: Proportion of samples that need to be retaken.

Knowledge: Number of tests suggested by laboratory personnel.

Responsiveness: Turnaround time for follow-up tests that do not require an additional draw.

Cost can be a dimension of performance in cases when the customer pays a variable amount for the service. In many cases, however, cost is a fixed or negotiated value rather than a measure of process outcome. That is, if a firm negotiates a purchase price with a supplier, and this price will not change over a period, this price is not considered a performance metric. However, in large supply chains, many negotiations take place routinely and therefore many cost elements do change over time. Hence, it is sometimes important to use cost as a dimension of performance. Many metrics act as surrogates for cost, such as the utilization of equipment or labor. However, its salience leads most firms to include cost as a performance dimension.

Certain features that are considered strengths of a business process should not be declared to be a performance metric. For example, the number of scientists holding a doctoral degree who work in a consulting company is a characteristic of the service, rather than a metric (i.e., it does not measure an outcome). Similarly, some facets of how the process is operated (however valuable) should not be considered a metric. For example, a call center that operates 24/7 can provide great service for customers. Here, availability during working hours can form the basis of a metric whereas the number of operating hours is a feature of the service process.

Customer satisfaction surveys can serve as supplements to performance metrics in important ways. Ideally, each performance dimension would have one or more satisfaction survey questions that address the dimension. Satisfaction survey results are not performance metrics themselves because they combine cost expectations with business process performance. Metrics represent an objective internal evaluation of performance, while satisfaction surveys are an external subjective measure. A business process can be meeting objectives based on metrics, but customers may not be satisfied. For example, a metric may be tabulated as the percentage of e-mail messages answered in 24 hours. The business process may achieve this goal 100% of the time, but customers may not be very happy because they expect answers sooner. The combination of performance metrics and satisfaction survey questions form an effective system for understanding performance.

Turnbacks, Mistakes, Close Calls, and Complaints

A business process manager should appreciate that, although they are best avoided, mistakes represent opportunities to make improvements. When mistakes do occur, they are often found before the customer notices the error. This event can be referred to as a *turnback*. A turnback occurs, for example, when a marketing analyst notices that data provided by a survey was completed by a biased mix of customers, and stops the report from being delivered. Cost would be incurred for redoing the survey but the customer would not be aware that the mistake was made. A mistake that does affect the customer is referred to as an *escape*. An escape would occur, for example, if the marketing analyst's report was delivered to the customer who noticed the error. This type of mistake is more costly to the organization than a turnback because customer satisfaction is affected.

Although the penalties for making mistakes can be high, they can also lead to the identification of underlying problems. Action can be taken to eliminate these problems from occurring in the future. It follows that *close calls* (near mistakes) offer even better opportunities for improvement because no customers are affected and little extra cost is incurred. In most organizations, however, close calls are not routinely reported. For example, if a new marketing assistant begins to develop a biased survey mechanism and this is discovered during a causal discussion with a peer over lunch, the biased survey would not have been administered. By not reporting this close call, an opportunity would be lost to correct the standard procedures used to identify the target survey audience and the mistake has potential to reoccur.

The U.S. Federal Aviation Administration operates a voluntary system for tabulating and reporting turnbacks, escapes, and close calls based on information provided by pilots, air traffic controllers, flight attendants and other airline workers and contractors. Those reporting incidents can do so anonymously and the reporter is immune from punishment. The success of this system is evidenced by the impressive safety record of major U.S. airlines. Other industries, especially healthcare, have taken strives to create similar systems. The organizational infrastructure at the firm level needs to support these initiatives. It should encourage the reporting of mistakes and close calls, and guarantee that those reporting these incidents are not punished. In fact, they should be rewarded.

At the department level, the use of simple sticky notes can facilitate the reporting of mistakes and close calls. Workers who encounter any mistake or close call would write it on a sticky note and post it in a central location. Periodically, a meeting would be held where the notes are organized in categories (i.e., moved to a set of columns, with one category per column). Then, the longest column of notes, which corresponds to the mistake or close class that occurs most frequently, would be addressed. Ideally, its root cause would be identified and eliminated. This system has been successfully employed in a research & development facility, and helped to eliminate time wasted finding equipment, correcting unclear reports, and ensuring accurate proposals. [1]

Customer complaints are also important to monitor. Although they seem similar to escapes, they should be treated differently. An escape is a mistake that is objectively identified by the customer; complaints are typically subjective. For example, consider an environmental health and safety (EH&S) department that creates monthly reports to executives (their internal customer). An important dimension of performance is accuracy. If a customer notices that a calculation is incorrect and they complain to the EH&S manager, this occurrence should be considered an escape. Alternatively, if a complaint is made that a EH&S employee was slow to return a call, this event would be classified as a complaint because expectations regarding response time are subjective. The analysis of customer complaints would follow the same methods as the analysis of performance metrics. These methods, covered in Chapter 11, will help avoid reaction to "loud voices" that may not be worthy of immediate attention.

Theory of Mistakes

It is useful to discuss how and why mistakes happen when managing a business process. W. Edwards Deming (1990–1993) claimed that 94% of mistakes should be blamed on the system (e.g., the culture, practices, incentives, training, and other management-controlled factors) and only 6% should be blamed on an individual worker (e.g., due to indifference, sabotage, or laziness). [2] Although these percentages were not based on a thorough scientific investigation, they are useful as a general philosophy. The system is the most important factor affecting the likelihood of mistakes, and therefore focusing on root cause rather than blame is the preferred approach to dealing with (and learning from) mistakes.

The fallacy associated with placing blame on workers can be illustrated by reading the accident investigation board's report on the 2003 space shuttle Columbia accident [3], which stated:

It is our view that complex systems almost always fail in complex ways, and we believe it would be wrong to reduce the complexities and weaknesses associated with these systems to some simple explanation. Too often, accident investigations blame a failure only on the last step in a complex process, when a more comprehensive understanding of that process could reveal that earlier steps might be equally or even more culpable. In this Board's opinion, unless the technical, organizational, and cultural recommendations made in this report are implemented, little will have been accomplished to lessen the chance that another accident will follow.

In his landmark book, *Human Error* [4], James Reason describes the following three categories of errors as associated with a business process.

Skill-based Mistakes

Skill-based mistakes, also called slips or lapses, happen in situations where the activity was not performed properly but they are not due to an extraordinary task or to a worker lacking the proper knowledge. Although the fault may lie with the worker, it is important to consider system-imposed root causes such as fatigue (e.g., extremely long work hours), distractions (e.g., when attention is diverted), or tedium (e.g., repetitive boring tasks). Therefore, the initial reaction to blame the worker would not be warranted.

Many of these mistakes stem from the 94% system-based causes that Deming described. Management should not make unrealistic assumptions about the ability of workers to perform accurate tasks while working long shifts. They should be careful when requiring workers to stop normal activities to work on an emergency or other extraordinary issue. When workers return to the original job, some specific issues may have been forgotten. These occurrences are known as *firefighting* and can occur too frequently in some firms. Finally, some tasks, such as screening attendees entering an event, make it difficult for humans to maintain full concentration.

Rule-based Mistakes

Rule-based mistakes are those that are due to an extraordinary task that falls outside of the normal work scope of the business process, but not due to inadequate worker knowledge. More specifically, the process has the knowledge to deal with the extraordinary task, but the approach to the task has not been specified. This would happen at a call center where a new innovative product or service is offered. Call center representatives have the training to understand the issues raised by callers, but were not given specific details about the new products. Hence, they fail in their intent to assist callers effectively.

Often, workers attempt to complete the extraordinary activities by attempting to find a similar situation where an approach exists. This subjective methodology leads to inconsistencies in how the task is performed across workers. In addition, the approach is inadequate when no prior situation is comparable. A new set of procedures needs to be devised for the situation at hand.

All rule-based mistakes stem from the 94% system-based causes that Deming described. To help eliminate these mistakes, cooperation is important across departments of the firm. In addition, flexibility should be built into standard work processes. Servers in restaurants are often allowed to give a discount to customers when any problem occurs during their meal, regardless of the problem type. Another approach is to specify an expert who should be consulted when a customer request exceeds typical parameters. It would be important for extraordinary requests to be tabulated because, over time, they may become normal. This phenomenon occurs when the services offered by a business process evolve over time.

Knowledge-based Mistakes

Knowledge-based mistakes are those that are due to the lack of process knowledge in the presence of an extraordinary task. Because the process has not been designed to deal with the situation, substantial retraining may be necessary. For example, the implementation of a new IT system necessitates training of workers involved in all business processes that interact with the system. In more extreme cases, the hiring practices of the business process manager should be reconsidered. For example, if an auditing firm takes on clients in a new industry sector, some workers with background in that field would need to be acquired.

Knowledge-based mistakes fall within Deming's estimated 94% system-based mistakes. Eliminating these mistakes would require more extreme measures compared to rule-based mistakes because the process (including workers – but not exclusively) needs to be redesigned. New information systems may be required, workers with different educational backgrounds may be needed, or other process characteristics may need to be changed. In the early days of the Internet, for example, many cafés supplemented their food and drink offerings with Internet access (i.e., Internet cafés). However, customers were often dissatisfied because employees lacked understanding of how the Internet worked.

Swiss Cheese Analogy

Mistakes do not always cause customers to be dissatisfied for a number of reasons. First, a mistake may be unimportant to the specific service output, such as when an error appears in an accounting statement but the executive making use of the statement does not include that figure in their analysis.

Second, some mistakes may be identified by other workers within the firm, such as when a worker creating a price quote notices that a physical characteristic specified by an earlier process activity exceeded the range of its possible values. Third, customers may not notice the mistake, such as when a miscalculation of a product forecast occurs.

When mistakes result in customer dissatisfaction, it is often due to a combination of mistakes in a pattern knows as *Swiss cheese*. When randomly stacking several slices of Swiss cheese, it is unlikely that one would see through the entire stack. For the customer of a business process to be dissatisfied: (a) a mistake would be made, (b) the worker would not notice the mistake, (c) workers in subsequent processes would not notice the mistake, (d) the customer would notice the mistake, and (e) the customer would be concerned about the mistake.

As a result of the Swiss cheese concept, mistakes often go unnoticed. The likelihood of the mistakes may increase over time, making it more and more likely that customers will eventually be affected (i.e., the holes on the slices of cheese become larger). In extreme cases, customers may be physically or mentally injured, causing the firm great harm. This concept reinforces the benefits of reporting mistakes and near misses, even when they do not reach the customer.

Customer Satisfaction Surveys

The level of customer satisfaction depends on both process performance and customer expectations. Therefore, in addition to performance metrics, a comprehensive performance management system must include a means to determine customer perceptions of performance. Performance metrics are internally derived, and they provide an objective measure of performance (e.g., what is the average waiting time for customers?). However, they are not impacted by customer expectations. Customer satisfaction represents the combination of performance and expectations (e.g., are customers satisfied with the waiting time?). Satisfaction is typically measured using a customer satisfaction survey. As a stand-alone metric, customer surveys are vitally important, but the system works best when both the subjective satisfaction measures and the objective performance metrics are considered.

The design of a customer satisfaction survey should start with a list of performance dimensions. For each dimension, one or more survey questions should be included on the survey. Each question should be clear and unambiguous. Examples of a poor question would be:

- Was your interaction with the cashier good? (What about the interaction is good – its timeliness? its accuracy? the friendliness of service providers?)
- Did the call center representative answer your question accurately in a short time? (Mixes two dimensions – timeliness and accuracy.)

- Were you satisfied with the technician's personality? (Personality is a vague term that should be more clearly defined – respectful? friendly? courteous?)

It is common to see marketing-oriented questions on a satisfaction survey, such as the customer's annual income, but these questions can add bulk to the survey and discourage some customers from completing the survey.

Satisfaction Survey Design

The design of a customer satisfaction survey would appear to be a simple matter of developing a list of questions and a set of multiple-choice answers. Problems arise when a survey is poorly designed, ineffectively administered, or inappropriately analysed. For example, a medical center's in-patient customer satisfaction survey consists of 4 pages that includes 13 entries of personal information, 107 questions, and 14 requests for written comments. Given a common rule of thumb that a customer is more likely to complete a survey if it will take less than 3 minutes, this survey may not result in sufficient sample size for effective analysis.

The survey should start with a brief introduction, which includes its purpose, how it should be completed and submitted, and any special notes regarding its completion. No performance dimension should be left without a question. From a performance analysis standpoint, there is little need to ask questions that do not pertain to a performance dimension. These questions would add to the completion time and would not be critical for gauging customer satisfaction.

The list of questions should focus on customer perceptions of performance. For example, consider monitoring of satisfaction for the dimension "responsiveness." A question phrased as: "Rate your satisfaction with responsiveness when answering your e-mails" would be suitable. A poor satisfaction survey question would be: "On average, how long does it take for us to answer your e-mails?" This is a poor question because it implies that the firm does not monitor response times and it gives no information on the customer's actual satisfaction.

Each question will include a set of potential responses (called the question's *response format*). Although time is saved by using the same response format for each question, care must be taken to ensure that the response choices make sense relative to the question being asked. The goal is to avoid imprecision because customers cannot clearly distinguish among the choices. Consider this seven choice scale: Exceptional – Excellent – Very Good – Good – Fair – Poor – Very Poor. To be effective, customer need to distinguish between very similar choices (e.g., exceptional vs. excellent, or very poor vs. poor). To help ensure effective choices, a survey developer should be confident that two customers with the same level of satisfaction would choose the same response.

Effective surveys often employ a customized set of responses for each question that reduce the potential for imprecise responses. For example, a question regarding "cleanliness" (e.g., "rate the cleanliness of our facility") may be more effective if response choices were: filthy, a little dirty, relatively clean, and spotless, rather than response choices: very unsatisfied, moderately unsatisfied, moderately satisfied, or very satisfied. Often, the middle category is listed as "average," which is problematic because it mixes absolute definitions (very poor, poor, good, and excellent) with a relative scale (average). This scale assumes that the average washroom has cleanliness somewhere between good and poor. But what if the customer's experience is that most washrooms are dirty and that this one is about average? Should she choose "poor" or "average"? It may also be better to indicate choices without associated text, such this scale: ☹ ☺ ☺ .

Asking an "overall satisfaction" question should be done with caution. In reality, this question would be a means to validate the list of dimensions and the scope of the questions. For example, if the other questions all showed satisfaction, but overall satisfaction was less than positive, then either a dimension is not being accounted for or a dimension has questions that do not effectively measure satisfaction. A major risk of the overall satisfaction is that it is tempting to simplify decision making by looking only at the data for these questions. The firm would lose the ability to better understand root causes of customers' satisfaction and may miss opportunities to solve problems before they become especially severe.

In summary, when designing an effective customer satisfaction survey, the following considerations are important: (a) include at least one question corresponding to each dimension of performance, (b) avoid inclusion of any questions that do not enhance an understanding of satisfaction (such as marketing-related questions), (c) do not ask customers to contribute ideas that will not be considered, (d) keep the survey as short as possible (a suitable target is three minutes or less), and (e) make the survey easy to complete. Other precautions related to the administration of surveys include: (a) design more open-ended surveys for smaller customer groups, (b) be sure not to allow a few "loud voices" to dominate the analysis of surveys, (c) include at least one question for each performance dimension, and (d) make each question concise and unambiguous.

Integrated Performance Management

Many factors determine whether or not a customer is satisfied with the outcomes of a business process. These factors can be categorized in many ways, including one that is based on performance gaps as illustrated in Figure 10.1, called the *Service Quality Model.* [5] The model is based on surveying a diverse group of practitioners. A great deal of consistency was found among the groups surveyed and therefore the model appears valid.

The five gaps shown in the model can be described as follows:

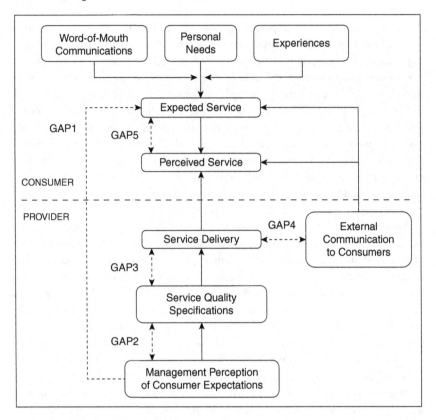

FIGURE 10.1 Service Quality Model

- GAP1 grows when the multi-dimensional nature of performance is not well understood. Often, the performance management system does not evolve as customer expectations change, or the system is based on a framework that is inconsistent with the type of service offered. For example, invoices may be accurate but too complex for customers to understand, or reports may require customers to do additional work to make reports more useable.
- GAP2 grows when changing customer needs are not well understood. For example, a business process manager may set a goal of a 24-hour or less response time to respond to customer e-mails but customers may desire faster responses. This gap also grows when customers desire change without corresponding changes in how the business process is delivered.
- GAP3 grows when service is provided that is inconsistent with internal requirements. This gap could grow because of inadequate capacity (or other inadequate allocation of resources), obsolete technology, time wasted on non-value-added activities, inconsistent training, or other major process changes such as downsizing or outsourcing.

- GAP4 grows when a service provider promises more than can be delivered. For customers who are external, these promises may be made through media advertising or other communications, such as newsletters or e-mail blasts. For services with internal customers, this gap is less relevant although a business process manager may make unattainable promises to avoid short term embarrassment or to earn favor with the firm's executives.
- GAP5 is the result of all other gaps. This gap is the most important gap, but it is difficult to identify its root causes in a timely manner. When this gap grows, the business process manager would expect a higher number of complaints from customers, although research has shown that most unhappy customers do not complain.

The main gaps that are measured in a quality management system are GAP3 and GAP5. GAP3 is measured by internal performance metrics and by tracking mistakes and close calls. Analysis of this gap makes up most of a performance management system. GAP5 is measured by customer satisfaction surveys, but this gap can also be monitored by complaint handing systems. The analysis of performance data as well as customer satisfaction data needs to account for random variation, using methods that help the business process manager find root causes. These methods are covered in Chapter 11.

Summary & Key Takeaways

Monitoring performance of a business process is more challenging than many practitioners appreciate because of the idiosyncrasy of each service. Customers' judgement of performance needs to be documented before monitoring can begin. Performance metrics should be coupled with customer survey questions so that each performance dimension is accounted for. Although mistakes are usually not the fault of employees, they need to be tracked so that the root cause can be identified and eliminated. Reporting close calls is also encouraged. In summary, the key takeaways from Chapter 10 are:

1. Performance metrics need to be aligned with customer desires. They are derived from the multiple ways with which a typical customer defines value, called dimensions of performance. When effective, metrics help managers precisely evaluate performance relative to all facets important to customers.
2. Problems (delays, mistakes, rework, etc.) should be recorded so that they can quickly be addressed and do not become bigger problems. Close calls should also be recorded, because this can prevent future problems from happening.
3. For each dimension of performance: (a) an internally-derived performance metric, (b) the tabulation of mistakes, complaints, and near misses, and (c) an externally-derived customer satisfaction survey question should be in place.

4. Customer satisfaction surveys should measure how performance is perceived by customers, which is affected by their expectations. A question should exist for each performance dimension, but the survey should not take long to complete.

Discussion Questions

1. A quality analyst for a financial advising office suggests that the following performance dimensions apply to customers seeking financial advice: (a) courtesy, (b) privacy, (c) convenience, and (d) friendliness. Which of these dimensions is probably unnecessary and what dimension should be added?
2. A materials testing process evaluates plastic parts for the presence of heavy metals. The four key performance dimensions are: (a) accuracy, (b) timeliness, (c) knowledge, and (d) responsiveness. List one performance metric for each dimension.
3. A business process writes proposals for a firm's consulting services, based on requests for proposal (RFP) from potential clients. The four key performance dimensions are: (a) conformance to the RFP, (b) timeliness, (c) clarity, and (d) responsiveness to questions. List one performance metric for each dimension and list one customer satisfaction survey question (with response format) corresponding to each performance dimension.
4. A troubleshooting help desk assists customers of a utility with energy-related problems. The four key performance dimensions are: (a) completeness, (b) timeliness, (c) clarity, and (d) courtesy. List one performance metric for each dimension and list one customer satisfaction survey question (with response format) corresponding to each performance dimension.

References

1 Arnheiter EA, Cocco J Loctite Corporation. *Richard Ivey School of Business, Case Study* 902D19, 2003.
2 Deming WE. *Out of the crisis.* Cambridge, MA: MIT Center for Advanced Engineering Study; 1986.
3 Columbia accident review board. *CAIB report (Volume I).* Washington, DC: National Aeronautics and Space Administration; 2003. Aug.
4 Reason J. *Human error.* Cambridge, UK: Cambridge University Press; 1990.
5 Parasuraman A. A conceptual model of service quality and its implications for future research. *Journal of Marketing (Pre-1986).* 1985; 49(000004):41.

11

STATISTICAL MONITORING OF PERFORMANCE

Variation

The biggest challenge when evaluating data for a performance metric is the presence of *random variation*. Variation in process outcomes will exist, even when no changes are made in the process. To illustrate random variation with the most basic example, consider the process of flipping a coin, where the outcome of interest is the percentage of heads. If the coin is flipped 100 times each day, the percentage of heads will vary day by day. This is random variation as it occurs even though the process (i.e., the likelihood of heads) is unchanged. Similarly, if a bank's loan approach rate was 50%, the percentage of loans approved each month would vary even when the loan approval process did not change. Therefore, changes in the monthly loan approval percentage does not imply that the likelihood of a loan being approved has changed.

A quality system should tabulate and analyse performance metrics, then report results in an action-oriented fashion. The set of performance metrics should be analysed periodically, whether that be on a daily, weekly, or monthly basis as determined by the nature of the process. Assuming that performance data are unbiased, the challenge in these analyses concerns random variation of process outcomes. The analysis should use mathematical formulas to predict the range of process outcomes that would be due to random variation. The analysis of variation is based on theories concerning their nature and causes.

Walter Shewhart (1891–1967), a pioneer in the field of quality research, classified sources of variation as falling into one of two categories [1]:

(a) When the process is unchanged, outcomes will vary according to their *natural variation*, which has many *common causes*. For example, the occurrence of the outcome heads or tails depends on the common causes associated with speed that the coin is flipped, rotational velocity, distance to the landing surface, etc. Unless the magnitude of natural variation is excessive, we generally do not attempt to list or quantify the common causes of variation. A system to monitor performance needs to be cognizant of the level of variation that is due to common causes. Changing the process under these conditions can often increase the level of variation. This action is called tampering with the process and should be avoided. [2]

(b) When the process changes, it is because other sources of variation have entered the process. Shewhart referred to these sources of variation as having *special causes*. These causes are also known as *assignable* causes because a process manager should identify the root cause of this variation (i.e., they should "assign" a root cause). The process change may be beneficial, detrimental, or neutral to the process. In all cases, identifying the assignable cause will assist the process manager. If the process is better, the process manager can learn from these situations. If the process is worse, the manager can seek to identify the problem and improve the operation of the process. If the process change is neutral (neither good nor bad), these situations also present a learning opportunity. For example, a change in the loan approval process may be due to younger professionals moving into a neighborhood. These customers may not possess the down payment normally required, but the firm may want to consider revising loan approval criteria for these potentially valuable customers.

A system is required to support a business process manager who needs to make decisions based on performance data. The system needs to distinguish between common cause and special cause variation. When special causes exist, the data analysis system should provide insight that can help the manager quickly identify root causes of the process change (i.e., its assignable cause). These systems employ a methodology known as *Statistical Process Control* (SPC). The two most important concepts that underlie SPC are process stability and process capability:

*   A *stable* process is unchanged over time. Performance outcomes from a stable process will vary due to common causes of natural variation. Their range of variation can be predicted using mathematical equations. Statistical control charts are used to determine if a process is stable.
*   A *capable* process meets its objectives. Objectives can be internally imposed (e.g., by the firm) or externally derived (e.g., by regulators). Analysing process capability is only possible when the process is stable, because otherwise its performance is not predictable. A formal procedure called a *process capability analysis* (PCA) is completed to determine if a stable process is capable.

A process can be stable relative to certain performance metrics and unstable relative to others. For example, if bank tellers are well qualified but some bank tellers are friendlier than others, a process may be stable with respect to accuracy of transactions but unstable with respect to friendliness of service providers.

The Deming Philosophy

W. Edwards Deming (1900–1993) was an American statistician who had a profound influence on business management, both in the U.S. and internationally. In 1950, at the invitation of the Japanese Union of Scientists and Engineers (JUSE), Dr Deming introduced his philosophy of management to Japanese industrialists. After being influential in Japan (especially at Toyota Motors), Deming went on to become a highly regarded consultant whose philosophies underlie modern quality management. Dr Deming is referred to by many individuals as the father of the third wave of the industrial revolution. The first wave involved the use of factories and modern machinery (e.g., Eli Whitney and the cotton gin); the second wave dealt with mass production (e.g., Henry Ford and the assembly line); and the third wave is characterized by the use of statistical methods to improve quality (e.g., W. Edwards Deming and SPC). Deming remains popular in Japan as evidenced by JUSE's continued awarding of the *Deming Prize*, a coveted international business award.

Deming's teaching became popular in the U.S. after a 1980 television broadcast called "If Japan can ... Why can't we" which introduced Deming and his philosophies to a national audience. Through the 1980's, Deming was a sought-after speaker at conferences and a consultant for corporations. His teachings emphasized that management was responsible for creating a process-oriented quality system and that managers should stop blaming employees for quality problems. He railed against many traditional thoughts, such as the idea that to improve quality costs would increase (he preached that, if quality improved, costs would decrease). Deming's teachings inform today's contemporary quality systems such as Total Quality Management (TQM) and Six Sigma.

Deming's philosophies (along with statistical methods he enthusiastically attributed to Walter Shewhart) are included in his landmark book, *Out of the Crisis* (1986). The book contains his *14 Points for Management* and *The Deadly Diseases*. Among Deming's 14 points for Management is the following: "Cease dependence on inspection to achieve quality; eliminate the need for inspection on a mass basis by building quality into the product in the first place." Although many readers may assume that he was referring to goods, this concept applies equally to services. It stresses the need to move from detecting mistakes to creating processes that eliminate mistakes from happening. Management's focus should move from inspections to a more action-oriented focus on understanding and improving processes.

Process Thinking

Deming was an early proponent of a concept called *process thinking*. This approach focuses on using performance data to understand and improve processes, which differs from a focus on outcomes alone. Process thinking recognizes that good processes generate good outcomes. It is action-oriented in that it seeks to understand how and why processes behave in the way they do. It is more complicated than outcome thinking because of the existence of random variation in process outcomes. In fact, Deming once stated "Understanding variation is the key to success in quality and business."

Deming often demonstrated the impact of variation and the flaw of an outcome-focused approach with his "red bead game." This manual simulation illustrates the challenges that random variation introduces when analysing process quality. In the red bead game, a large container consisting of both white and red beads represents a process, each bead represents a unit of process output, and a red bead represents a defective product. A paddle with 50 slots is used to randomly select 50 beads from the large container, representing a week of production. The number of red beads in the sample of 50 beads is recorded. This procedure of drawing 50 beads is repeated to generate performance data over a period of many weeks.

Described in this way, it is clear that the weekly defect rates will vary due to natural variation while the process itself is stable. The simulation is generic but it can represent any number of different outcomes, including any metric that is described as a proportion. Examples include the proportion of reports delivered on-time, loans approval percentages, employee attrition rates, hospital patient mortality, and percentage of interviewees hired. In fact, it can represent any performance metric that is expressed as a ratio with the numerator (number of times an event occurred) and denominator (total number of customers or jobs).

As the weeks progressed in the red bead game, Deming would amuse his audience by acting as an unenlightened manager. When the occurrence of red beads increased (i.e., more defects produced), he would scold the volunteer assigned to play the role of production manager. Conversely, when the occurrence of red beads decreased (i.e., less defects produced), he would pat the production manager on the back and congratulate him. The audience, being well aware of the lack of a process change, would appreciate the humor. But more importantly, they would understand the significance of the message – the data changed but the process remained the same.

As the red bead game illustrates, systems of rewards and punishments based on random variation will at best be a waste of time. Deming described the result of outcome thinking as workers shifting from serving customers to "serving the numbers." According to Deming, it fails to recognize that performance is mostly dictated by the system, not the individual employees. It spreads fear within an organization, encourages rivalries among departments, and eventually causes the performance metrics to be "gamed" (i.e., artificially manipulated). It leads to internal competition and a focus away from customers and their needs. An effective analysis of performance outcomes would use a process thinking approach.

Implementing Process Thinking

To implement a process-oriented analysis approach consistent with the Deming philosophy, a framework suggested in Figure 11.1 would be implemented. After performance metrics are determined for each key dimension of performance, performance data are collected. At predetermined intervals of time, a statistical control chart would be created. These charts, described below, determine if the process is stable relative to the metric analysed. If the control chart concludes that the process is unstable (the "Is the Process Stable?" NO branch) a root cause investigation would be initiated. The control chart itself forms an excellent basis for beginning this investigation because it shows how the performance data varied over time. In most cases, the timeframe that led to the conclusion of instability would be isolated.

For stable processes, the capability of the process to meet stated goals (e.g., benchmarks, conformance rates, etc.) is then evaluated. This step is usually performed at specified points in time, generally not as frequently as data are added to the control charts. If the process is not capable (the "Is the Process Capable" NO branch) an improvement project would be contemplated. These efforts

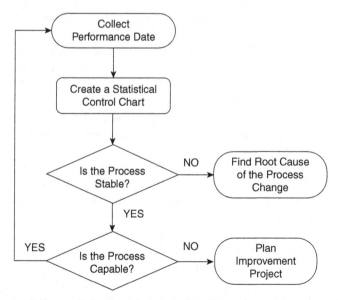

FIGURE 11.1   Framework for Process-Oriented Performance Management

are comprehensive and use a standard project management framework as described in Chapter 12.

Analysing Process Stability

A statistical control chart determines if a process is stable, and forms the core of the process-oriented approach using SPC. Although they have been used for decades, control charts remain an essential component of contemporary quality systems (e.g., Six Sigma) and they are encouraged by accrediting and certification bodies (e.g., the ISO 9000 quality standards). Most practitioners use software or Excel templates to create and evaluate control charts. A brief but conceptual mathematical background is provided below.

Control charts are displayed as a time series graph, with performance data combined into *subgroups*, and *control limits* based on the expected level of natural variation. Usually the subgroup represents one period of time, such as a week or a month. Every control chart includes a *center line*, which displays the average value of subgroup data. They all include a lower control limit (LCL) and upper control limit (UCL) that represent the range of variation existing for 99.7% of subgroup values. In other words, they provide the expected range of subgroup data. Sometimes, intermediate 1- and 2-sigma limits are shown to assist with the control chart's interpretation.

Proportion (P) Charts

Because an exhaustive coverage of control charts is not practical for this book, one specific type of control chart that applies to most business processes is described below. As the name implies, a *Proportion (or P) Chart* is used to evaluate the stability of a process that generates proportion data similar to the data generated in the red bead game. These data are called proportion data because they have a numerator and denominator that falls between 0.0 (0%) and 1.0 (100%). Proportion data require that the performance metric classifies the process outcome (generically) as a *success* or *failure*. Each subgroup proportion represents how often the success occurred. In these cases, the success need not represent a desirable event.

Although only of theoretical interest to some readers, the natural variation for proportion data are described by the binomial probability model and, if the subgroup size is large enough, the pattern of common cause variation will follow a bell shape consistent with the normal distribution. To be a valid P chart, the average number of successes in a subgroup must exceed about 3 and that the average number of failures in a subgroup must also exceed about 3. The center line for a P chart is equal to the average subgroup proportion called $\bar{p}$ (pronounced p-bar). The lower and upper control limits may be constant (when the subgroup size is constant) or vary from subgroup to subgroup. Equation

11.1 shows the formula for calculating the lower and upper control limits for a subgroup i of a P Chart that has a subgroup size equal to n_i. It is noteworthy that, as the subgroup size increases, the range of expected variation decreases.

$$\bar{p} \pm 3\sqrt{\frac{\bar{p}(1 - \bar{p})}{n_i}} \tag{11.1}$$

Consider the following data collected from a HR department, representing the percentage of time an e-mail was not answered within 24 hours. Because each value falls into one of two categories (late or on-time response), the data are referred to as proportion data and the proper control chart is a P Chart. Each week represents a subgroup of performance data. A *SPC Template* that includes P Charts is included in this book's eResources, along with a video describing its use. The weekly performance data (e-mails not answered within 24 hours) are shown in Table 11.1. The user enters each subgroup's data – the subgroup size and the number of

TABLE 11.1 Data for Late Response to E-Mails

Subgroup Number	Subgroup Size	Subgroup Occurrences	Subgroup Proportion
1	42	15	0.357
2	37	11	0.297
3	37	14	0.378
4	40	10	0.250
5	43	12	0.279
6	39	5	0.128
7	42	9	0.214
8	42	7	0.167
9	43	5	0.116
10	44	7	0.159
11	42	4	0.095
12	39	12	0.308
13	40	4	0.100
14	35	9	0.257
15	45	11	0.244
16	43	14	0.326
17	42	7	0.167
18	44	5	0.114
19	37	10	0.270
20	45	7	0.156
21	42	9	0.214
22	38	2	0.053
23	44	12	0.273
24	40	9	0.225

occurrences of the event of interest (i.e., the "success"). For example, in Week 1, 42 customers sent an e-mail and 15 of them were not answered within 24 hours. The validity of a P chart requires that the average number of on-time responses and the average number of late responses in each week both exceed 3. This assumption is satisfied because, as evident in the data, the average number of e-mails not answered within 24 hours is at least 3 and the average number of e-mails answered within 24 hours (e.g., 27 in Week 1) is at least 3.

The P Chart in Figure 11.2 was created from these performance data. The solid horizontal *center line*, showing the overall average proportion of e-mails replied to within 24 hours, is 21.3%. The solid control limits change from subgroup-to-subgroup because the subgroup size changes in each week. For example, the limits are somewhat wider in Week 2 (37 e-mails received) compared to Week 1 (42 e-mails received). That is, the expected variation during a one-week period is determined based on the number of messages received in that week. Similarly, the dished 1-sigma and 2-sigma limits vary across subgroups. Although the possible range of proportions extends from 0 to 1 (i.e., 0% to 100%), the P Chart vertical exist is always adjusted to "zoom in" on the variation.

Interpretation Rules

A set of rules, called the Shewhart (or Western Electric) rules, is used to interpret a control chart. [1] The rules identify patterns that would not be expected for a stable process. They are based on the fraction of points expected to fall within 1-sigma limits (about 67% of values), within 2-sigma limits (about 95% of values), within 3-sigma limits (about 99.7% of values), and either above or below the center line (about 50% of values on each side). The recommended

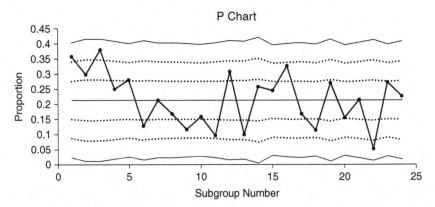

FIGURE 11.2 P Chart for Late Response to E-Mails

Shewhart rules for detecting an unstable process are listed below. A process should be declared to be unstable if any of the following occur:

- Any point outside of the 3-sigma limits,
- Two of three consecutive points outside of 2-sigma limits (in the same direction),
- Four of five consecutive points outside of 1-sigma limits (in the same direction),
- Eight consecutive points on the same side of the center line, or
- Ten of eleven consecutive points on the same side of the center line.

If a Shewhart rule is violated, the recommended course of action is to find the assignable (i.e., root) cause of the process change (this may be a good, bad, or neutral change). In Figure 11.2, the first and third data values fall beyond 2-sigma limits, the Shewhart rule "two of three consecutive points outside of 2-sigma limits (in the same direction)" has been violated. At this point, an investigation would commence to determine the assignable cause. Because an effective data collection scheme would include notes of any occurrences that may affect the process, there should be some hints on the data collection sheets. In this case, let's assume that in Week 4, a software upgrade had been made that included multiple reminders of e-mail messages that had been in queue longer than 12 hours. This feature was not in place before Week 4.

After confirming that the software upgrade was the root cause of the process change, the P Chart is actually illustrating the operation of two processes – the process before the change and the process after the change. Because the process before the change no longer exists, those data should be removed from the data set. The revised P Chart is shown in Figure 11.3. The P Chart shows the empty places for Weeks 1–3, reminding the analyst that those weeks were no

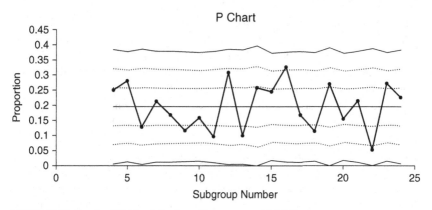

FIGURE 11.3   Revised P Chart for Late Response to E-Mails

longer used. In the revised P Chart no violation of Shewhart rules is apparent. Therefore, this process would be considered stable, with a center line of 19.6%.

Sometimes a P Chart includes a Shewhart rule violation and an assignable cause is found and removed, but the remaining process data include less than about 18 subgroups. In these cases, the P Chart can be revised but not analysed. Confirming stability requires that more time passes so that additional data can be collected.

Once a process is declared stable, the resulting information should be presented in precise terms. It would be correct, but not informative, to state: "the average on-time response rate was 19.6% over the past 21 weeks." Because the purpose of the analysis is to predict current (and hence future) process performance, it would be better to state: "the likelihood of an on-time response for this department is about 19.6%." In fact, by declaring the process stable, this likelihood applies both to the past and to the future. Although Weeks 11 and 12 have very different on-time response rates, the *likelihood* of a late response was 19.6% in both of those weeks. The difference in these data was due to natural variation. In other words, the data changed but the process remained the same.

The process-oriented approach does not focus on individual outcomes unless they are extraordinary (i.e., unless there is a violation of the Shewhart rules). For example, in Week 12, 32.6% of the responses were late, which appears much higher than the 19.6% average percentage. Although this point falls beyond 2-sigma, it is within 3-sigma limits. With a total of 21 data plotted on the P Chart, it would not be unusual for a few points to fall between 2- and 3-sigma limits. Hence, the 32.6% rate for a stable process that averages 19.6% late responses is not surprising, given the number of e-mails answered in each week.

Note on Analysing Satisfaction Surveys

Customer satisfaction surveys make use of a variety of response formats. For example, some questions ask for a yes/no response (e.g., "Are you satisfied with our response time to your e-mail messages?"). Other response formats present a list of qualitative choices (e.g., very dissatisfied, somewhat dissatisfied, neutral, somewhat satisfied, and very satisfied). Still other response formats use a numerical scale that is often a Likert scale because qualitative choices are translated to numbers (e.g., very dissatisfied = 1, somewhat dissatisfied = 2, and so on).

A problem with many of these response formats is their lack of precision. For example, if two customers with the same opinion may choose different responses, then the survey is imprecise. Putting this concern aside, the analysis of stability may proceed using a P Chart. The P Chart can be used to analyse any survey because, in every case, responses can be categorized as a "success" or "failure." For example, consider the case where a group of 50 customers took a survey and their responses to the question "Rate your satisfaction with our response time to your e-mails" generated the following results:

Very Dissatisfied: 1 customer
Somewhat Dissatisfied: 5 customers
Neutral: 10 customers
Somewhat Satisfied: 22 customers
Very Satisfied: 12 customers

In this case, 34 customers can be categorized as satisfied (either somewhat or very). This is a proportion of 68% of the 50 customers surveyed. The P Chart would then be an effective tool for determining if the satisfaction of customers followed a pattern consistent with a stable process. If so, the likelihood that a customer is satisfied with the response times would be estimated.

Analysing Process Capability

A stable process will have predictable outcomes, but it may or may not be capable of meeting its objectives. Determining if a process is *capable* requires a methodology known as a *process capability analysis* (PCA). A PCA can be done only for stable process because an unstable process is not predictable. For metrics classified as a proportion, the objective would be to determine an acceptable likelihood of a "success," which will be referred to as a benchmark. Example benchmarks include a 15% (or less) likelihood of not answering an e-mail within 24 hours, a 72% loan approval likelihood, and a 0.3% (or less) likelihood of a hospital-acquired infection per patient-day.

Determining the benchmark for a performance metric can be done in many ways, including: (a) a comparison with a historical likelihood (e.g., last year's likelihood of success), (b) an internally-imposed likelihood (e.g., an improvement over last year's likelihood of success), or (c) an externally-imposed benchmark based on customer contracts, regulatory requirements, industry standards, or peer organization performance. A benchmark should be consistent with customer needs, and it should play a role in the continuous effort to proactively improve the business process. Care must be taken to avoid imposing unrealistic requirements on a process that previously met its objectives. The business process manager should remember that the system determines performance and that expecting improvements by simply motivating employees to work harder can be counter-productive.

Externally-imposed benchmarks can be derived from a variety of sources. For call centers, researchers at Purdue University designed extensive questionnaires for call center managers to input their call center performance data, which have been consolidated into a database. In return, call center managers receive reports that compare their performance with other participants (www.benchmarkportal.com). The American Purchasing Society publishes its annual

Research and Procurement Benchmarking Report based on information from monthly and annual benchmarking surveys (www.american-purchasing.com). The Society for Human Resource Management compares organizations across 27 industries and various sizes relative to their HR practices (www.shrm.org). And, the Institute of Internal Auditors provides a benchmarking report that compares an audit department's size, experience, and other metrics against the averages of similar organizations and peer groups (www.theiia.org).

Benchmark information that is obtained from external sources usually provides reports that compare a business process to a large group of peer organizations. Although providers of these benchmarks often generate many statistical analyses and displays, in reality the only information that is important to a PCA is a benchmark likelihood of success. For a hardware seller's contact center PCA, the required information for evaluating their abandonment rate is the average abandonment rate for all hardware sellers. In this section, it is assumed that the benchmark is based on a large number of peer organizations, and therefore it is not subject to random variation.

From a statistical perspective, the PCA would determine if the outcomes experienced by a business process were consistent with the benchmark. Because the business process data is subject to random variation, the analysis would need to account for the sample size of the performance data. In this context, business process performance is "consistent" with the benchmark if the differences observed between its stable outcomes and the benchmark could be due to random variation. This analysis requires the use of a statistical confidence interval (CI).

A CI represents a range of likelihoods within which the *true likelihood* corresponding to the outcome will fall (usually with 95% confidence). It uses the same statistical methodology as margin of errors in political polls. For example, if 1000 voters are asked to choose between candidates A and B, the poll may indicate that 52% of voters favored candidate A. It would also report that the poll's margin of error was plus or minus 3%, meaning that the likelihood of all voters preferring candidate A falls within the range 49% to 55%. This result is sometimes referred to as a *statistical dead heat* because it is possible that either candidate could win the election. Here, one could state that the data in the poll are consistent with a benchmark of 50%. Equation 11.2 provides the formula to calculate the 95% CI for proportion data, where N is the total of all subgroups found on the P chart and $\bar{p}$ is the center line for the stable P chart.

$$\bar{p} \pm 1.96\sqrt{\frac{\bar{p}(1-\bar{p})}{N}} \qquad (11.2)$$

The procedure for performing a PCA for proportion data is described in Figure 11.4. It is recommended that a PCA be performed annually, although it can be performed more frequently. The PCA would start by confirming that the performance metric can be expressed as a proportion, and that the process is stable by implementing a P Chart. The PCA procedure terminates when the process is unstable because future outcomes would not be predictable.

For a stable process, a CI will be created containing the true likelihood of success. This step is necessary because even though the center line of the stable P Chart estimates likelihood, it is based on a sample and therefore it is subject to random variation. Once the CI is determined, the benchmark likelihood is compared to the CI. If the benchmark lies within the business process's CI, then one would conclude that the process performance is consistent with the

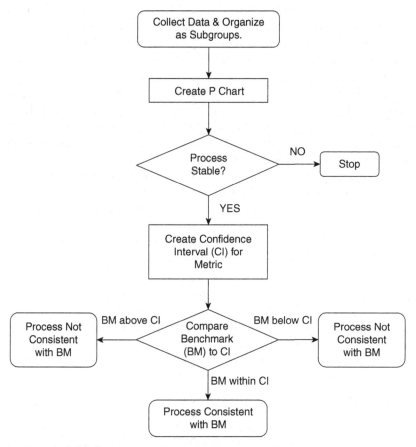

FIGURE 11.4 PCA for a Process Generating Proportion Data

benchmark. This determination does not constitute proof that the benchmark is met, only that it cannot be proven to differ from the benchmark.

If the benchmark falls outside of the business process's CI, then we would conclude that process performance is inconsistent with the benchmark. Depending on the definition of the performance metric, this event constitutes proof that process performance is either better than or worse than the benchmark, although in some cases no clear distinction can be made. For example, if the performance metric is the number of e-mails not answered within 24 hours, then lower values represent better performance. Alternatively, if the metric is defined as the percentage of satisfied customers, then larger values are better. Finally, if the metric is a bank's loan approval rate, it may not be clear whether larger or smaller values are preferred, but the bank would be interested to know that their processes are inconsistent with the benchmark.

For example, assume that the bank's loan application process is stable and operates with an estimated approval rate of 84.8% (i.e., the centerline in its P Chart). The average approval rate for the State in which they operate (i.e., the benchmark) is 86.2%. Let's assume that the CI for the bank's actual loan approval likelihood extends from 82.8% to 86.8% (i.e., the margin of error is plus or minus 2.0%). In this case, we would conclude that the bank's application process is consistent with the benchmark of 86.2%. In these cases, no action would be required other than documenting this information. If the benchmark rate had been lower than 82.8% or higher than 86.8%, then the bank would be inconsistent with the benchmark, and an investigation would be undertaken to determine if action is warranted.

In some cases, when performance is inconsistent with a benchmark, management should be sure that the benchmark is suitable. The benchmark may be unreasonable or circumstances may make the benchmark irrational. For example, a benchmark goal for on-time completion of tasks may not be reasonable for new innovative services. In general, if the process is proven to be worse than the benchmark, then four possibilities should be considered:

(a) Can the process be changed to improve its performance?
(b) Is the benchmark appropriate and, if so, can it be adjusted?
(c) Should extraordinary controls be placed on the process while process improvement options are considered?
(d) Should the process operation be discontinued?

Example PCA

A scenario was presented earlier in this chapter, where a data set consisting of the proportion of e-mails not answered within 24 hours was analysed. The P Chart in Figure 11.2 was produced using these data, then Figure 11.3 was created after discovering that the process was unstable, finding the root cause, and removing the first three weeks of data. At this point, we have established that the process is stable and that the estimated likelihood that an e-mail will be responded to within 24 hours is 19.6% (the center line of the P Chart). During Weeks 4–24, a total of 869 e-mails were received (total number of calls received over the stable period).

We will assume that a suitable benchmark response rate is identified and that the average response rate for a large group of similar firms is 15%. The PCA results are shown in Figure 11.5, using the *SPC Template*. The main inputs (Estimate of Proportion "Successes" and Sample Size That Determined Estimate) were automatically linked to the P Chart. The 0.15 benchmark is entered by the user and the 95% default confidence level for the CI can be changed if desired. The PCA analysis indicates that there is a 95% chance that the true likelihood of an e-mail not being answered within 24 hours at this firm is between 16.9% and 22.2%.

Process Capability Analysis Template	
(Enter Values in Shaded Areas)	
Calculations area ONLY VALID when the process is <u>stable</u>.	
Estimate of Proportion "success"	0.195627
Sample Size That Determined Estimate	869
Enter Benchmark Outcome (if any)	0.15
Degree of Confidence	95%
Confidence Interval (Low):	0.169253
Confidence Interval (High):	0.222001
Conclusion to Capability Analysis:	**Performance Exceeds Benchmark**

FIGURE 11.5 Benchmark Analysis of E-Mail Response Data

The benchmark likelihood of 15% falls below the CI (i.e., it is below the lower CI value of 16.9%). Hence, the performance of this business process is not consistent with this benchmark. Because it is always better to answer calls in shorter timeframes, we would conclude that this process falls short of meeting its benchmark and therefore action should be taken. Because the process is stable, the lack of consistency with the benchmark is systemic and not associated with any particular time period. The analyst should start by confirming that the 15% benchmark is suitable for this department. Assuming that the benchmark is appropriate, then a formal process improvement project should be initiated that aims to reduce the percentage of e-mails not answered within 24 hours. This project would follow the procedures covered in Chapter 12.

Summary & Key Takeaways

Monitoring performance of a business process enables a manager to determine if objectives are being met or when changes have occurred that need attention. Effective analysis of performance data can identify problems and assist in finding their root causes. It can eliminate the tendency for process managers to react to performance data that vary due to normal variation when the business process is unchanged. In summary, the key takeaways from Chapter 11 are:

1. Business process managers should understand variation. In particular, they should know that outcomes will change even when the process is unchanged. This mantra is key to effectively evaluating performance data to set the stage for appropriate action (or inaction).
2. Stable processes are unchanged – if they generate acceptable results they should be left alone.
3. Control charts are effective at determining if a business process is operating in a stable fashion.
4. Unstable processes should be identified quickly and the root cause addressed.
5. A stable process will generate predictable results that should be evaluated using a statistical confidence interval to determine if output meets suitable benchmark values (while considering the effect of random variation).
6. Stable processes that are unacceptable require improvement projects because their issues are systematic. Unstable processes need to be made stable before they can be compared with a target or benchmark.

Discussion Questions & Problems Set

1. A professor once stated: "When evaluating process outcomes, managers need to understand that the data can change even when the process remains the same." Explain this statement.

2. Would paying a high school teacher a bonus if his or her class's average test score equals or exceeds a standard set by the government to fit with Deming's philosophy? Explain.

3. Each month, customers are asked a few questions about their satisfaction until 50 customers respond. Over the past 1.5 years, the monthly results (number of customers satisfied with the business process relative to its accuracy) were: 46, 43, 35, 38, 41, 43, 36, 32, 38, 43, 42, 37, 42, 43, 47, 36, 37, and 36. Create a P Chart and determine if the process is stable.

4. Each month, customers are asked a few questions about their satisfaction until 50 customers respond. Over the past 1.5 years, the monthly results (number of customers satisfied with the business process relative to its usefulness) were: 49, 48, 44, 49, 46, 50, 48, 50, 46, 45, 48, 48, 50, 48, 49, 47, 46, and 45. Create a P Chart and determine if the process is stable.

5. Each month, customers are asked a few questions about their satisfaction until 50 customers respond. Over the past 1.5 years, the monthly results (number of customers satisfied with the business process relative to its privacy) were: 40, 34, 40, 35, 32, 39, 39, 43, 38, 35, 38, 34, 37, 38, 40, 37, 46, and 45. Create a P Chart and determine if the process is stable.

6. Each month, customers are asked a few questions about their satisfaction until 50 customers respond. Over the past 1.5 years, the monthly results (number of customers satisfied with the business process relative to its clarity) were: 46, 44, 47, 45, 44, 41, 47, 46, 44, 45, 43, 48, 47, 47, 46, 48, 47, and 42. Complete a PCA to determine if the process performance is consistent with a benchmark likelihood of 92%.

7. Each month, customers are asked a few questions about their satisfaction until 50 customers respond. Over the past 1.5 years, the monthly results (number of customers satisfied with the business process relative to its responsiveness) were: 40, 39, 41, 40, 41, 44, 43, 46, 44, 48, 49, 48, 47, 44, 49, 48, 49, and 48. Complete a PCA to determine if the process performance is consistent with a benchmark likelihood of 95%.

References

1 Shewhart WA. *Economic control of quality of manufactured product*. New York: Van Hostrand; 1931.

2 Deming WE. *Out of the crisis*. Cambridge, MA, USA: MIT Center for Advanced Engineering Study; 1986.

12

BUSINESS PROCESS IMPROVEMENT

Process Improvement

In their quest to keep customers satisfied, most organizations practice process improvement. These efforts can take many forms and their motivations differ. Example motivations include to improve quality, to avoid litigation, to cut costs, or to increase customer satisfaction. A triggering event often takes place that motivates the need for process improvement, such as a costly mistake, an embarrassing error, or poor results of a process capability analysis. Some organizations use formal systems for process improvement while others' efforts are more ad hoc. Many certification and accreditation systems require that an organization formally document their process improvement system. These systems would include the triggering mechanism, the project management approach, and how improvement recommendations are implemented and sustained over time.

Although process improvement systems vary across organizations, they generally seek to improve their product or service using elements of Lean and/or Six Sigma. While definitions of Lean and Six Sigma vary, it is fair to say that when properly implemented both have met with considerable success. It is also clear that they offer greater potential when applied in tandem. Here, guidelines for the application of Lean Six Sigma in business process improvement are recommended. These guidelines consist of a disciplined, project-based approach that ensures effectiveness of improvement efforts. They are useful to managers responsible for a wide range of business processes including those targeted to either internal or external customers.

The moniker *continuous improvement* is often used to describe formal efforts to improve business processes. The reality is that most substantial process improvement is done in discrete and incremental steps, as an outcome of a *process improvement project*. Instituting a formal process improvement program with worker involvement can provide great benefits. Workers are closest to customers and usually know more about the operation of a process than their managers. A rigorous process improvement system can serve to consistently reinforce the notion that workers have two important jobs – doing their work and improving how their work is done.

The intent of this chapter is to describe a process improvement system based on elements of Lean and Six Sigma. It is robust and follows a prescribed mandate and structure. The system ensures that important problems are attacked using a sound and consistent methodology. It is designed to avoid pitfalls common to efforts that address symptoms, rather than causes, of problems. A consistently applied process improvement approach enhances the effectiveness of project teams and allows for the sharing of project results across the organization. But sustaining these efforts requires a culture that actively supports process improvement in both words and actions.

This chapter introduces readers to core process improvement concepts embedded in Six Sigma (including the DMAIC framework) and Lean (including Kaizen). Although Lean and Six Sigma have many elements in common, it is important for practitioners to understand where they can differ in important ways. Readers should also be aware that many successful organizations refer to their process improvement approach using other names, and some do not name their approach at all. Thus, the coverage below may be modified to account for organizational differences, as long as the core methodologies are sound. In Chapter 13, recommendations are made concerning how the program should be initiated, concentrating on important infrastructure and implementation concerns.

Six Sigma & DMAIC

Six Sigma originated at the Motorola Corporation in the United States with credit generally attributed to Bill Smith (1929–1993). The problem Smith addressed stemmed from quality-related returns due to increased product complexity. That is, although a set of "good" manufacturing processes may be sufficient for a simple product, "superior" manufacturing processes are necessary when products are more complex. The reason for this phenomenon is purely mathematical – the more "opportunities for defect" (OFD), the lower the final product quality because the product has more ways to be defective. For example, if the defect rate for each opportunity is 3 per 1000 and the final product includes 1000 OFD, final products will average 3 defects. In order for the final product to have only 3 defects per 1000 sold, each OFD would need to average only 3 defects per million opportunities. This rate of about 3 defects per million constitutes what is known as 6-sigma quality.

Although the goal of 6-sigma quality is based specifically on the manufacturing characteristics at Motorola, it has become widely adopted as a quality standard for both products and services. The techniques of Six Sigma, many of which have been used traditionally by statisticians and quality engineers, include many statistically-based methods. They include statistical control charts, process capability analysis, design of experiments, regression analysis, analysis of variance, hypothesis testing, and other well known methodologies. A key contribution of Six Sigma is its framework that seeks to apply these methods within a well organized project rather than through a haphazard collection of analyses.

Six Sigma is part of a natural evolution of quality systems based on the Deming philosophy and the contributions of Shewhart and others. Many of these systems were originally known by a variety of names, such as Total Quality Management (TQM) or Continuous Quality Improvement (CQI). Today, Six Sigma places less emphasis on the 6-sigma quality metric and tends to emphasize quantifiable financial success. Along with the formal project-based framework, it also includes a highly structured training regimen. Training is based on certifying individuals as "belts" (green belt, black belt, master black belts, etc.). Obtaining Six Sigma certification from an organization, such as the American Society for Quality, is an effective way for a young professional to obtain a credential enabling them to become more competitive in the career marketplace.

The formal Six Sigma improvement project structure is called DMAIC (Define-Measure-Analyse-Improve-Control). Similar structures have been used before (e.g., in the 1930's Walter Shewhart developed a system that evolved into the Plan-Do-Study-Act cycle). DMAIC is considered by many practitioners to be the primary reason for Six Sigma's success because it enforces a high degree of discipline and commonality in project organization, problem solving tools, software, and terminology. The DMAIC steps are summarized below (a more detailed framework is detailed later in this chapter):

- *Define:* Describe the problem, state the project's purpose, specify the process boundaries, identify key stakeholders, identify customers, choose the project team, list relevant metrics, indicate important risk factors, and develop a project plan. The result is a concise problem statement and project charter.
- *Measure:* Gather information on the current process, develop a process map or flowchart, describe process inputs and outputs, collect relevant data and summarize using statistical calculations and displays, and confirm accuracy of measurement systems. The result is a description of the current process with a focus on the problem at hand.
- *Analyse:* Evaluate process maps and data to identify wasteful activities, instances of unacceptable quality, identify root causes of problems, and

confirm using data analysis methods. The result is a thorough evaluation of the current process with a focus on where improvements should be targeted.

- *Improve:* Use available methods to list potential corrective actions, choose one or more improvement ideas, develop the revised approach (including benefits, costs, and risk factors), evaluate alterative plan implementation or pilot. The result is a set of recommendations for problem solution along with their justifications.

- *Control:* Based on the final recommendation, design a plan for ensuring that the changes are sustained, including training plans, data collection routines, quality tracking mechanisms, and statistical analysis procedures. The result is an action plan for confirming and sustaining the improvements.

Although the DMAIC framework is described in this chapter, other similar frameworks can lead to effective results as long as they enforce a standard approach using sound methodologies that are repeatable across improvement projects. The application of Six Sigma for business process improvement would downplay reducing variation using statistical methods in favor of reducing errors during the delivery of services. As discussed below, many firms combine the formal structures of Six Sigma with the more intuitive approaches typically associated with Lean management.

Lean & Kaizen

Lean organizations employ a process improvement methodology called *Kaizen* (in Japanese kai means "to take apart", and zen means "to make good"). Kaizen is usually interpreted to mean "change for the better" or "continuous improvement." A Kaizen project, or Kaizen event, would typically consist of an accelerated 1 to 5 day intensive project. The project team would include managers and employees, along with a facilitator who was traditionally called the *sensei*. It needs top management strong support because the project team may need the cooperation of others within a short timeframe. In organizations that practice Kaizen successfully, managers also participate in improvement projects on a periodic basis. With Kaizen, a quick "good" solution is valued over the "best" solution which may take more time to accomplish.

As contrasted with the Six Sigma approach of minimizing variation, Lean improvement projects typically seek to remove wasteful activities that compromise the ability to satisfy customers. Recalling that wasteful activities are defined based on customer needs, explicit motivation to justify improvements based on financial considerations is downplayed. That is, projects are chosen using a more robust set of criteria. Womack and Jones [1] introduced many practitioners to Lean, including a five-step application guide:

- *Identify value:* This definition needs to encompass the totality of how typical customers ascertain the value of a business process's output. It encompasses all customer dimensions of performance, as well as the process's ability to adapt to changing customer needs. It sets the stage for the analysis of the process from the perspective of customers rather than the producer.
- *Map the value stream:* A display is created to understand all activities that take place while delivering the service. The display may take many forms, as long as it shows activities that create value and those that are wasteful. It should include connections with customers and interdepartmental interactions. Once the current display has been created, a detailed analysis would be conducted that identifies where process waste can be removed or customer value increased.
- *Create flow:* All of the activities that add value would be organized to minimize interruptions during processing. These activities should be capable, available, and adequate. Activities that do not add value would be removed to the extent possible in the context of the Kaizen event's timeframe and scope. New activities that add additional value can be considered.
- *Create pull:* The process should be configured so that all work is initiated by customer demand. This step is only required for manufacturing operations, where inventory would be reduced and actual demand would trigger production. Because services cannot be inventoried, almost all services are naturally initiated when a customer need exists. Therefore, this step is unnecessary in a business process improvement project.
- *Seek perfection:* The steps above should be repeated until all waste is removed from the process and the customer experience is optimized. Because firms constantly develop new or redesigned products and services, the reality is that wasteful activities will always exist. Hence, this step is more of a philosophical underpinning – a business process manager should never assume that the business process is perfect.

Lean Six Sigma Process Improvement System

Despite their disparate roots, it is clear that the Six Sigma's DMAIC and Lean's Kaizen frameworks encompass many common features. Their strategic aim is to maintain or improve competitiveness and/or growth through superior and ever-improving customer satisfaction at competitive costs. Executives play a key role in both systems because they need to be actively involved in the program's implementation and operation. Many of their tools and techniques are similar. They both include basic root cause analysis, problem solving, process analysis, and data analysis techniques. Employee involvement is critical in both systems, because employees are trained and encouraged to contribute to problem solving, and to identify problems as they occur. Finally, although both were initially focused on manufacturing, they can and have been applied to other industries (e.g., service, government, healthcare, and education) and to business processes.

But it is equally clear that differences exist. Kaizen projects are completed in a few days, with a team working full time on solving the problem. DMAIC projects are more deliberate. They may take weeks or months to complete, using a more thorough approach. Kaizen projects focus on improving customer service by minimizing wasteful practices, while DMAIC focuses on improving customer service by minimizing errors. Project selection for Kaizen is somewhat holistic in its desire to remove wasteful activities that hinder their ability to serve customers, even when immediate financial benefits are unclear. DMAIC project selection is more pragmatic based on a desire to reduce costs or increase revenue. Kaizen analysis techniques are geared towards intuitive displays, root cause analysis, and mistake proofing, while DMAIC is geared towards statistical data analysis, controlled experiments, and mathematical optimization.

It is easy to envision several varieties of *Lean Six Sigma*. A version offered here would be characterized as follows. The Lean influence would cause the organization to: (a) maintain an understanding of both internal and external customers' needs and desires, (b) seek to maximize the value-added content of all processes, and (c) constantly evaluate employee incentives to ensure their alignment with system-wide performance objectives. The Six Sigma influence would cause the organization to: (a) stress data-driven decisions that are based on facts rather than opinions, (b) devote resources to solving problems that present significant challenges to business success, and (c) implement a consistent, highly structured project-based improvement regimen.

A Lean Six Sigma project – geared towards service or business process improvement – would use the DMAIC framework, but attempt to complete each step as quickly as possible, emphasizing Lean methods. A standard five step approach is recommended and described below.

Project Initiation

Careful planning of a process improvement project would start before the project commences. Successful projects are motivated by valid concerns, they employ project teams that include all key stakeholders, and they are supported by management. For example, some projects fail because an important stakeholder played no role in its initiation or because of unaddressed internal politics. For inexperienced project teams, not including a skilled facilitator may cause difficulties. Therefore, structured approach is recommended for selecting projects and assembling the project team.

There can be many reasons to initiate a process improvement project. In early stages of process improvement system implementation, solving problems that affect employee wellbeing can be an effective focus. These projects give workers practice in applying process improvement methods, and they help leadership solidify support for future projects. Later, projects would be chosen based primarily on direct or indirect business impacts. Example criteria for project foci include impacts on shareholders (e.g., profit enhancement); on customers (e.g., faster service); on suppliers (e.g., better communication); on employees (e.g., safer workplace); on governments (e.g., adherence to regulations); or on the surrounding community (e.g., reduced environmental impacts).

Project benefits should be quantified to the extent possible. In this regard, three categories of benefits exist. The first and best way to justify a project is based on its financial benefits. They include projecting cost savings (e.g., by eliminating the need to replace a retiring worker) or revenue enhancements (e.g., by extending the service offering and thereby increasing prices). Project benefits can also include those that are quantifiable in other ways. Therefore, the second best way to justify a project would include quantifiable but non-financial benefits. For example, more clearly formatted reports would decrease the number of questions asked by clients and therefore the decrease in the number of questions can be estimated. These estimates give decision makers an idea of the scale of the potential improvements and add to the credibility of the project organizers. Finally, other benefits may be intangible, which constitutes the third best way to justify a project. Intangible benefits, such as more engaged employees, better community relations, or improved relationships with regulators, are suitable. But, these benefits would rarely be justification for project initiation without other financial or other quantifiable benefits.

The establishment of performance targets can be useful to the project team. These targets create a focus on either incremental or substantial performance improvements. But, many projects should be considered successful even if the target improvement is not achieved. Therefore, care must be taken to eliminate any sense of punishment or disappointment if targets are not met. Otherwise, to avoid failure, the team may resort to artificial manipulation of the "numbers." In fact, administrators should be careful not to classify any project as a failure as long as the project team worked diligently on the improvement effort (because learning took place that will be valuable for the next project).

The project team should be large enough to encompass key stakeholders of the business process but not so large as to hamper its effectiveness. Among the group of about 6–12 members, the project team should include: (a) an experienced facilitator; (b) at least one representative from each department through which the operation flows; (c) front line employees who understand how the process currently operates; (d) one or more administrators who understand the context within which the service operates, including organizational, financial, legal, environmental, and political contexts; and (e) at least one customer, if customers are internal.

Project Execution

The project will have a planned timeline that is based on the project team's availability and the problem scope. The project may follow a Kaizen format, completed in 1–5 days with the team devoted full time to the project. Or, the project may be executed over weeks or months with the team devoted part time to the project. A third alternative that combines the first two options would be the imbedding of a kaizen activity within each phase of DMAIC. This alternative allows for the gathering of information between sessions and can maximize the effectiveness of each project phase. The activities included in each phase of the project are described below. Detailed methods found within each phase have been described earlier in this book; the corresponding chapters are indicated.

Define – Create Problem Statement and Customer Value Definition (Chapters 2–3)

The *define* phase of an improvement project starts with the development of a precise project definition or problem statement. Here, the problem is defined and the project objectives are delineated. The scope of the process under study is also specified (i.e., where it starts and ends). Using a standard format, the problem statement would also include major constraints, key metrics, improvement targets, and the role of each team member. It is useful to review the list of stakeholders and modify the team's composition if necessary to remove future barriers.

As described in Chapter 3, the team needs to develop a concise understanding of the so-called "voice of the customer." The customer value definition is multi-dimensional and often subjective. Consider a tax collection process with two main customers. The first customer is the taxpayer. This customer evaluates performance based on accuracy (an error-free tax bill), timeliness (receiving the bill in time to make a payment), convenience (a payment option that suits their needs), courtesy (pleasant interactions when calling or visiting the office), and responsiveness (quick question resolution). The second customer is the municipality. This customer evaluates performance based on timeliness (prompt deposit) and accuracy (error-free processing).

In order to define value accurately, it is sometimes necessary to speak with a sample of customers, especially external customers. One-on-one or small group sessions are typically more effective than surveys, which require brevity in order for customers to complete them in sufficient numbers and can add development time to the project. More open-ended information also allows for the uncovering of issues with which the team was unaware. For example, a tax office improvement project may invite a group of citizens for lunch and ask for their input. These sessions would not require the entire project team. The facilitator must be careful to keep the discussion focused on defining value and exposing problems, while exploring gaps in the present service offering.

Measure – Create a Process or Consumption Map and Collect Associated Data (Chapters 4, 6, and 11)

The *measure* phase begins with the creation of a business process map. For projects targeted to customer experience improvements, a consumption map is also useful. These displays help the project team develop a common and complete understanding of the business process and/or the customer experience. It is important that each display include every activity that takes place, including those that are wasteful from a business process standpoint or undesirable from a customer perspective. The complexity of the process map should be kept manageable and not include unnecessary information, such as activities that rarely occur.

Other useful displays include: (a) a spaghetti chart that shows how the process flows physically through a facility, (b) a time value map that highlights the process lead time and its value-added portion, or (c) a fishbone diagram that lists root causes of a problem using a hierarchical structure. Multiple displays can be especially helpful. For example, a combination process map and spaghetti chart can show the relationship among the process steps as well as how the process flows physically within a facility. These displays enhance the team's ability to appreciate the interactions among activities that cross departmental lines and the need to work together more effectively. The value of a process map cannot be overstated.

As process improvement programs mature, their use of data increases. Without the benefit of data, a project team risks making recommendations based on inaccurate perceptions. Check sheets [2] can be used to collect data in ways that help identify important characteristics. For example, consider a project to reduce delays in obtaining information from other departments. A data set could include the date of each delayed request with facility layout showing the offending departments. This data set may uncover previously unknown facts, such as delays corresponding with other departments' important deadlines.

Analyse – Identify Problems and Significant Waste (Chapters 4 & 6)

The *analysis* phase evaluates the current process and/or customer experience. Although process maps, consumption maps, and data will often highlight areas of concern without excessive analysis, the project team should systematically identify process steps that do not add value. They should also highlight delays and other frustrations that customers experience. Consider a process that reports OSHA recordable data that internal customers use to track accidents. Waste in the business process may include: late delivery of information, employees walking to pick-up forms, and reworking an incorrect data analysis. The consumption map may show that customers sometimes experience late reports causing them to miss deadlines or unclear explanations causing them to call with follow-up questions.

Many of the seven tools of quality described by Ishikawa can be helpful for the analysis of data. [2] Pareto charts can be used to display the problems that need the most attention due to their disproportionate impacts. Scatterplots are effective for displaying relationships between two data sets, and control charts can help identify timeframes where problems occurred most frequently (in the context of the natural variation of the data). Control charts can be used to analyse data (including performance metrics) to determine if a problem is systematic or sporadic.

Once a significant form of process waste or customer inconvenience is identified, the project team must be careful to address its cause rather than its symptoms. The Five Whys is very helpful for "drilling down" to root cause. As an example, consider the case of excessive errors in documents an audit department sends to regulators. A response to a symptom would be having a manager check all documents prior to their submission to the regulator. But this inspection will add cost and time, and may not significantly reduce errors.

Improve – Find Ways to Eliminate Waste and/or Add Value (Chapters 5 & 7)

The *improve* phase transitions the project team to the generation of ideas for making improvements based on the main concerns identified in earlier phases. For many business processes, basic improvement techniques often provide great opportunity for significant performance enhancement, due to the prevalence of "low hanging fruit." The ideas will generally include Lean methods (poka-yoke, standard work, visual controls, or 5S), self-service, or other process changes. A disciplined project structure ensures that recommendations are derived from an objective analysis rather than by an individual's or the group's opinion. A challenge often faced by the facilitator is keeping each team member engaged and actively participating, while at the same time focusing the discussion on relevant ideas.

Narrowing down a large number of improvement ideas requires evaluating or rating each idea based on two sets of criteria. One set of criteria would concern the projected benefits. The benefits of each idea should be projected for all customers across every dimension of value. The second set of criteria would concern projected costs. The costs of each idea would include implementation time, ease of implementation, risk of creating new problems, required resources, implementation cost, complexity of operation, required training, probability of stakeholder acceptance, and required computer system modifications.

It is tempting to consider improvement ideas that involve the use of information technologies, such as hand held devices or software modifications. But the team must be careful to avoid the automation of waste. If automation is considered, it is imperative that representatives from departments that would be responsible for its creation and maintenance be consulted. Indirect costs, such as training and maintenance, must be considered as well as the capability of the users, including customers.

Care must also be taken to avoid focusing on streamlining paperwork flow. With a structured approach, the team should recognize that the purpose of the service is not to transmit paper, but to transmit information. Problems can be mitigated by considering redesign of the paperwork to serve two purposes – reduce waste in the service process and provide better value for customers. For example, a hospital invoice can be redesigned to make payment instructions clearer and to simplify descriptions of the treatments that the patient received.

Control – Develop Implementation and Follow-up Plan (Chapters 10–11)

The *control* phase of DMAIC involves the development of plans to track implementation progress, collect data on subsequent performance, and discover the return of previous problems or the existence of new problems. This phase is often overlooked or downplayed, but it is critical to sustained success. Performance data may take as many as three forms. First, metrics could be placed within the system to measure objectively how well the system performs. Second, customer surveys could be developed and used to measure customers' perspectives of performance. These data should be analysed using statistical control charts. And third, a feedback mechanism could be initiated to identify problems as they arise.

The feedback mechanism for identifying problems should be quick, easy, and non-judgmental. Highly visual representations are useful to communicate the existence of problems to employees and managers, and to separate recurring problems from isolated events. For example, employees could write each problem they experience onto a sticky note, which would then be placed onto a centrally located display board. It is important that the note contain a problem, not a solution and not an assignment of blame. Periodically, the notes would be retrieved, the problems tabulated, and the staff would meet to discuss solutions.

Discipline during this phase also helps to sustain process improvement efforts by ensuring project closure, and by guaranteeing that the project team's efforts have produced change for the better. Two recommendations should be considered: (a) a standard six-month or one-year project team meeting could be scheduled for each improvement project, where recommendations would be revisited, their success analysed, and modifications considered; or (b) a centrally located database or spreadsheet could also be maintained, containing important information for each project, such as its goals, its results, and its implementation timeframe.

Project Communication

An often overlooked element of a process improvement program concerns publicizing its existence. Information about process improvement projects and their impacts on the firm's performance should be communicated to administrators responsible for the service process, employees affected by the project, and other administrators or customers affected by the project. The specific forms of communication could vary depending on the targeted group or individual.

Early in the project, the creation of a short "elevator speech" is recommended so that each member of the project team can communicate a common theme to coworkers and others. It would be a less formalized version of the problem statement, but very brief and communicated in conversational form. The elevator speech can help to serve an internal public-relations purpose by exposing employees to ongoing projects and reinforcing their usefulness and transparency.

Brief periodic status meetings should also be considered. They would be targeted to key leaders and affected administrators who are not members of the project team. Keeping all decision makers informed is critical because it eliminates unfortunate "surprises" due to unforeseen circumstances. Communication of project results to the leadership team would typically involve both an oral presentation and a written report. Project results should be widely available in a visible and convenient way. Options include physical placement predominantly in the facility, placement on the organization's computer system, or placement on a public Internet site. A large storyboard, for example, could be displayed predominantly in a lobby, cafeteria or another popular location routinely frequented by visitors or employees.

Summary & Key Takeaways

Although a process improvement system promotes continuous improvement, it does so in discrete steps based on a series of process improvement projects. To be effective, a methodology needs to be adopted to ensure that projects follow a formal structure. This structure also helps familiarize participants with reasons why improvements are sought and how recommendations are made. In summary, the key takeaways from Chapter 12 are:

1. Kaizen is an approach to process improvement that seeks good results quickly, focusing on minimizing wasteful practices.
2. DMAIC is an approach to process improvement that uses a deliberate, often quantitative, structure that seeks to improve the firm's profitability.

3. Lean Six Sigma can be used as a framework that effectively combines the Kaizen and DMAIC structures.
4. A process improvement project can be motivated by many objectives, including those that are financially quantifiable and those that are more intangible.
5. Process improvement projects can fail if a project team does not take action to ensure that improvements are sustained.
6. Communicating results of improvement projects to all stakeholders (employees, customers, suppliers, etc.) helps to encourage more participation.

Discussion Questions

1. In a process improvement program, what methodology works best: Lean, Six Sigma, or Lean Six Sigma?
2. In a Lean Six Sigma project, in what stage of DMAIC would you measure the potential business impact of the project? What types of impacts would be considered and how would they be expressed?
3. In a process improvement system based on Lean Six Sigma, why is top management support required in words and actions? How can this be accomplished?
4. In a Lean Six Sigma project, what stage of DMAIC is most often not done?
5. Why is communicating the results of a process improvement project important? How can it be accomplished?

References

1 Womack JP, Jones DT. *Lean thinking*. New York, USA: Simon and Schuster; 1996.
2 Ishikawa K. *Guide to quality control*. 2nd ed. White Plains, NY: Quality Resources; 1986.

13

SUPPORTING INFRASTRUCTURE FOR PROCESS IMPROVEMENT

Process Improvement Is Easy ... and Difficult

The most important aspects of business process improvement involve well known and relatively easy to understand techniques, such as process mapping and Lean methods. Their implementation tends to be visually oriented, and consistent with common sense and the frugality of people. They are neither mathematically sophisticated nor do they exist within an IT-dependent environment. In fact, it can be said that most service-related process improvement methods are aimed at simplifying a problem rather than implementing a complex solution. For example, reducing the lead time for service deliver can make developing an IT-based job tracking method unnecessary.

Everyone in the organization can, and should, contribute to process improvement. Workers are responsible for both doing the work and assisting in improving how the work is done. Leaders recognize that the best ideas for improvement often derive from the service provider. Utilizing the intellect of every employee is critical in the development of effective work methods, and in eliminating potential resistance to change. For this reason, it is imperative that all workforce-related decisions align with this desire, such as issuing a promise that no layoffs will occur as a result of a process improvement project to which workers contribute.

It may seem puzzling that the implementation of improvement systems, such as Lean or Six Sigma, often achieve less success than hoped. But, many challenges stand in the way of effectiveness. Simplifying a problem can require hard work and necessitate organizational changes. Legacy performance incentives can conflict with achieving cross-departmental cooperation. Examples include purchase price reduction goals, bonuses based on the quantity of jobs completed, and resource utilization targets. The desire to simply copy success from one type of product to another can lead to misapplication of techniques. Notably, service applications require an approach that differs from manufacturing, as discussed earlier in this book. Moving too quickly to a system that removes inspections or other verifications before substantially eliminating waste can lead to problems that affect customers and discourage continued efforts.

Most successful process improvement programs have been allowed to evolve and mature over a sustained time period. In these cases, the active participation of management is required, both in words and actions. Case studies of successful programs have shown that those managers who truly understand the approach are more likely to succeed. In some cases, the leaders themselves contribute significantly to employee training. Their commitment is required during times where business pressures may otherwise cause decisions that go against intended or stated improvement principles.

Silo Mentality's Impact on a Price Quoting System

Consider the price quoting system that is the responsibility of the sales department, but requires inputs from the design, operations, marketing, and logistics departments. In many organizations, these functions are managed as *silos*, meaning that their performance is measured based on parameters that the leadership deems critically important given their core responsibilities with the firm. For example, the following characteristics may be measured in each of the functions that play a role in the price quoting system: sales (e.g., customer retention, sales growth, lead conversion), marketing (e.g., lead generation, customer acquisition, brand awareness), operations (e.g., unit costs, resource utilization, delivery times), design (e.g., number of patents, hours billed, first-pass yield), and logistics (e.g., shipping costs, on-time delivery, order accuracy). Except for the sales department, which is positively impacted by successful price quoting, other functions would not be incentivized to cooperate.

One may visualize a firm as consisting of a vertically-oriented system resembling grain silos found on a farm. Most business processes flow horizontally through more than department, with customer satisfaction dependent on each involved function. If the performance management system does not recognize this reality, the business process is challenged to be effective. In the case of price quoting, the lack of incentive to contribute to price quoting will likely result in delays. That is, workers in the supporting functions will lack a sense of urgency when requests are received from the sales department.

Respect for People

The two pillars of the Toyota production system are continuous improvement and *respect for people*. [1] Continuous improvement is achieved via *kaizen, genchi genbutsu* (finding facts at the source of a problem) and *challenge* (maintain a long term vision to solve problems with courage and creativity). Respect for people is achieved via *teamwork* (stimulating personal growth by collaborating with others) and *respect* (building mutual trust by understanding each other and taking responsibility). It has been estimated that 80% of Toyota's improvement suggestions come from line personnel and that 10% come from Kaizen events. Once a product is in production, it has been estimated that about 90% of all suggestions for process improvement and cost reduction come from the plant floor and their team member engagement process. [2]

Practitioners should understand that sustained improvement is only possible when employees at all levels actively participate. Often, resistance to change occurs when those affected by changes do not agree that change is warranted. Often, they are correct – especially when managers take it upon themselves to solve problems without worker involvement. When employees play a role in the improvement effort, they are much more likely to experience a sense of ownership and actively strive to make the changes successful. They often generate the best ideas for service process improvement because they are closest to customers, and their ideas are often practical and easy to implement.

The workers who are closest to customers are often among the lowest paid workers in a firm. These workers have a disproportionate effect on customer satisfaction. Receptionists are often the face of the firm because every visitor to a facility interacts with them upon their arrival. Employees who take orders or schedule appointments with customers can also impact the way customers perceive the empathy exuded by the firm. Call center representatives offer another appropriate example, especially because many call centers are outsourced to low-wage providers.

In many cases, higher-paid employees who design or affect the quality of a business process are not aware of problems because they do not interact with customers on a routine basis. A university professor designs courses and provides classroom instruction, but often a teaching assistant (TA) interacts directly with individual students. In this example, the TA is the employee who responds to questions about topics that the professor presented in a confusing manner. Lower paid mechanics perform repairs on problems of which the highly paid product designer may not be aware. Many of these problems are those that could be solved with a minor redesign. In legal processes, paralegal or legal assistants will talk to clients more often than their more highly paid bosses. They would be aware of the day-to-day challenges faced by customers while they navigate a complex legal system.

Leadership and the firm's infrastructure play a big role in the successful implementation of a process improvement program. In a healthy organization, all employees would be willing and able to contribute to improvement efforts. To this end, organizations with successful process improvement programs tend to make a "no layoff" guarantee. This is a promise that no employee will lose their job as a result of an improvement project (the promise would not extend to layoffs necessitated by business downturns or other unexpected disruptions). The goal is to foster a culture of cooperation. This aim is consistent with what Deming stated in his 12th Point: "Remove barriers that rob the hourly worker of his right to pride of workmanship."

The Corporate Structure Dilemma

The modern corporate structure was created by Alfred P. Sloan (1875–1966) at the American automobile manufacturer General Motors (GM). Sloan referred to GM's corporate structure as "decentralized operations with coordinated control." This approach created a hierarchical structure with divisions, such as finance, legal, sales, marketing, purchasing, manufacturing, personnel, research, and engineering. Each division would be led by a director with the expertise appropriate to their division. These directors would simultaneously oversee their division's activities while meeting objectives of the corporation by following strategic mandates from the firm's executive leadership.

Sloan's corporate structure precludes the need for the firm's executives to understand the nuances of every activity. It places responsibility on experts to manage business processes in the myriad of technical and non-technical disciplines – engineers manage engineering processes, IT professionals manage IT processes, etc. This structure can be looked upon as a set of silos where divisional performance can be measured both locally (within the division) and more broadly. Although not the intent, local incentives can take precedent over higher level objectives mainly because local performance is easier to measure. This structure can result in inefficiencies caused by conflicting incentives and internal competition. That is, it implicitly encourages a fallacy that optimizing the parts will naturally optimize the whole.

A typical example that illustrates what can go wrong in a corporate hierarchical structure is associated with the purchasing department. A common performance metric for purchasing materials, purchase price variance (the difference between the budgeted and actual aggregate purchasing costs), which encourages purchasing managers to buy materials at the lowest prices. In fact, the business process for choosing suppliers often requires a purchasing associate to make a special case for choosing a supplier that does not offer the lowest price among those bidding for the work. As a result, quality problems can occur within other departments that make use of the materials, due to inadequate quality or delivery performance. It is unlikely that these problems would be traced back to the original purchasing decision. Busy purchasing associates would find choosing the cheapest supplier to be more efficient from both a timing and a blame standpoint.

Another aspect of modern organizational structures that can compromise a manager's ability to effectively operate a business process concerns employee layoffs. Because of the sensitivity of this activity, managers and workers will not be given advanced warning of the pending layoff that will affect their jobs or those that work under their supervision. Operating a business process with fewer workers without advanced warning will cause significant inefficiencies. In these cases, the consequence can be chaos with the remaining workers struggling to serve customers without a clearly defined process in place. Quickly re-engineering the process in these circumstances will likely be ineffective and have a detrimental effect on customers.

The solution to the dilemma concerning decision making for hierarchical organizations may be found by considering what would happen in a smaller firm. In these firms, decision makers tend to be more aware of the *whole* (i.e., the consequences of every decision on every part of the organization). For example, consider a firm that paints commercial buildings, where the shortage of an important chemical additive causes the price of paint to increase. At a smaller firm, the decision of whether or not to purchase less expensive paint would give equal measure to its effect on paint finish quality. Although future bids will need to account for higher costs, ongoing jobs may need to be accomplished as a diminished profit. These managers would likely be aware of losing customers by buying paint that causes a substandard paint finish.

For larger firms with a hierarchical divisional or departmental structure, integrating processes would avoid myopic incentives in favor of those that are based on the firm's performance. Some firms have replaced many divisionally-based financial incentives with profit sharing schemes, where performance of the firm dictates each worker's bonus salary. Default decisions (e.g., choose the lowest priced bid unless a special case is made) would also be abandoned. Rather than designing performance systems that make it easier for upper management, systems should be designed that requires upper management to embrace the complexity of their business. All decisions should consider the totality of effects so that the "whole" is optimized.

Unions

Worker unions exist in many firms. Some unions are *trade unions* because they represent a job category of workers who are employed across many firms. Other unions are *company unions* because they represent workers within a firm across a range of jobs. For example, workers at Toyota in Japan are members of a company union, while members of the United Auto Workers are trade union members. In some firms, long standing grievances and animosities have created an antagonistic environment, especially in the case of trade unions. Because a trade union's success is not directly impacted by the success of the firms that employ its members, poor relations within a firm can become exacerbated.

Perhaps the most important impediment to change are strict work rules and job classifications. In fact, any setting where workers have distinct and clearly delineated sets of responsibilities can be a challenge. For example, many trade unions enforce rules that limit flexibility whereby some workers cannot pro-actively perform a task that is outside of their job classification. This rule applies to seemingly simple tasks. These rules, if strictly adhered to, can limit the ability of management to make process changes. On the other hand, poor management decision making (in particular their disrespect of worker's rights) have created the setting for union deployment.

Business process improvements can take place in union settings. In fact, in any setting, workers will only participate enthusiastically when they personally benefit from the improvements. Although this concept may sound self-serving of workers, it is an aspect of human behavior that should not be ignored. In order to get the union "on board" with a process improvement focus, honesty and commitment are necessary. Managers should not use process improvement to achieve an explicit goal of reducing costs because most costs associated with a business process are derived from workers' wages. Although process improve-ments can have a profound effect on productivity (i.e., generating more output for less cost), cost cuts should be achieved by labor attrition or transfers to other departments. Improvements can also be created by adding additional value for customers without adding costs.

Managers need to consider the union to be a partner when process improvements are considered. Union workers are close to customers and appreciate the opportunity to express their ideas to improve the satisfaction of their customers. After all, they often have the unpleasant task of listening to customer complaints and correcting mistakes. Research has consistently shown that better internal quality improves job satisfaction. A union worker will also appreciate when their job is saved by a better process. Managers should be dili-gently focused on adding value for customers, and should realize that their workforce knows best how to achieve success. In fact, to show their appreci-ation, some firms place union members in charge of conducting plant tours so that members can showcase their ability to improve how work is done.

Organizational Infrastructure Recommendations

A firm's organizational infrastructure is defined by its facilities' locations, departmental configuration, lines of authority, methods of communication, management philosophy, employment policies, and culture. This infrastructure impacts how information flows and how decisions are made. An ineffective infrastructure can cause potentially valuable initiatives to fail. For example, when quality management practices evolved to a more process-oriented focus (as described in Chapter 11) some firms did not change their employment pol-icies to be consistent with the needs of the new paradigm. Firms that continued to pay workers on a piecework basis (according to the quantity of parts produced) conflicted with the realities of the process thinking approach that seeks to quickly identify and solve quality problems.

For a process improvement program to be sustainable, the firm's leaders need to be consistent in their messages to stakeholders. They need to exude the patience to withstand early complications and maintain a focus on implementing the program properly. In most successful programs, the leadership team plays a role in training by providing some of the classroom instruction and participating in improvement projects. Most importantly, they need to create an environment that motivates workers to participate in making processes perform better.

This challenge has been studied for process improvement programs implemented in public services, which may be the most difficult environment to implement these initiatives. [3] The following four recommendations will help a firm create a sustainable organizational infrastructure for process improvement to thrive.

Develop a Sound, Consistent, and Robust Methodology

A plethora of consultants, universities, and associations provide training on process improvement, with each suggesting that their approach is superior to others. But, research has shown that successful organizations incorporate many viable alternatives. These programs represent an alphabet soup of names and acronyms, often a combination of Lean and Six Sigma, such as Lean Six Sigma (LSS) or Lean Sigma (LS). Some use more traditional names, such as Continuous Quality Improvement (CQI) or Total Quality Management (TQM). Other methodologies are based on the International Standard Organization (ISO) 9000 standards for manufacturing, the Joint Commission Accreditation for Healthcare, and the Malcolm Baldridge National Quality Award (MBNQA) criteria for all types of firms. Many international firms base their process improvement programs on a local standard, such as the European Foundation for Quality Management (EFQM) Excellence Award, the China Quality Award, Prêmio Nacional da Qualidade (Brazil), and the Philippine Quality Award.

The establishment of any rational philosophy along with a viable methodology is required for sustainable success. The philosophy should be easily understood but not reduced to clichés. It must create a consistency between talk and actions by ensuring that organizational incentives align with the program's intentions. In many cases, changes will need to be made within the firm based on the recommendations made below.

The methods associated with the program need to be those that make sense for the type of business and the knowledge-base of employees. For example, a method that is heavily informed by statistical methods should not be implemented in a firm whose employees are not quantitatively oriented. Training needs to be consistent with the chosen methodology and provided in a just-in-time manner. It should include first-hand experience in applying the methods covered to solve real problems. This approach enables employees to immediately apply the concepts and techniques covered. The methodology, however, cannot be viewed as inflexible. It should be allowed to evolve as circumstances change, such as during times of leadership turnover.

Build Trust by Removing Fear

Changes forthcoming within an organization will be accompanied by apprehension among workers and managers. In fact, resistance to change has spurned a management discipline known as *change management*. This idea should be considered in context, however, because there are certainly times in one's personal life where change is resisted. It is usually true that, in these cases, the individual considers the alternative to be less desirable than the current situation. The change may cause the individual to work harder for the same result, or they may simply believe that the alternative is not better than the current situation.

The failure of Frederick Taylor to fundamentally change business practice by implementing standard work before World War II may be attributed to his lack of worker involvement in developing the new work practices. With management dictating the new procedures, workers felt (often correctly) that management did not understand customer needs as much as they did. An effective approach to implementing a process improvement program would be the realization that no one will participate unless they foresee a personal benefit were the new initiative to be implemented.

Leadership should directly address potential fears that will accompany the implementation of a process improvement program. The main fears of most workers are concerned with job insecurities, including the potential layoffs or being punished for reporting problems. Firms that have been successful in implementing process improvement maintain a policy that no layoffs will occur as a result of a process improvement project. They make this guarantee in a clear and unambiguous statement.

The importance of jointly implementing ideas that changes should have a personal benefit for each worker while removing fear from the organization can be illustrated with examples involving trade unions. In the city of Fort Wayne, an improvement project reduced the cost of a city service so that it compared favorably with a similar private service, eliminating union and individual employee concerns regarding potential privatization. [3] At the manufacturer Wiremold, the union participated in implementing kaizen approaches to process improvement. Their success stemmed from the actions of a new leadership team that ensured all workers, including union members, would benefit from the new Lean implementation. [4]

With labor costs dominating the budget of a business process manager, it would be reasonable to ask how cost savings can be realized without employee layoffs. With employee attrition rates averaging about 15% in the United States, workers rendered unnecessary due to a process improvement can be transferred to better positions with the firm. These positions are in constant supply. Although some retraining may be necessary, employees who are already familiar with the products, services, and culture of the firm require less orientation. They can immediately contribute to improvement projects in their new position with little to no additional training.

An interesting approach would be to consider starting an improvement project just before a current worker is scheduled to depart, either to another job within the firm or outside the firm. For example, a business process operated by six employees with one retiring worker can be the subject of an improvement project to decrease the number of workers required to perform the service. The management needs to be careful to not simply allocate more work to the remaining employees, but to maintain the same level of work while retaining activities that do not add value for customers.

Initiate Long Term Cultural Change

In many firms, leadership uses internal competition to motivate worker productivity, such as choosing as employee of the week the service worker who earns the highest scores on customer satisfaction surveys. Although this type of incentive system can be abused by gaming (e.g., serving the numbers rather than serving customers), a pervasive sense of competition across departments or functions can also exist. This latter form of competition occurs when budgets are increased or resources are allocated as a form of zero-sum game with winners and losers.

Because service processes cross departmental or function lines, an overtly competitive environment can exist. In order to most effectively implement a process improvement program, a culture of cooperation, rather than competition, needs to be maintained. Incentives associated with functional silos can hamper the ability of the business process to operate effectively. For example, monthly sales force goals can result in a disproportionate number of orders being placed towards the end of each month. These orders can become burdensome to business processes that schedule work, handle orders, or organize shipments. Every manager and employee needs to be incentivized to optimize the whole rather than just their part of the firm's activities. For example, if every worker receives a year-end bonus based on the firm's overall profit, the incentive would not exist for one department to optimize its own operations to the detriment of the firm's success.

Changing an organization's culture cannot be done quickly. Many employees are well aware that previous initiatives failed and they may, in fact, have played a role in selling the program to their peers only to have the program discontinued. A sense of "this too shall pass" permeates some organizations, resulting in workers reacting in passive-aggressive ways. Leadership needs to avoid this phenomenon by action. They need to create an environment where problems are identified and solved, without assigning blame to individual employees who are likely not the root cause of the problem. The preferred approach can be illustrated by a quote from H. Ross Perot (1930–2019), former General Motors executive, who stated:

> I come from an environment where, if you see a snake, you kill it. At GM, if you see a snake, the first thing you do is go hire a consultant on snakes. Then you get a committee on snakes, and then you discuss it for a couple of years. The most likely course of action is – nothing . . . We need to build an environment where the first guy who sees the snake kills it.

The new culture should incentivize workers to report problems and near misses, so that they raise awareness can be solved. Supervisors must allow workers to devote attention to improving their work in addition to doing their work. This change requires the creation of performance metrics that support this reality. Each worker should be incentivized to participate in improvement activities – and they should want to participate rather than be forced to participate. As mentioned earlier, each worker should perceive a personal benefit from their participation. Finally, because any new program will incur some mistakes during implementation, leadership needs to "stay the course." Gradual implementation will allow time to carefully evolve the system in response to successes and challenges that are unique to each organization.

Publicize the Program to All Stakeholders

An often overlooked aspect of program success is ensuring that relevant stakeholders are informed about its goals, limitations, methods, and accomplishments. All workers need to be exposed to the program because they need to be willing and enthusiastic participants. Shareholders need to be aware that some short-term costs may increase as more time is devoted to improvement efforts, and that these efforts will eventually have positive impacts on competitiveness. Future program participants will develop a knowledge of how improvement projects proceed and the types of problems that can be solved. For other stakeholders, such as regulators, suppliers, customers, and local communities, the goodwill the program creates can have indirect benefits.

Publicizing the program should start early to help create support for the program among stakeholders, although leadership needs to be avoid promising too much too quickly. The stakeholders should be kept informed as the program develops and matures. Without exaggeration, this information should include the tangible and intangible benefits that each stakeholder will receive. It is critical to show that internal commitment exists at three levels – leadership, middle management, and workers.

An easy way to create visible manifestations of projects would be using posters or other visible media, placed predominantly in a common work area. Posters describing successful projects could be placed in the lobby of the facility, the worker cafeteria, or in the hallways near affected departments. Workers would be able to better understand the program, and they will see the methodology employed. With a consistent methodology, the visible approach will help to train workers. They will see that their friends or peers have participated, and they will talk to them about the projects. Ideally, they will want to have their name associated with one of these posters.

Summary & Key Takeaways

A firm's commitment to a sustained process improvement program must go beyond slogans, banners, or motivational speeches. Business process managers should focus on utilizing the minds of their workers to not just do their work, but to engage in improvement efforts. Sustaining a program that continuously seeks improvements that remove wasteful activities and increase value for customers requires a supporting organizational infrastructure. In summary, the key takeaways from Chapter 13 are:

1. Applying process improvement methods appears easy on the surface, but leaders should be aware that underlying organizational issues can impact the ability to successfully implement these useful methods.
2. A system for process improvement should motivate participation by those front-line workers who deliver services to customers because they are the best sources of improvement ideas.
3. Leadership should be aware that hierarchical corporate structures and labor union relations can hinder the ability of a firm to improve business processes, but these challenges can be overcome.
4. To be effective, an organization should choose a process improvement approach that best matches their types of processes and skills of their employees.
5. Leadership should ensure that employees do not fear being laid off when a process is improved or being punished for reporting problems.
6. A culture that supports cooperation and limits internal competition is essential for success, because service processes usually cross functional lines.
7. Publicizing the program in early stages helps build support and publically communicating project results helps maintain sustainable process improvement.

Discussion Questions

1. In Toyota's production system, what does "respect for people" refer mainly to: managers, customers, or employees? Explain.
2. In a process improvement program, does a "no layoff" pledge mean that employees have permanent jobs unless they choose to leave the company?
3. What are some factors that should be considered when adopting a specific process improvement methodology?
4. In a process improvement program, why is it important to remove fear from an organization?
5. When implementing a process improvement program, what types of cultural change may be necessary?
6. Why is it important to publicize a process improvement program to internal stakeholders? What methods can be used?

References

1 Liker JK. *The Toyota way*. New York: McGraw-Hill; 2004.
2 Protzman C, Whiton F, Kerpchar J, Lewandowski C, Stenberg S, Grounds P. *The lean practitioner's field book*. New York: CRC Press; 2016. 15 p.
3 Maleyeff J. *Improving service delivery in government with lean six sigma*. Washington, DC: IBM Center for The Business of Government; 2007.
4 Emiliani BL. *Better thinking, better results*. Connecticut, USA: Center for Lean Management; 2003.

14

BUSINESS PROCESS OUTSOURCING

Business Process Outsourcing

A firm's leadership often concludes that costs can be saved or value increased by assigning the responsibility of operating a business process to another firm. The term *outsourcing* is used to denote placing responsibility for a business process with another service provider (often called a supplier). The location of the outsourcing organization can be anywhere, including in the same facility of the customer firm or in another country. The term *offshoring* is used when the business process is performed in another country. There may be cases where an offshore business process remains under the control of the original firm but is moved to a location that is far away from its customers.

Outsourcing a service makes the most sense for services with deductive rules because rules-based service activities are easily taught. Examples include verifying account information in a billing process, entering data into an IT system, or paying an invoice. Greater skills are needed for services that make use of inductive rules, such as the checking for fraud in a credit card transaction. These activities are based on pattern recognition skills, which can also be taught to those with the requisite backgrounds. When more tacit knowledge is needed (i.e., when rules are not easily defined), effective outsourcing is more difficult because tasks are more subjective. They can even vary somewhat based on specific customer needs. Examples include the tacit knowledge needed to evaluate an intangible quality of a job candidate or the clarity of a business proposal.

The insurance industry uses outsourcing for many of its business processes. Typical outsourced business processes include those associated with underwriting, issuing policies, billing policyholders, preparing insurance certificates, overseeing policies, managing commissions, adjudicating claims, and reporting financial performance. Outsourcing these services assures that all policies adhere to regulatory standards and that crucial information is included and accurate, including declarations, coverages, and exclusions.

Processes considered by a firm to be non-core activities are routinely outsourced. Outsourcing decisions concerning these processes should not be undertaken without due diligence, because they can impact the quality of many business processes. For example, the management of facilities such as offices and data centers is typically outsourced to a third party, including services like security, maintenance and building operations. These processes impact the comfort of workers and often include interactions with visitors. Therefore, their impact can be hidden from obvious view of managers.

Many professional services are outsourced because their demand is not sufficient to justify operating the business process in-house. It is common for many firms to outsource legal services. Smaller firms may outsource business processes associated with bookkeeping, account reconciliation, and tax preparation. Some companies outsource marketing processes such as survey design, data analytics, market research, advertising, lead management and sales. Those processes that can be standardized across firms, such as human resources or payroll, are also good candidates for outsourcing. A good example would be the review of an online publications' comment section to remove inappropriate comments. Offshoring is common for these types of processes when they are labor intensive.

Business Process Offshoring

A firm considering the offshoring of a business process should be confident that its technology infrastructure is reliable, including IT systems and communication mechanisms. With the expansion of the Internet in the early 1990's, offshoring was initiated at many organizations to take advantage of low labor costs. Initially, India was the most popular location for offshoring IT services. Subsequent expansion to other countries and other process types followed including many eastern European countries that were formerly under Soviet influence. Initial applications included low-end technology-based services, such as troubleshooting call centers, basic application software, maintaining IT infrastructure, and software maintenance. Subsequent applications expanded to other types of call centers, internal administrative services, healthcare services, and others. For example, payroll and accounting services are now often accomplished by offshore entities that include related services such as payroll tracking and analysis, and tax document preparation and distribution.

An interesting example in legal, insurance, and healthcare firms involves transcription. These processes require a great deal of knowledge that includes language skills (to understand dictation), medical terms, insurance processes, industry codes, etc. Workers are paid higher wages than other offshored business process service providers. In fact, many transcription service providers are themselves well-educated professionals. Given the importance of communicating in the language preferred by the firm, there has typically been a set of favored locations for offshoring of communication-sensitive processes, which differ by country. Examples include many English speakers in India, Mexico, and the Philippines; many German speakers in Romania and Poland; many Japanese speakers in China; and many French speakers in North Africa.

Many offshored business processes are completely transparent to external customers. They include routine transactional services (e.g., transaction processing, benefits, testing, accounting, payroll, accounts payable, invoicing, and basic tax returns) and some professional services (e.g., software development, engineering, design, hiring, legal, troubleshooting, analytics, R&D, call centers, and marketing). Others, perhaps most notably call centers, are less transparent. Dell, for example, faced a "Bangalore backlash" from customers who perceived their move to offshore call centers to be a cost-cutting move that decreased quality of information exchanged during troubleshooting calls. As a result, Dell offered domestic call center services to its customers who were willing to pay a fee for this perceived service improvement.

As a way to achieve some of the benefits of offshoring, but with better results, "insourcing" is common. In these cases, the supplier performs the work on site rather than at an international location. An especially relevant example concerns application programming (and similar IT services). These arrangements are similar to consulting or contractual relationships, except that the workers are foreign nationals who work under a temporary work visa. These workers would be paid lower wages than domestic counterparts, although decision makers typically need to account for transportation and living expenses.

In a counter-intuitive way, more recent technological advances have made offshoring of certain processes unnecessary. This tendency is especially apparent for rules-based services that can be automated, such as account verification that can be done using imaging capabilities. More complex processes, which require pattern recognition skills, are also automated to various degrees of success. They tend to use software applications that are based on machine learning, artificial intelligence, or neural network technologies. For example, synthetic speech technologies can be used to replace a call center representative. Other examples include credit card fraud detection and legal dispute resolution.

Offshoring Quality

Firms that seek to reduce costs by outsourcing or offshoring a business process often fail to consider how all customer performance dimensions will be affected. This decision-making mistake is especially common when customers are internal. Ignoring communications-related performance dimensions is especially common. Although the ability to speak required languages well is usually considered, the ability to communicate in a timely and effective manner can be overlooked. With great distances that encompass both geography and culture, communication in supplier-customer relationships is often ineffective. For example, consider offshoring IT services. Prior to the service being offshored, locally located IT service providers could speak frequently with internal customers, including over lunch or during breaks. Offshoring IT services requires that the tacit knowledge needed for accurate results can be provided when the service providers are many time zones away from their customers.

Another important dimension of performance that can be overlooked is competency. Offshoring suppliers of a service need to possess the rigorous qualifications that are required to perform a complex service. In the U.S., a healthcare professional would be certified by a variety of educational, professional, national, and regional governing bodies. In addition, it is likely that the individual would be vetted using a personal interview that may include one or more days and numerous individuals. If a professional healthcare service, such as radiology or medical transcription is offshored, vetting service providers moves primarily to documentation from sources that may not be entirely consistent with the firm's specific needs. These challenges can be overcome by establishing relationships with governments and universities in locations targeted for processional service outsourcing.

When making decisions that concern offshoring professional services, the "empathy" performance dimension should not be overlooked. For example, an offshore radiologist who analyses a MRI will likely not be familiar with the patient whose image is being analysed. But the service could face quality-related risks if the analysis would have been improved with knowledge of the patient's medical history or other clinical symptoms. In radiology, trust would also be important because customers will likely be fellow physicians who need to rely on a colleague with whom they have no personal relationship. Therefore, an evaluation of consumption maps and dimensions of performance should be a critical element of offshoring decisions, especially for business processes that deliver a professional service.

Risk Identification

Although Lean methods are very effective at reducing uncertainties associated with operating a business process, outsourcing and offshoring introduce uncertainties that are difficult for a firm to control. Uncertainties that are not eliminated will create risks to the business that have a detrimental effect on its customers. The discipline of *risk management* is concerned with identifying and prioritizing each risk factor, then taking proactive action to avoid the risk or mitigate its effect.

The first component of a business process risk management system is identifying all the potential events and circumstances that can adversely affect business process performance. In other words, the analysis starts by finding what can go wrong. It is useful to think of these risks as ordinary or extraordinary, which are commonly separated into operational (ordinary) risks and disruption (extraordinary) risks. This separation helps to apply risk management strategies and risk mitigation approaches. It is also consistent with a popular internal versus external classification of risks.

The accumulation of a complete list of risks that can affect a business process should start by consulting a master list of common risks. The following list, combined into five groups, is based on a combination of risks listed in [1–3] as they would apply to a business process:

- Technological/Operational (e.g., anticipated demand changes, capacity constraints, quality problems, technology failure/downtime, software failure, emergence of a disruptive technology, contract terms, communication/IT disruptions, technology obsolescence, inadequate controls, barriers to change, lack of due-diligence, Internet congestion, slow updates, poor problem solving).
- Social/Community (e.g., labor shortages, strikes, accidents, employee turnover/absenteeism, human errors, union/labor disputes, reputation, negative media coverage, perceived quality, cultural conflicts, fraud, sabotage, acts of terrorism, malfeasance, decreased labor productivity, poor worker conditions, political instability, pandemics, other ethical challenges).
- Natural/Hazard (e.g. fire, severe weather, hurricanes, tornados, flood, drought, earthquake, tsunami, epidemic, famine, avalanche, climate change effects, other natural disaster).
- Economy/Competition (e.g., interest rate fluctuation, exchange rate fluctuation, commodity price fluctuation, price and incentive wars, bankruptcy of suppliers, stock market collapse, global economic recession, inadequate capital, market downturns, substitutes, demand changes, falling prices, other globalization effects).
- Legal/Political (e.g., liabilities, noncompliance, law suits, barriers to entry, governmental restrictions, tax liabilities, new regulations, lobbying from customer groups, corruption, bribery, instability overseas, intellectual property infringements, confiscations abroad, war, trade disputes, tax structures, customs risks, other human rights violations).

Risks that cause disruptions are especially problematic. These risks are caused by less predictable events that are often not in the firm's control. Management of disruptive risks is generally more challenging than it is for operational risks. Their identification can be incomplete due to ignorance of key uncertainties. This is especially true for international facilities, including cultural impacts (see the section below on culture). Similarly, the assessment of disruptive risks is made difficult because the frequency of these events is generally rare, but their impacts can be great. This is the case, for example, with disruptions attributed to natural disasters. On the other hand, once identified and assessed, mitigation of disruptive risks can be fairly easy to accomplish, albeit with consideration of costs (as discussed below).

A *risk management system* (RMS) identifies and assesses both existing and potential risks, formulating potential risk responses, implementing risk mitigation, and measuring and monitoring progress. Given the diversity of business processes and the complexities of global corporations, the RMS is intended to provide direction and guidance without prescribing a precise approach that may not match every firm's circumstances. The RMS usually has the following sections: (a) risk identification, (b) risk assessment, (c) risk mitigation, and (d) risk monitoring.

Risk Assessment

After identifying outsourcing risks, each should be evaluated relative to its likelihood, potential severity, and how effective internal controls will be at eliminating or mitigating their impact. Qualitative approaches provide quick determinations about what action may be appropriate when dealing with the risk. Those risks having a low likelihood and minor potential severity can be handled on a casual basis without significant or costly action, such as the purchase of insurance against the associated disruption. Those risks having a higher likelihood or severe potential impact (or both) should be given careful consideration. They are candidates for comprehensive or more costly avoidance or mitigation strategies.

Although the terms likelihood, severity, and detection are well known, they all represent quantifiable characteristics that would be defined similarly across firms or individuals. *Likelihood* is the probability that the identified risk will occur. Some disruptive risks, such as the risk of a shutdown due to a hurricane, would be estimated based on historical trends. These risk factors typically have an annual likelihood (i.e., the likelihood of a disruptive hurricane this year is 3%). *Severity* is the expected impact if the identified risk occurs. The impact can range from minor (e.g., a few hours to connect portable power generators) to severe (e.g., loss of power for several days eliminating the availability of important IT systems). *Detection* is the probability that internal controls will discover the risk factor and eliminate or greatly reduce its effect.

Many frameworks have been created for action planning based on risks and their impacts. They generally share an important characteristic: highest priority is given to the risks that can have the most devastating impact on the enterprise. Therefore, priority is assigned based on the combination of likelihood of occurrence, its impact if it does occur, and the chance that internal controls will be ineffective. A basic framework, which is used by Lean and Six Sigma practitioners, is referred to as *failure modes* and *effects analysis* (FMEA).

Failure Modes and Effects Analysis

FMEA determines priorities associated with risk by examining each *failure mode* and quantifying its potential for disruption based on its severity, occurrence probability, and detection probability. A failure mode is a potential cause of a disruption in the operation of a process. When applied to a business process, failure modes would include causes related to unavailable workers (e.g., sickness, injury, or strike) or inaccessible IT systems (e.g., power failure, cyberattack, or Internet interruption). FMEA sets priorities for each failure mode based on the following three variables:

- Occurrence (O) – What is the likelihood of an occurrence?
- Severity (S) – How significant are the effects if they do occur?
- Detection (D) – Will internal controls identify the failure before it affects customers?

The FMEA calculations are relatively simple. Quantification of each input (severity, occurrence, and detection) is done using a scale between 1 and 10, where 1 is the best case and 10 is the worst case. Many definitions have been suggested for these ordinal scales; the best approach uses a common scaling across the organization. For *occurrence*, a typical FMEA framework will assign a value of 10 to a "extremely high" likelihood, down to a value of 1 to signify an "almost impossible" likelihood. For *severity*, a FMEA will assign a value of 10 to "dangerously high" down to a value of 1 to signify a "negligible negative" impact. For *detection*, a FMEA will assign a value of 10 to a "very remote" (chance of detecting the failure) down to a value of 1 to signify "almost certain" detection.

A risk priority number (RPN) is calculated for each failure mode based on its likelihood, severity, and detection. The RPN is an indicator of the concern a business process manager should have relative to each failure mode. The RPN is calculated as the product of Severity, Occurrence, and Detection (RPN = O × S × D). RPN will range from 1 (no worries about this failure mode) to 1000 (extremely significant worries about this failure mode). For example, if a failure mode had scores of 6 (likelihood), 8 (severity), and 2 (detection), its RPN would be equal to 96. Typically, numbers approaching 1000 are rare, so the focus is those failure models with the highest RPN.

Table 14.1 shows an example FMEA for a financial auditing process, simplified for brevity. In this case, the highest RPN is associated with the client's being unavailable. Although this failure mode's severity is less than many of the other failure modes, it is much more likely to occur without internal detection. When responding to the FMEA results, the business process

TABLE 14.1 Example FMEA for Financial Audit Process

Failure Mode	Effect	O	S	D	RPN
Unavailable Audit Supervisor	Cannot supervise team	4	4	10	160
Unavailable all Audit Staff	Need to find replacements	4	2	6	48
Flu/Epidemic	Project cannot proceed	2	6	4	48
Power Failure	Cannot access transactions	2	9	8	144
Cyberattack	Client Privacy at Risk	1	10	5	50
IT Breakdown	Cannot access transactions	5	5	6	150
Client Unavailable	Cannot confirm transactions	9	4	6	216
Client Commits Fraud	Work stops for investigation	1	10	8	80
Client Mistakes/Ignorance	Delays work on audits	8	3	2	48
Accounting Rules Change	Requires retraining of staff	4	8	2	64

manager needs to choose a threshold RPN that would declare a failure mode worthy of attention. For example, it may be determined that a RPN of over 200 be given immediate attention and that a RPN above 100 be given some attention. In addition, any failure mode with a severity score higher than a critical value (e.g., 7) could be included on a list of failure modes deserving attention, regardless of its occurrence or detection scores.

Many accreditation and certification bodies require a methodology similar to FMEA. These systems would be designed to identify or anticipate potential problems. The requirement would also extend to documenting project improvement processes and risk mitigation strategies. Unfortunately, some firms treat this requirement as a nuisance and "go through the motions" of performing a FMEA but not making use of it as a risk management tool. FMEA has proven to be an effective tool for understanding potential failures, but it is meaningless if not implemented properly.

Risk Avoidance & Mitigation

Risks are either accepted, avoided, or mitigated. Accepting a risk would be a reasonable approach if its RPN is less than the threshold deemed worthy of attention and its severity score is low. This decision can also be impacted by the totality of the FMEA results and the resources available. *Risk avoidance* is most appropriate for failure modes that have a high RPN or a high severity score, especially when the means to detect the risks are lacking. Risk avoidance is often accomplished by creating a policy that restricts certain business process designs or decisions. The firm may require that certain business process not rely on IT systems to operate, such as a process that provides real time information of customers concerning critical health or safety information. Examples include the operation of an airline, rapid transit train, or a medical device. The firm may also restrict locations for outsourced suppliers due to potential turmoil or unreliable infrastructure.

Risk mitigation refers to actions that reduce the likelihood or severity of a failure mode. They often make use of the Lean methods, such as a poka-yoke device and other methods described in Chapter 5. For example, installing and maintaining smoke detectors in an office suite's kitchen will reduce the likelihood of damage caused by a fire. These methods are less effective for removing uncertainty associated with externally-derived events, such as a natural disaster or political upheaval. The quality management methods in Chapters 10–11 are also helpful for mitigating risk. In these cases, care must be taken to ensure that metrics are being collected in an unbiased manner, and that analysis is timely and proactive. For example, skill-based mistakes can be minimized when the parent firm's trainers travel to an offshore location to deliver training programs.

Risks can also be mitigated by transferring the impact to others, albeit with consideration of ethical implications. Externalizing risk is often fraught with moral or ethical concerns. When offshoring a business process in countries with universal healthcare, the firm should not ask workers to perform unsafe or potentially unhealthy tasks due to the realization that the resulting health-care costs would not be the responsibility of the firm. A better way to transfer risk is through the purchase of insurance, such as professional liability insurance, property insurance, workers' compensation insurance, product liability insurance, and business interruption insurance.

Risk monitoring refers to the procedures used to track the progress of avoidance and mitigation strategies, and to periodically re-evaluate failure modes by reapplication of the FMEA method. The risk monitoring procedure would confirm that progress is being made to reduce chances of operational glitches or process disruptions. This phase of a RMS can be overlooked because it requires time and effort to execute. Thus, it works best when the activities of risk monitoring are not invasive and relatively infrequent. The methods of performance metric development and analysis (described in Chapters 10 and 11) are useful in this regard.

Impact of International Cultures

Culture is a defining characteristic of humanity. It should be a consideration when choosing an offshore supplier of a business process and when managing offshore personnel. Culture consists of beliefs, traditions, attitudes, and norms, and encompasses art, history, language and ways of expressing oneself. Cultural characteristics serve as a mechanism for adapting to the complexities of living and working by establishing a common set of behaviors, thoughts, and actions across members of a social group. A culture changes slowly over time as the group's circumstances change and the need to adapt becomes evident. This evolution would be affected by natural events including environmental factors. In this way, groups find comfort in maintaining the stability of old traditions while evolving to new realities.

Cultures can also be changed in more profound ways by external extraordinary events. These events may consist of catastrophic natural calamities but more often they will be motivated by man-made incidents. Changes to political systems or laws are man-made events that can profoundly change aspects of a culture. For example, the transition from a capitalist to communist system (or vice-versa) will cause culture changes that may affect workplace behaviors. Laws associated with human rights or lifestyles can also have important effects. The culture of workers in a business process can be affected by significant changes to the rules that regulate how a process operates. It can also be affected by modifications in management philosophies and incentive systems. Some of the results may be temporary, but others can have effects that last for generations.

Defining a specific culture is always difficult and imprecise, but this exercise should not resort to stereotyping. Stereotypes are short-cut beliefs that often attribute negative characteristics to others. They are attributed to groups of people based on unsubstantiated beliefs, such as superstitions and other forms of prejudice. Because the observer is affected by his or her own culture, background, and experiences, their judgments are subjective. However, this is not to suggest that there are no absolutes or established values.

To be successful in a global economy, the thoughts and actions of business process managers should not merely tolerate cultural differences. They should embrace those differences and build sustainable relationships with their offshore suppliers. Managers should start by learning about international cultures, by studying history, and speaking directly with numerous individuals at potential sites, especially workers. Managers should become aware of how workers and managers at a potential supplier approach business issues and challenges. It is particularly important for business leaders in developed countries to view other cultures as different from – but not inferior to – their own.

When offshoring a business process, the misunderstanding of cultures adds more uncertainty to an already risky endeavor. The impact of culture is addressed in a case study by Arnheiter [4], who describes activities that took place at a jet engine maintenance and repair facility in Singapore. The facility, called Eagle Services Asia (ESA), was a joint venture with U.S.-based Pratt & Whitney (P&W) Aircraft and Singapore Airlines. P&W's business system included many elements of Lean production that it expected all of its suppliers and partners to implement.

Upon startup at ESA, the mostly Chinese and Malaysian workers were not familiar with Lean methods, and there appeared to be a reluctance to embrace these methods. In particular, P&W noticed hesitancy by workers to become involved with the improvement project framework known by the Japanese term *kaizen*. After some study, the P&W managers realized that the reluctance stemmed from a historically contentious relationship with Japan. A number of modifications that suited the local Malaysian culture were made. Among other changes, a name change was made from kaizen to *Majulah Induction* (Majulah means "the way forward" in the Malay language). Other changes were also made to other terminology and approaches. The ESA facility was eventually awarded a P&W Employee Fulfillment Leadership Award due to its successful process management approach.

Summary & Key Takeaways

Business process managers often attempt to save money by using an outside supplier to operate a business process, a concept known as outsourcing. When the supplier is located in another country, the term offshoring is applied. Outsourcing and offshoring have financial benefits but present a myriad of risks. In summary, the key takeaways from Chapter 14 are:

1. Outsourcing or offshoring a service can be beneficial, but a firm should consider the effect on all important customer dimensions of performance, and the revised process's impact on the customer's consumption process.
2. The myriad of risks associated with outsourcing and offshoring can be categorized and listed. A risk management system is used to assess the levels of risk and develop plans for avoiding the risk or mitigating its effects.
3. Lean methods can be suitable for lowering the likelihood of a risk, but risks with potential for significantly negative impacts need to be handled in other ways.
4. When offshoring, a business process manager should pay close attention to the worker culture at the supplier location, while avoiding stereotyping. Adapting to local cultures can enhance effectiveness and avoid delays in implementing a successful offshore business process.

Discussion Questions

1. Find several examples of business processes that have been outsourced but not offshored.
2. Find several examples of business processes that have been outsourced and offshored.
3. List some examples of business processes with important customer dimensions of performance that would be effectively addressed by outsourcing.

4. List some examples of business processes with important customer dimensions of performance that would not be effectively addressed by outsourcing.
5. Give examples of how Lean methods that reduce uncertainty can actually increase risk in an outsourced or offshored business process.
6. Discuss some cultural differences that could affect how business processes would operate in countries you have lived and some actions that might be warranted.

References

1 Chopra S, Sodhi MS. Managing risk to avoid supply-chain breakdown. *MIT Sloan Management Review*. 2004; 46(1):53–61.
2 IBM. Supply chain risk management: a delicate balancing act. *IBM Business Services*, 2008.
3 Rainey DL. *Visionary strategic leadership: sustaining success through strategic direction, corporate management and high-level programs*. Charlotte, North Carolina, USA: Information Age Publishing; 2013. 231 p.
4 Arnheiter E. *Eagle services Asia*. Ivey Publishing; 2007. Case Number 9B07D019.

APPENDIX

Problem Set Solutions

Chapter 8

1. The resource utilization of the cashiers is 83.3%.
   The resource utilization of the sandwich makers is 62.5%.
   The resource utilization of the pickup station worker is 83.3%.
2. Yes, the target is 90% and the resource utilization of the director during a month where two proposals are required is 86.1%.
3. Three agents are needed.

Chapter 9

1. Solutions are listed below:

   a. For serious problems: $\lambda = 12$ per hour, $\mu = 3$ per hour.
      Average waiting time for serious problems: Not enough servers.
      For troubleshooting: $\lambda = 24$ per hour, $\mu = 6$ per hour.
      Average waiting time for troubleshooting is 0.02 hours.
      For non-complicated problems: $\lambda = 4$ per hour, $\mu = 5$ per hour.
      Average waiting time for non-complicated problems is 0.8 hours.
   b. For serious problems: $\lambda = 13.8$ per hour, $\mu = 3$ per hour.
      Need 6 servers for serious problems at 76.7% utilization and 0.11 hour average wait time.
      For troubleshooting: $\lambda = 27.6$ per hour, $\mu = 6$ per hour.
      Need 6 servers for serious problems at 76.7% utilization and 0.11 hour average wait time.
      For non-complicated problems: $\lambda = 4.6$ per hour, $\mu = 5$ per hour.

Need 2 servers for serious problems at 46.0% utilization and 0.05 hour average wait time.

2. $\lambda = 6$ per hour, $\mu = 1.333$ per hour

Nine servers are needed because, with 9 servers, 4.7% of customers will wait.

3. Solutions are listed below

a. For new purchases: $\lambda = 0.1667$ per minute, $\mu = 0.0625$ per minute. The average waiting time for new purchases is 38.4 minutes.

For troubleshooting: $\lambda = 0.4167$ per minute, $\mu = 0.1111$ per minute.

The average waiting time for troubleshooting is 3.3 minutes.

For billing inquiries: $\lambda = 0.25$ per minute, $\mu = 0.1667$ per minute.

The average waiting time for billing inquiries is 7.7 minutes.

b. Four servers would be needed for new purchases.

Five servers would be needed for troubleshooting.

Three servers would be needed for billing inquiries.

Chapter 11

1. The process is stable.
2. Average number of "failures" is too small for completion of a valid P chart.
3. The process is unstable because there are two consecutive points outside of 2-sigma limits in the same direction.
4. The process is stable. Performance is consistent with the benchmark, because it falls within the true likelihood confidence interval (0.889 to 0.927).
5. The process is unstable because there are five consecutive points outside of 1-sigma limits in the same direction and two consecutive points outside of 2-sigma limits in the same direction. Cannot compare an unstable process to a benchmark.

GLOSSARY

Activity   A process step. Many interconnected activities make up a business process; some are value-added and some are wasteful.

Assignable cause   The root cause of an event that introduces special cause variation to a process.

Better, cheaper, faster (BCF)   The three main ways that process is traditionally evaluated – the goal is high quality (better), at low cost (cheaper), and done quickly (faster).

Business process   The way that customers are provided value by transforming an input to an output that is not manufacturing-based; its customers are often found inside the firm.

Capable process   A business process that meets the objectives placed on it by the firm.

Capacity   The amount of work that a resource can do over a period of time, usually expressed as jobs per hour.

Capacity buffer   Extra capacity that is reserved in case demand is higher than the forecast.

Cause-and-effect diagram   Also called a fishbone or Ishikawa diagram, it is used to display potential causes of a problem using a hierarchical structure.

Center line   The average value of data plotted on a control chart.

Check sheet   A manual data visualization tool used to collect data using a format that assists in root cause analysis.

Close calls   When mistakes almost occur, this is important to notice to prevent the chance of mistakes in the future.

Common cause variation   The sources of variation that affect a stable process – this variation will have many causes, with each cause contributing a small amount to the overall natural variation of the process.

Confidence interval (CI) A range of values within which we would find a process parameter (e.g., the likelihood of success) with a specified degree of certainty, usually 95%.

Consumption map A process map that shows how the customer interacts with a service provider; it should display both activities and emotions.

Control chart A display that shows process data over time that is used to determine if the process is stable; it includes statistically-calculated limits of process variation and standard rules for interpretation.

Control limit A value that signifies an upper or lower bound of process output based on its expected level of natural variation while stable; there may be a lower control limit (LCL) and/or an upper control limit (UCL).

Critical incident approach The procedure of obtaining unbiased information from customers about how they evaluate the output of a business process.

Customer Any constituency that receives value from a business process; the customer may be external or internal.

Customer journey map A display that shows the actions of customers when consuming a service.

Demand The amount of work that a business process needs to perform.

Deming Prize An award given by the Japanese Union of Scientists and Engineers to an organization that acts in ways consistent with the Deming philosophy of management.

Detection In FMEA, it is the likelihood that internal controls will prevent a failure mode's impact from affecting customers.

Dimensions of performance The numerous ways in which a customer judges performance of a business process; similar to better, cheaper, faster but more specifically customized for each business process and customer combination.

DMAIC Acronym for "Define, Measure, Analyze, Improve and Control" – refers to a systematic approach to running a process improvement project; usually associated with a Six Sigma improvement project.

Escape Occurs when a defect or mistake is discovered by a customer.

External customers Customers who are not members of the firm.

Failure mode & effects analysis (FMEA) A structured approach that prioritizes numerous causes of poor quality by assigning a score for each cause based on its likelihood, the chance of internal detection, and the severity of its resulting.

Feasible A solution to a problem or capacity plan that would work, but may not be the best solution.

Fire-fighting Signifies the event of service personnel switching from job to job (or customer to customer) due to problems in other parts of a process.

Fishbone diagram Also called a cause-and-effect or Ishikawa diagram, it is used to display potential causes of a specific problem using a hierarchical structure.

Five S's (5S) A set of methods (sort, straighten, shine, standardize, and sustain) for organizing a workplace so that less time is wasted when performing work.

Five whys A procedure that consists of asking a sequential series of questions designed to drill down from problem symptoms to root cause.

Flow Describes the movement of people or information through a business process.

Flowchart A display that shows the flow of a business process using standard shapes to represent types of activities and arrows to illustrate flow.

Forecast error The difference between actual demand and predicted demand.

Genchi genbutsu The activity of going to the source of a problem to see it first hand, and to discuss issues with operating personnel.

Hidden costs Costs that are generated during the operation of a business process that are not precisely accounted for on financial statements.

Histogram A display using vertical bars to represent the frequency of where data fall over the range of values – it is used to determine the distribution of a process and is only valid for a stable process.

Internal customers Customers who are members of the same firm as the process owners.

Inventory buffer Products that are made in the weeks or months before demand is expected to account for demand uncertainty when capacity is limited or changing capacity is costly.

Ishikawa Diagram Also called a cause-and-effect or fishbone diagram, it is used to display potential causes of a specific problem using a hierarchical structure.

Kaizen Literally means "change for the better" but typically used to denote a short-term (one-to-five day) process improvement effort during which the project team works full-time on the project.

Kanban The use of information cards to signal when supplies or other material should be ordered.

Lead Time The total time a process takes to be completed from the start to finish – includes both value-added time and non-value-added (i.e., wasted) time.

Lean A methodology associated with the management of a business process whereby activities that do not add value for customers are identified and eliminated.

Lean Six Sigma (LSS) A process improvement program that combines elements of Lean production and Six Sigma.

Low hanging fruit A common term for problems that are easy to solve; they are typically identified in early stages of a process improvement program.

Markovian A set of assumptions associated with a M/M/s queuing system that has Poisson arrivals and exponential service times.

Mistake proofing Also known as poka-yoke, it is a mechanism that seeks to prevent problems and errors from occurring; examples include a simple checklist or color-coded forms.

Monte Carlo simulation   A methodology that uses computer code to mimic the operation of a system; it uses random number generators to determine the effect of uncertainty on the system's performance.

Muda   Also called waste, the term denotes an activity that does not add value for customers.

Natural variation   The variation that occurs when a process is stable.

Non-value-added activity   Also called a wasteful activity, it denotes an activity that does not add value for customers.

Occurrence   In FMEA, it is the likelihood that a failure mode occurs.

Offshoring   The business practice whereby work is assigned to an entity that is located in another country; the entity may or may not be owned by the parent firm.

Opportunity for defect (OFD)   Used to indicate a potential error that could occur during the servicing of a customer.

Optimal   Denotes the best of all feasible options available when solving a problem or planning capacity.

Outsourcing   The business practice whereby another entity is hired to perform work on behalf of a firm, because quality will be improved and/or costs reduced.

Pareto chart   The display of data relating to the occurrence of problems that highlights those having a disproportionately detrimental effect.

Performance metrics   A way of measuring how well quality is achieved relative to a specific dimension of performance.

Poka-yoke   Also called mistake proofing, it is a mechanism that seeks to prevent problems and errors from occurring; examples include a simple checklist or color-coded forms.

Process capability analysis (PCA)   A statistical analysis that compares the variation in stable process output to the goal set by customers or others.

Process flow   The sequence of process activities in the order that they are followed.

Process thinking   A framework for managing quality that focuses on understanding and controlling how jobs are done rather than focusing specifically on outcomes.

Process map   A display that shows the flow of a business process using standard shapes to represent types of activities and arrows to illustrate flow; it can show the interaction among departments effectively using "swim lanes" to represent each department involved with the process.

Proportion (or P) Chart   A control chart used to analyze the stability of a process that generates outcomes categorized as proportion data.

Poisson process   The pattern of customer arrivals that occurs when single customers arrive independently of one another.

Queuing model   A mathematical representation of a queuing system that, when certain assumptions apply, can predict queue sizes and customer waiting times.

Queuing system A process that includes customers arriving either at random or by appointment, then being served by a group of parallel servers; customers wait in a queue if all servers are busy serving other customers.

Random variation The differences in outcomes of a process due to common causes of variation that are expected to occur.

Random word generator A procedure for generating words that have no relationship to the solution of a problem; it is used to help a project team generate innovative problem solutions.

Regression analysis A statistical method that analyses data to determine the effect that certain explanatory (or controllable) variables have on process performance.

Resource efficiency An adjustment that is made to the capacity of a resource based on the percentage of time, usually unplanned, during which it is not serving customers.

Resource utilization The percentage of time that a resource (labor, equipment, tool, etc.) is serving customers, either planned or actual.

Respect for people Toyota's concept of shared appreciation among managers and workers for each other's talents and associated responsibility to make processes better.

Risk avoidance Preventing the impact of a risk factor by creating a policy that restricts certain business process designs or decisions.

Risk management system (RMS) A set of procedures that identifies risk factors, quantifies their priority, plans avoidance and mitigation strategies, and monitors future risks.

Risk mitigation Refers to actions that reduce the likelihood or severity of a failure mode.

Risk monitoring Procedures used to track the progress of risk avoidance and mitigation strategies; it periodically re-evaluates failure modes by reapplication of the FMEA method.

Risk priority number (RPN) In FMEA, it represents the priority of a failure mode; it is calculated as the product of its occurrence ranking, severity ranking, and detection ranking.

Run chart A display that shows process data over time that is used to determine if a process is stable; it helps to identify the cause of non-stable trends.

Scatter Plot A display for analysing data generated in pairs, typically used to show the relationship between two potentially related variables.

Sensei An individual who facilitates a process improvement project, usually associated with kaizen.

Severity In FMEA, the potential impact of a failure mode.

Service blueprint A process flowchart that explicitly separates direct interaction with customers (i.e., front room activity) from operations that take place away from customer view (i.e., back office activity).

Service process   A business process that is not classified as manufacturing, agricultural, or mining.

Service quality model   A framework that shows the five gaps that can exist when comparing the management of a process to expectations of customers.

Service science   An emerging academic discipline created in response to the need for organizations (businesses, industries, non-profits, governments, etc.) to better understand how to create, manage, and improve services for the benefit of consumers, internal entities, and external partners.

Setup   The process activities that take place between the completion of the last job and the start of the next job, when job types are changed.

Shewhart rules   Also called Western Electric rules, they consist of a checklist for determining if a process should be classified as unstable.

Sigma   A statistical term meaning "standard deviation"; it is a measure of variability.

Silos   The structure of divisions found in many corporations, where each division's performance is measured by metrics that apply specifically to the type of work performed in the division; this structure can sometimes encourage optimizing the "parts" while not optimizing the "whole."

Single-minute exchange of die (SMED)   A set of methods for reducing the downtime of a resource when changing over the process from one job type to another.

Six Sigma (6σ)   Originally a statistical measure, it is generally used to denote a quality system that seeks to improve the competitiveness of a firm by reducing variations in its processes that cause defective products or unacceptable services.

Spaghetti chart   A display that shows the layout of a facility with the process flow superimposed on the layout; it is used to highlight wasted movements.

Special cause variation   Variation that exceeds the common cause variation expected during the operation of a process; there must be an assignable cause of special cause variation.

Stable process   Describes a process that generates outcomes (i.e., data) that change due only to random variation (i.e., the process is unchanged over time).

Stakeholder   All individuals or organizations that are involved with a business process, such as suppliers, service providers, customers, and regulators.

Standard work   Refers to the structuring of a work task so that it is done similarly given similar circumstances; the resulting standard work procedure should include rules for allowing flexibility.

Statistical process control (SPC)   The set of statistical methods used to determine if a process is stable and, if so, whether it is capable of meeting objectives placed on its outcomes.

Subgroup   The number of entities (usually customers or jobs) contained in a set of data that represents one plotted point on a control chart.

Takt Time A calculation that determines the required cycle time for a process, used to determine minimum capacity requirements when applied to a business process.

Time value map A timeline supplemented with data that separates time into value added and wasteful categories; it typically includes a summary of total value-added time and total lead time.

Total Quality Management (TQM) The set of principles derived from (among others) the principles of W. Edwards Deming and the techniques introduced by Walter Shewhart; it was a popular quality system in the late 20th century and a precursor of Six Sigma.

Toyota Production System (TPS) The principles and techniques developed by Taiichi Ohno and Shigeo Shingo at Toyota Motors that forms the basis of Lean management.

Transformation Signifies how a business process changes inputs to outputs; service process transformations are physiological, locational, exchange, informational, and storage.

True likelihood The theoretical likelihood that a process will generate a successful outcome; it cannot be determined precisely but a confidence interval can provide its range of potential values.

Turnback When an error or mistake occurs that is detected before the customer notices its occurrence; in most cases, the job is performed again.

Utilization The percentage of time that a resource (labor, equipment, tool, etc.) is serving customers, either planned or actual.

Value Used to define actual or intended output of a business process in terms of desires, expectations, or needs of customers (both internal and external).

Value-added activity A task that takes place in a business process for which a customer would be willing to pay.

Value stream map A display that includes each step in a business process, often with data used to indicate activity durations and other process-related information.

Visual workplace A general term that refers to the use of displays and other highly noticeable means that communicates important process-related information to workers, managers, and customers.

Waste Also called non-value-added activities, it usually denotes time spent during service delivery in other than value-added ways.

Western Electric Rules Also called Shewhart rules, they consist of a checklist for determining if a process should be classified as unstable.

SUPPLEMENTAL READING

1   Barry LL. *Discovering the soul of a service*. New York: The Free Press; 1999.

2   Bettencourt L. *Service innovation: how to go from customer needs to breakthrough services*. US: McGraw-Hill; 2010.

3   Blokdyk G. *Continual service improvement a complete guide – 2019 Edition*. Emereo Pty Limited; 2019.

4   Britz GC, Emerling DW, Hare LB, Hoerl RW, Janis SJ, Shade JE. *Improving performance through statistical thinking*. Milwaukee, Wisconsin: ASQ Quality Press; 2000.

5   Edwards DW. *Out of the crisis*. Cambridge, Massachusetts: MIT Center for Advanced Engineering Study; 1986.

6   Edwards DW. *The new economics for industry, government, education*. 2nd Edition. Cambridge, MA, USA: MIT Center for Advanced Engineering Study; 1993.

7   Dodds S. *Three wins: service improvement using value stream design*. 2 ed. Chichester, U. K: Lulu.com; 2007.

8   Ehrlich B. *Transactional six sigma and lean service: leverage manufacturing concepts to achieve world-class service*. US: A CPC Press Company; 2002.

9   Emiliani ML. *Better thinking, better results*. Kensington, CT: The Center for Lean Business Management; 2003.

10   Gawande A. *Complications: a surgeon's notes on an imperfect science*. New York: Metropolitan Books; 2002.

11   George ML. *Lean six sigma for service*. New York: McGraw-Hill; 2003.

12   Graban M. *Lean hospitals*. Boca Raton, Florida: CRC Press (Taylor & Francis Group); 2016.

13   Harry M, Schroeder R. *Six sigma*. New York: Doubleday; 2000. 65.

14   Hayler R, Nichols M. *Six sigma for financial services: how leading companies are driving results using lean, six sigma, and process management*. NY: McGraw Hill Professional; 2006.

15   Ishikawa K. *Guide to quality control*. 2nd ed. White Plains, New York: Quality Resources; 1986.

16 Johnston R, Clark G. *Service operations management: improving service delivery*. Financial Times/Prentice Hall; 2008.

17 Liker JK. *The Toyota way*. New York: McGraw-Hill; 2004.

18 Liker JK. *The Toyota way to service excellence*. New York: McGraw-Hill; 2016.

19 Maleyeff J. *Improving service delivery in government with lean six sigma*. Washington, DC: IBM Center for The Business of Government; 2007.

20 Monden Y. *The Toyota production system*. (2nd ed.) Norcross, Georgia: Industrial Engineering and Management Press; 1993.

21 Ohno T. *Toyota production system*. Milwaukee, Wisconsin: Productivity Press; 1988.

22 Parker D. *Service operations management – the total experience*. 2nd ed. UK: Edward Elgar Publishing Limited; 2018.

23 Pyzdek T, Keller P. *The six sigma handbook*. New York: McGraw-Hill; 2010.

24 Reason J. *Human error*. UK: Cambridge University Press; 1990.

25 Sarkar D. *Building a lean service enterprise: reflections of a lean management practice*. FL. USA: CRC Press; 2017.

26 Scupola A, Fuglsang L. *Services, experiences, and innovation – integrating and extending research*. Cheltenham, UK. MA, USA: Edward Elgar; 2018.

27 Shewhart WA. *Economic control of quality of manufactured product*. Princeton, NJ: Van Nostrand; 1931.

28 Shewhart WA. *Statistical methods from the viewpoint of quality control*. Washington, DC: Graduate School, Department of Agriculture; 1939.

29 Shingo S. *A study of the Toyota production system*. Milwaukee, Wisconsin: Productivity Press; 1989.

30 Talbot C. *Theories of performance: organizational and service improvement in the public domain*. Oxford NY, USA; 2010.

31 Tetteh E. *Lean six sigma approached in manufacturing, service, and production*. Benedict M. Uzochukwu. USA: Virginia State University; 2015.

32 Womack JP, Jones DT. *Lean thinking*. New York: Simon and Schuster; 1996.

33 Womack JP, Jones DT. *Lean solutions*. Detroit: Free Press; 2005.

34 Womack JP, Jones DT, Roos D. *The machine that changed the world*. New York: HarperCollins Publishers; 1991.

INDEX

Printed in the United States
by Baker & Taylor Publisher Services